INTERNATIONAL LIBRARY OF THE
PHILOSOPHY OF EDUCATION

# PHILOSOPHICAL ANALYSIS AND EDUCATION

# PHILOSOPHICAL ANALYSIS AND EDUCATION

*Edited and with an introduction by*

REGINALD D. ARCHAMBAULT

Volume 1

Routledge
Taylor & Francis Group

LONDON AND NEW YORK

First published in 1965 by Routledge & Kegan Paul

This edition first published in 2010
by Routledge
2 Park Square, Milton Park, Abingdon, Oxon, OX14 4RN

Simultaneously published in the USA and Canada
by Routledge
52 Vanderbilt Avenue, New York, NY 10017

First issued in paperback 2012

*Routledge is an imprint of the Taylor & Francis Group,
an informa business*

© 1965, 1972 Taylor & Francis.

Notice:
Product or corporate names may be trademarks or
registered trademarks, and are used only for
identification and explanation without intent to infringe.

*British Library Cataloguing in Publication Data*
A catalogue record for this book is available from the
British Library

ISBN 13: 978-0-415-55946-1 (Set)
eISBN 13: 978-0-2038-6097-7 (Set)
eISBN 13: 978-0-203-86153-0 (Volume 1)

**Publisher's Note**
The publisher has gone to great lengths to ensure the
quality of this reprint but points out that some imper-
fections in the original copies may be apparent.

**Disclaimer**
The publisher has made every effort to trace copy-
right holders and would welcome correspondence
from those they have been unable to trace.

ISBN13: 978-0-415-65084-7 (PBK)

ISBN13: 978-0-415-56269-0 (HBK)

# Philosophical analysis and education

*Edited and with an Introduction by*
REGINALD D. ARCHAMBAULT

LONDON:
ROUTLEDGE & KEGAN PAUL

NEW YORK: HUMANITIES PRESS

*First published 1965*
*Second impression 1966*
*Third impression 1967*
*Fourth impression 1968*
*Reprinted, and first published as a*
*Routledge paperback 1972 by*
*Routledge & Kegan Paul Ltd*
*Broadway House, 68–74 Carter Lane,*
*London EC4V 5EL*
*Printed in Great Britain by*
*Alden & Mowbray Ltd*
*at the Alden Press, Oxford*

*ISBN* 0 7100 1021 4 (C)
*ISBN* 0 7100 7445 X (P)

TO CLAIRE

# Contents

# General editor's note

There is a growing interest in philosophy of education amongst students of philosophy as well as amongst those who are more specifically and practically concerned with educational problems. Philsophers, of course, from the time of Plato onwards, have taken an interest in education and have dealt with education in the context of wider concerns about knowledge and the good life. But it is only quite recently in this country that philosophy of education has come to be conceived of as a specific branch of philosophy like the philosophy of science or political philosophy.

To call philosophy of education a specific branch of philosophy is not, however, to suggest that it is a distinct branch in the sense that it could exist apart from established branches of philosophy such as epistemology, ethics, and philosophy of mind. It would be more appropriate to conceive of it as drawing on established branches of philosophy and bringing them together in ways which are relevant to educational issues. In this respect the analogy with political philosophy would be a good one. Thus use can often be made of work that already exists in philosophy. In tackling, for instance, issues such as the rights of parents and children, punishment in schools, and the authority of the teacher, it is possible to draw on and develop work already done by philosophers on 'rights', 'punishment', and 'authority'. In other cases, however, no systematic work exists in the relevant branches of philosophy—e.g. on concepts such as 'education', 'teaching', 'learning', 'indoctrination'. So philosophers of education have had to break new ground—in these cases in the philosophy of mind. Work on educational issues can also bring to life and throw new light on long-standing problems in philosophy. Concentration, for instance, on the particular predicament of children can throw new light on problems of punishment and responsibility. G. E. Moore's old worries about what sorts of things are good in themselves can be brought to life by urgent questions about the justification of the curriculum in schools.

There is a danger in philosophy of education, as in any other applied field, of polarization to one of two extremes. The work could be practically relevant but philosophically feeble; or it could be philosophically sophisticated but remote from practical problems. The aim of the new International Library of the Philosophy of Education is to build up a body of fundamental work in this area which is both practically relevant and philosophically competent. For unless it achieves both types of objective it will fail to satisfy those for whom it is intended and fall short of the conception of philosophy of education which the International Library is meant to embody.

R. S. P.

# General editor's preface

Nearly ten years ago Reginald Archambault spent a period in England looking into what was going on in philosophy of education and talking to philosophers about the subject. As a result he was able to put together this collection of essays to which both pure philosophers and philosophers of education contributed. It was the first English collection of essays on philosophy of education written from the 'analytic' point of view. There has been a steady demand for this book since it was published and some of the essays have been widely influential.

Philosophy of education has now become firmly established in England as a branch both of educational theory and of philosophy, and Reginald Archambault's collection marks an important early stage in this steady process of development. So when the International Library of Philosophy of Education was founded it seemed appropriate to include in it a reprinted edition of this early collection.

R. S. P.

# PREFACE

All of these essays were written expressly for publication in this volume. They represent a sincere desire on the part of the participants to contribute substantially to, and thereby to help define, the philosophical study of education. I am especially grateful to them for their interest, their effort, and their thorough co-operation.

The publication of this book has been possible only through the direct and indirect contributions of many.

I should like to thank Paul Woodring, the distinguished American philosopher of education, for his belief in the importance of bringing philosophers and educationists closer together in confronting their common concerns.

My thanks go, too, to the Ford Foundation, for a grant for a trip to England to study the relations between philosophy and education in that country, a trip which made possible the production of this book.

R. S. Peters was particularly helpful in his suggestions regarding the scope of the book, and the authors who might contribute to it. He was also of great assistance in arranging for its publication.

Finally, my special thanks go to Gladys Beaty and Judith Roberts for their help in the mechanics of preparing the manuscript.

R. D. A.

*Grinnell, Iowa*
*U.S.A.*

# INTRODUCTION

WHEN D. J. O'Connor published his small, but original and influential volume, *An Introduction to the Philosophy of Education*, in 1957,[1] he cast some grave doubts on the adequacy and validity of contemporary theories in education. He also noted the prevalent confusion regarding the nature of philosophy of education and its rôle in educational theory. Since that time there has been a great deal of attention paid to these questions, both by educationists with a concern for philosophical issues, and by philosophers with a fresh interest in educational problems. In fact, the tendency toward self-analysis among scholars interested in education has become so widespread that it sometimes seems that we shall never see the issues for the *meta-problems*. However, during the past decade some very important gains have been made as a result of these investigations. Perhaps the most important of these is the recognition of the complexity of the field of education and the futility of any attempt to arrive at a notion of educational theory based exclusively on the model of theories in science. For the field of education is broad, ranging in its concerns from simple problems of tutoring to questions of desirable curricula for the secondary schools, from the efficacy of teaching machines to the limitations of Socratic method, from the methods of teaching grammar to criteria for success in moral education. And the disciplines that must be drawn upon in seeking solutions to this wide range of multi-faceted problems are several.

Educational theory is concerned with three major kinds of investigation. The first is the scientific study of factors relevant to an understanding of present problems. These are, chiefly, studies in psychology and sociology. A second kind of study is historical analysis, which attempts to provide perspective on current concerns

## Reginald D. Archambault

by looking at analogous situations in the past, or by projecting hypotheses on the genesis of present problems. A third mode of investigation is the philosophical. Its major aim is to make clear those factors which are susceptible to investigation by the other disciplines, to explore and explicate the philosophical premises underlying investigations in these other areas, and to attempt to shed light on the issues involved in complex educational problems, especially those which relate to questions of value.

One major deficiency in recent attempts to clarify the nature and function of educational theory is the failure to recognize both the complexity of the field and the varieties of disciplined investigation that must be used within it. To say, for example, that educational theory is pseudo-scientific because its hypotheses are not sufficiently supported by objective evidence, or because its constructs are not susceptible to objective test, is to fail to recognize the rôle of education as a vital, purposive activity, the aims and procedures of which must be open to analysis and justification. As such, it cannot now, because of its procedural limitations, or in the future, because of its value connections, accept the rôle of being *merely* scientific. Education is a humane study, and as such, it must reflect the uncertainties, the paradoxes, and the unanswered value questions characteristic of other studies in the humanities. However, it should also attempt to clean its stables, and recent criticisms of education by influential laymen and scholars have served as a stimulus in that direction.

A major deterrent to progress in educational theory in general, and the philosophy of education in particular, has been the tendency on the part of educational theorists to attack problems of wide scope by using very general principles and methods, and hence to arrive at 'theories', or at least propositions about education that seem to have very little relevance to such concrete considerations as aims, curriculum, and teaching. This has not always been true. Plato did not merely paint with a wide brush. His *Republic* is not only replete with specific details which might inform educational practice; it also presents some important distinctions regarding knowledge, understanding, and experience that are directly relevant to educational practice. The same could be said for Aristotle, Comenius, Herbart, and Dewey, to name only a few. However, many of these authors tended to deal with educational problems in terms of an 'ideal educational situation' (as L. R. Perry would put it), if not a Utopia. This ideal situation usually seems to differ drastically from that of

2

the concrete present. This may be due to one or more of several different factors: the ideal model may be philosophically unacceptable because of the metaphysical, epistemological, or ethical assumptions on which it is based; it may be psychologically unsound because of its misinformed or inadequate notions of learning, individual differences, or human development; it may be sociologically unacceptable to adherents of democratic social organization because of its views on elitism or social caste and class. Classic educational theories, then, although they are often in themselves consciously and directly relevant to specific problems, are not acceptable *in toto*. However, there seems to be a great deal of value in them which would be wasted if they were totally rejected. This consideration has led to two important tendencies in modern educational theory and philosophy of education.

The first is concerned with educational theory broadly conceived. It is the tendency toward eclecticism. One might accept Aristotle's characterization of the intellectual and moral virtues, yet reject his teleological explanations; Plato's line of cognition might be considered valid, but his notion of 'experience' shoddy. Hence various elements are borrowed from philosophers of greatly divergent character. These are usually formed into a hodge-podge called a 'synthetic philosophy of education'. The result is frequently disappointing, not necessarily because it is an admixture, although this is sometimes true, but more often because of another deficiency: the principles on which the synthesis is based are usually so vague, so loose, or so lacking in justification as to call into question the validity of the whole construct. Or another deficiency is evident: in attempting to deal with *all* problems of education through a cluster of broad principles loosely organized, the theoretical statements, although apparently consistent, are in fact vacuous, for they permit no clear applications to practice or even to the broadest policy making.

The last deficiency is not confined to eclectic theories of education, but is prevalent in most other modern theories of education, be they philosophical or broadly theoretical, prescriptive or descriptive. In individual philosophical treatises on education this takes the characteristic form which J. B. Wilson finds so appalling: the treatment of broad questions regarding 'the good life', 'the ends of education', the 'development of character', etc. The questions raised, and the answers offered are so general as to be ambiguous at best and

3

## Reginald D. Archambault

fruitless at worst in improving educational policy or practice. In the second order treatment of these philosophies of education in text books and courses in education, there is also a characteristic technique. This consists in categorizing the philosophies according to the metaphysical, epistemological, or ethical presuppositions that seem to underlie similar theories. Hence, philosophies of education are designated as belonging to the 'school' of 'idealism', 'realism', or 'experimentalism'. The assumptions here are that these basic philosophical positions have clear and definite differences based on their views of the problems of philosophy *per se*, and that clear implications for educational practice of the most specific kind can be drawn from each position, thus making possible a contrast at the practical as well as the theoretical level. One can work down from theory to practice or back to theory from practice, once the full position is known. ('Experimentalism' implies non-stationary school furniture; 'realism' implies rigid regimentation, passive pupils, and authoritarian teaching methods.)[2]

### CHANGING CONCEPTIONS OF PHILOSOPHY

The basic confusion here results from a failure to be clear on the relation between theory and practice. Yet this is in turn related to another, more fundamental consideration: the function of philosophy *per se*. It might be argued, however, that the failure of philosophy of education is due to a much more simple cause: that those educationists who have engaged in speculation concerning philosophical issues in education were usually utterly lacking in any adequate training in philosophy, regardless of how that might be defined. In recent history this has, alas, too often been true. The growth of the 'professional movement' in education prompted a separation of educationists from other scholars. Those interested in philosophy *of education* were primarily concerned with practical educational problems, and often considered philosophy as an adjunct to this kind of investigation. In order to add an aura of respectability to the endeavour, classical theories were taught, but often with only a superficial understanding of the complex views of the theorists. Hence the oversimplified classification into 'schools' and 'typical positions'.

Of course, not all philosophers of education have been untrained in philosophy or unknowledgeable about it. Yet, even many of the

4

more sophisticated have held a view of the function of philosophy, in relation to education, which nourished further vagueness and ambiguity. The function of philosophy was to provide a directive for life, to distinguish the first rate from the inferior, to give students 'something to believe in'. Students were often expected to 'learn' philosophy rather than to *do* philosophy.

Recent trends in philosophy, have, of course, given a completely different direction to the discipline. These trends are complex, reflecting conflicts among philosophic camps (the clash between 'emotivists' and 'rationalists' in ethics is a clear example), divergent directions between groups of philosophers (the continental existentialists and the English and American analysts), and differences within certain factions (for example the logical positivists and the linguistic analysts). Yet, leaving aside for the moment the obvious difference in emphasis that characterizes the existentialist position, there is considerable similarity among the views of many contemporary philosophers, at least with regard to certain notions of the functions of philosophy: its function is, at least in part, to make clear the diverse factors that are involved in complex issues of major theoretical import. This involves a strong emphasis on analysis, both logical and linguistic. This further entails, generally, a great deal of attention to the elimination of ambiguity, and specifically, a treatment of limited, clearly discernible issues, which are often drawn from common experience: hence an emphasis on the analysis of ordinary language, and the treatment of common practical puzzles. The rôle of philosophy is seen as a much more modest one in that only limited solutions, or perhaps merely clarifications of severely limited problems are sought.

The indictment of 'pure analysis' by L. A. Reid in the first essay in this volume is one indication of the concern on the part of many contemporary philosophers (including, in many instances, the analysts themselves) regarding the limitations of analysis and the need for a clearer and stronger rôle for philosophy in informing vital decisions. There is a fear on the part of many that philosophical speculation has become arid: that it has, in developing a more sophisticated method of study, unwittingly divorced itself from its proper and traditional concerns—an investigation of central problems, including value considerations, that underlie the tragic concerns of life. It is not difficult to discern the existentialist influence here.

5

*Reginald D. Archambault*

Now, the study of philosophy of education has been left relatively untouched by these new trends until quite recently. Within the past few years there have been some small but significant attempts to use the methods of modern philosophical analysis in investigations of issues in education. These have taken two forms. Some of these have been only accidental contributions to educational philosophy, for their major purpose was to deal with problems in ethics, epistemology, or aesthetics, using educational situations or issues as a context for exploration. Analyses by R. M. Hare[3] and P. H. Nowell-Smith[4] in England, and Max Black[5] and R. B. Perry[6] in America have made important contributions in this fashion. This practice is, of course, not at all new. It would be difficult to say whether Plato's *Republic* is merely an educational tract used as a convenient vehicle for presenting his more basic philosophical ideas, or whether Plato chose education as a focus because of its intrinsic importance. The intimate relation between philosophy and education has a long and distinguished history from Plato through Dewey.

The second form that the philosophical analysis of education has taken is the direct attempt to use philosophical techniques in order to clarify problems in educational theory. A major pioneering effort in this direction was C. D. Hardie's book,[7] written over twenty years ago. This book soon went out of print, for educationists were not ready for it and philosophers were not interested in so specialized an analysis of education. In the mid-nineteen-fifties there developed a fresh interest in this kind of treatment of philosophy of education, and this interest has continued to the present.[8] It is now clearly discernible as a major trend in philosophy of education, if not a dominant one.

The reasons for the growth and sustenance of this trend toward more direct philosophical investigations in education are several. The first stems from the changing conceptions, among philosophers themselves, of the proper scope and function of philosophical analysis. There was a growing concern among many, prompted in part by the arguments of the existentialists, that the analytic movement had become too precious and too 'antiseptic'. The demise of emotivist ethics, for example, had begun; the severely limited criteria of meaning postulated by the logical positivists were seen to be seriously deficient. More positively, analytic philosophers began to turn to interesting practical problems as a context for the investigation of ethical and epistemological questions, or as a vehicle for developing techniques of analysis. T. D. Weldon, for example, employed these techniques in the treatment of theoretical constructs in politics.[9] R. S. Peters turned to psychology as a source of issues for analysis.[10] It was not surprising that someone should turn to the field of education, and it was D. J. O'Connor who did it. Even in studies whose aims were to treat philosophical issues *per se*, there was an increasing tendency to use practical contexts as a taking off point, for this satisfied the philosophers' quests for specificity and relevance to important concerns, theoretical though they might be. In this context it comes as no shock to note that a 'pure' philosopher such as Ryle not only uses simple pedagogical puzzles as a means of describing the intellect, but calls, at the end of his highly influential book, for 'a branch of philosophical theory concerned with the concepts of learning, teaching, and examining. This might be called "the philosophy of learning", "the methodology of education", or, more grandly, "the Grammar of Pedagogy".'[11]

These tendencies within philosophy itself, combined with the common concern over education following Sputnik I, prompted a fresh look at the problems of the philosophy of education. Again, this took two forms. One was the use of techniques of analysis by practising philosophers of education. This trend was stimulated in America by Israel Scheffler,[12] a philosopher who was strongly influenced by modern English analysis. It has continued and grown to the present day. The difficulty here is that there are few educationists who are adequately trained in philosophy. Many, however, are 'retooling' themselves. The second, begun metaphilosophically in the now famous issue of the *Harvard Educational Review* in 1956,[13] consisted of 'pure' philosophers turning their attention and techniques to the analysis of educational problems. There have been some remarkable contributions made in this fashion, and there is some evidence of increased activity in this area: R. S. Peters, a 'pure' philosopher, has, for example, taken the chair in philosophy of education at the University of London. Unfortunately, however, interest in education by competent non-educationist philosophers has been relatively sparse.

*Reginald D. Archambault*

## PHILOSOPHY OF EDUCATION

Philosophy is, of course, always the philosophy *of* something: the philosophy of art, of science, of politics. Philosophy has a traditional subject matter. It is primarily concerned with problems of epistemology and ethics. In the investigation of issues in aesthetics, or the philosophy of religion, these issues themselves serve as a focus for the investigation of more basic problems of knowledge, meaning, and the values that underlie them. Yet it is not its subject matter that distinguishes philosophy from other disciplines. It is its aims, its concerns, and its manner of investigation. Again, these factors are consistently present in philosophical investigations regardless of the specific issues under consideration—be they political, religious, or scientific. For these reasons the study of philosophical problems in these areas is special, because of the focus and context of study, and yet fundamentally similar to investigations in other branches of philosophy. Since the problems of education offer a rich field for philosophical analysis, and since education is such a complex, vital, and value-laden activity, it would seem that the study of philosophy of education might be a legitimate, valid, and valuable study, worthy of the attention of working philosophers. Recent developments have lent some support to this view.

I spoke earlier of the need to clean the stables. This is particularly pressing in educational theory, for the eclecticism and broad, synthetic treatments have spawned vagueness, ambiguity, pseudo-problems and pseudo-explanations, vacuous principles and impractical prescriptions. These are characteristic of writings in the philosophy of education. This is due to the enormity of the field and the failure, on the part of workers in the philosophy of education, to recognize or to use the gains made in recent philosophy. For these reasons, issues in education are in need of rigorous analysis. Yet education is a vital activity of even greater importance than ever before. Its problems are immediate and real. This factor is quite important, for it makes it imperative for us to avoid chucking whatever hay there may be into the dust-bins. It is not even sufficient to clean the stables thoroughly. This should not imply that analysis in itself is not of great value. Nor should it imply that philosophers of education must engage in prescriptions—either broad or specific. I merely suggest that the educational enterprise goes on, and that those analyses and clarifications that emerge from the philosophical investigation of central educational issues must

8

necessarily affect and inform educational decisions. The fact that investigations in the philosophy of education stem from vital and real problems and purposely or inadvertently contribute to the treatment of them, is a great advantage, for it is a deterrent to frivolous speculation. The philosophy of education should not, and must not, have as its aim the solution of immediate practical problems. This kind of social engineering, which characterized the philosophy of progressive education, reflects a complete misunderstanding of the function of philosophy, or any other liberal discipline for that matter, in contributing to society. The philosophy of education must help make clear those factors that are relevant to making wise decisions in education. It cannot make them. Yet it must keep the live context in mind.

### THE PRESENT VOLUME

This leads us, then, to a brief statement of the rationale for, and the purposes of the present volume. We have spoken of the lack of deliberate activity, on the part of professional philosophers, in the field of educational theory. If gains are to be made, not only in the investigation of philosophical issues in education, but also in the clarification of the function and nature of philosophy of education, the professional philosophers are obviously equipped to help in this task. Only an artificial separation of the study of education from the practice of philosophy has prevented many of our better philosophers from doing this. We have spoken too of the need for a movement in the other direction: for the educationists to develop more sophisticated investigations through the use of modern philosophic techniques. Both types are represented here. The major purposes of the volume, then, are (1) to demonstrate the results that can be obtained when central educational problems, limited though they might be, are analysed in a disciplined philosophical manner; (2) to encourage further activity of this kind, and hence greater co-operation between educationists and philosophers, and hopefully, some progress in the solution of problems; (3) and finally, to help to define, in a fresh way, the function and nature of philosophy of education, not by edict or proclamation, but through examples presented in the form of specific analyses of central educational issues by working philosophers, be they educationists or not.

Let us consider, then, the actual text that we have here. We have said that the problems of education are many and complex. The contributors to this volume deal with a great many of them, both directly and indirectly: the aims of education; the definition of moral education; the function of educational theory; the rôle of educational philosophy; the meaning of teaching; and many more. The work has a loose form of organization and a kind of unity and continuity. The unity is based on two factors: the kinds of problems discussed and the method of discussing them.

The central problems of educational theory, some of which are named above, are, since they are highly complex, susceptible to a wide variety of approaches and treatments. Hence, for example, we find that the question 'What ought the aims of education to be?' is discussed quite directly in *every* essay in this volume. There is, then, a similarity of material.

Yet, and much more important, there is also great similarity of *manner* in these essays. There is certainly no consensus among these authors on the ultimate definition of the nature and function of philosophy, or of its scope of investigation. As mentioned earlier, Professor Reid's essay is in part an attack on 'mere analysis', Peters' is a plea for much wider, if not exclusive use of it. Yet there is *working* agreement on the way in which philosophers can fruitfully *talk about* educational issues. Reid's essay is strikingly similar in approach and technique to that of Peters. I do not want to make too much of a good thing. There are obvious differences in technique. Professor Hirst's essay is much more comprehensive than most, dealing with a great variety of problems by relating them to central unifying principles. Professors Griffiths and Perry are somewhat sceptical of the fruitfulness of this approach. Nevertheless, there is a remarkable basis for *understanding* that runs through these essays. Robert Hutchins referred to educational philosophizing as the '*Great* Conversation'. Most of the contributors to this volume would reject such a grandiose label. Yet it is evident that there is an informed, disciplined and serious exchange of views here among men who are able to understand each other. This has not often occurred in past discussions of educational philosophy.

What makes this conversation possible is an implicit agreement in principle to talk about relatively concrete and tangible problems by using the accepted methods of philosophy. That in itself is a significant achievement.

Those two similarities help to organize and unify the book. A third factor gives the book structure of sorts: this is the general type of educational problems dealt with. The first two essays, by Reid and Best, deal, in their own ways, with a similar problem: the *meta* question concerning the nature of educational theory in general, and the rôle of philosophy of education in particular. The papers by Perry, Peters and Hirst form a unit, for each of them is primarily concerned with describing what education consists in. Perry's attempt is to define what an educational situation is, in actuality, as contrasted with what it is usually considered to be, as an ideal. Peters attacks the broader issue of the definition of 'education' by attempting to get at the *essence* of the concept and then relating it to such notions as aims and manner. Hirst's approach is yet more comprehensive. He examines the concept of a liberal education, and in the process relates his notion of that idea to the structure of knowledge and the nature of the academic disciplines.

A third unit is made up of the next three essays in the volume. They are all concerned with teaching. Corbett's essay deals directly with a description of what the teaching of philosophy, properly conceived, consists in. In the process he presents several principles that are relevant to a wide range of other teaching situations. Wilson proposes a major distinction between two types of learing: that which is essential to a human being, and that which is not. He concludes that the manner of instruction and its consequent facilitation of communication is the key consideration in any discussion of teaching. Atkinson turns to moral instruction as the crucial case for defining a true teaching situation.

The paper by Griffiths makes a unit of itself, for its scope is broad, and in the course of the discussion he treats, in a systematic and comprehensive fashion, the central issues raised in all of the other papers, either directly or by implication. This makes it a fitting closing paper for the volume.

There are, of course, many other relations among these articles. Corbett, too, is concerned with the definition of philosophy, Atkinson, Hirst and Griffiths with the relation between general and specific skills, and so on. And there are controversies, or potential controversies based on general or specific disagreements. The book begins with a conflict between Reid and Best regarding the proper function of philosophy of education; it ends on a note of conflict with Griffiths' suggestion that the general qualities of mind, which most of the authors maintain can be engendered through the academic disciplines, are possibly non-existent.

There is also considerable agreement on certain central principles.

## Reginald D. Archambault

It would be boring to catalogue these areas of agreement. But one or two are particularly worthy of mention. One is the importance, in the minds of many of these authors, of the notion of *manner* in education. This is a relatively new concept in the philosophy of education, and its popularity is indicative of the general tendency to frame discussions of purposive processes in terms of clearly discernible activities, rather than abstract *a priori* categories. The tendency to employ this notion is, in a sense, symbolic of the total approach that characterizes this volume. There is also considerable agreement among several of the authors on an analogous notion: that teaching for generic skills is, at best, highly suspect, since these are difficult, if not impossible to define. This too is indicative of a broader tendency: to reject, or at least put to question any suggestion of automaticity, be it in the form of engendering values through free, unhampered development, or in postulating definite relations between certain subjects and certain desirable skills, or in the suggestion that knowledge of the good leads necessarily to moral action.

There are many other areas of agreement within these essays: the emphasis on the activity and freedom of the learner as a proper condition and aim of education; the rejection of the institutional model of an educational situation for the more fruitful model based on the relation between teacher, pupil, and subject; the emphasis on knowledge as skill, rather than merely propositional knowledge. But one is particularly worthy of note. Most of these philosophers *have* decided to *prescribe*. Their prescriptions are very limited and quite modest indeed, but they have decided to tell us, if only in part, what they believe education should consist in.

Regarding these prescriptions there is, of course, great disagreement. There is disagreement, too, regarding the distinctions, assumptions, and principles on which these prescriptions are based. And there are many questions that remain unanswered. Griffiths ends his essay, the last in the volume, in stating that specific skills must be taught for specifically. But this raises the whole issue of how we can ever get our knowledge of one thing to transfer to anything else, and whether we can fruitfully discuss economy in curricula. If this volume stimulates further disciplined investigation into problems such as these, it will have fulfilled one of its major purposes.

*Grinnell, Iowa, U.S.A.*  REGINALD D. ARCHAMBAULT
*November, 1964.*

# Introduction

## NOTES

1. D. J. O'Connor, *An Introduction to the Philosophy of Education* (London: Routledge and Kegan Paul, 1957).

2. Sidney Hook, in the new edition of his *Education for Modern Man*, states it this way: 'The view that a philosophy of education represents merely an application to the process of education of philosophical truths antecedently won is demonstrably false for most philosophies of education; when true it represents their superficiality and irrelevance to actual educational concern' (New York: Knopf, 1963), p. 52.

3. R. M. Hare, *The Language of Morals* (London: Oxford at the Clarendon Press, 1952), pp. 56–78.

4. P. H. Nowell-Smith, *Ethics* (London: Unwin, 1954).

5. M. Black, 'Education as Art and Discipline', *Ethics*, LIV, No. 4, 1944, pp. 290–4.

6. R. B. Perry, *Realms of Value* (Cambridge, Massachusetts: Harvard University Press, 1954).

7. C. D. Hardie, *Truth and Fallacy in Educational Theory* (London: Cambridge University Press, 1942).

8. Recent studies in philosophy of education by educationist philosophers have been dominantly analytic. See for example: B. O. Smith and R. H. Ennis, *Language and Concepts in Education* (Chicago: Rand McNally, 1961); I. Scheffler, *The Language of Education* (Springfield, Illinois: C. C. Thomas, 1960); H. W. Burns and R. H. Beck (eds.), *Philosophy of Education* (New York: Ronald Press, 1962).

9. T. D. Weldon, *The Vocabulary of Politics* (London: Penguin Books, Ltd., 1953).

10. R. S. Peters, *The Concept of Motivation* (New York: The Humanities Press, 1958).

11. G. Ryle, *The Concept of Mind* (New York: Barnes and Noble, 1949), p. 318.

12. I. Scheffler, 'Toward an Analytic Philosophy of Education', *The Harvard Educational Review*, XXIV (Fall, 1954), pp. 223–30.

13. 'The Aims and Content of Philosophy of Education', *Harvard Educational Review*, XXVI (Spring, 1956). This, in turn, was prompted, significantly, by a symposium in the journal of the American Philosophical Association, by H. S. Broudy and K. Price, on the aims and content of philosophy of education, *Journal of Philosophy*, LII (October 27, 1955).

# THE NATURE AND FUNCTION
# OF EDUCATIONAL THEORY

PROFESSOR Reid's essay is a fitting first piece for this volume, not only because it reflects the experience gained through many years in his Chair of Philosophy of Education at the University of London, but also because of the scope of the piece, and the author's courage in presenting his views on the nature and function of educational theory and the rôle of philosophy of education in it. His strong plea is for greater co-operation between educationists and professional philosophers, on the assumption that improvement in the quality of educational theory and practice would result, even if these cannot be measured by the instruments of science. His stroke is wide, and covers the range of many *meta* issues that impinge on educational theory, including the rôle of philosophy, a definition of the term, and the application and limitations of any theory of education.

Dr. Best's essay is, in one sense, considerably less optimistic. He considers two major divisions of educational theory. Discussing educational psychology first, he points to the many value assumptions that underlie current theories in educational psychology, assumptions which are seldom made explicit and still less often given substantial justification. He finds this same difficulty in much philosophy of education, yet he does not stop there. Taking issue directly with Reid, he argues that the rôle of philosophy in education should be a relatively limited one, aimed at bringing about modest improvements, through analysis, in the special sciences that bear on education, rather than the generation of broad statements on such general notions as 'the aims of education'. In this different sense, his analysis is mildly optimistic.

# PHILOSOPHY AND THE THEORY
# AND PRACTICE OF EDUCATION

## L. Arnaud Reid

WHAT I would like to try to do is to state, as clearly as I can, after the reflections and discussions of fifteen years as Professor of Philosophy of Education at London, the nature of philosophy of education as I see it, its relation to what is called 'educational theory', and the relation of both to the practice of education. By doing this I hope to be able to answer, in part at least, certain criticisms of philosophy of education which are frequently made from different quarters. It is said, for instance, that education can perfectly well stand on its own feet without the help of philosophy, that educational theory is autonomous and does not need philosophy. Anyhow, philosophers, it is well known, never agree. The progress of philosophy is just stumbling from one bog into the next. Philosophers are sowers of the seed of doubt and uncertainty. Away with them to their ivory towers! Let practical common sense and experience guide our thinking about education.

From a different quarter, from a section of the philosophers themselves, come other protests. It is said that the business of philosophy nowadays is purely the analysis of meaning and that this has nothing whatever to do with influencing practical action. The aim of philosophy is understanding, or clarification, and not reform. Philosophers are no longer to be regarded as the guide of humanity, in education or anything else. Moreover, if someone were to argue that the philosopher as a human being may have some desire to do at least what he can to leave the world a little better than he finds it, a common contemporary philosopher's reply would be that there is not the slightest reason to suppose that his philosophical reflections

—say upon some aspects of the problem of values—would render him in any way more competent to pronounce or advise on practical affairs. Indeed, if one grants for the moment that philosophic reflection might have some effects upon practice, the effects might possibly be bad. Elaborate philosophical reflection on questions of value might lead the philosopher off the rails, so that his conclusions were more misleading and dangerous than the risks of practical common sense. Or again, there may be the repetition of the objection that philosophy may lead to scepticism, and so, indirectly, may paralyse the power of practical decision. Finally, there is the objection (both popular and philosophical) that the claim that the study of, say, philosophy of education can be of practical educational benefit is one which it is impossible to confirm in any remotely scientific way. In the first place, in the human sciences generally, controls are very difficult if not impossible to establish accurately. Secondly, even if two groups of teachers could be set up, one as a control for the other, it would be impossible to show that any claimed benefits of the study of philosophy of education in one group were, in fact, due exclusively to that study and not to other factors. This is always a difficulty, even in testing the practical efficacy of scientific (say, psychological) theory in education. But in the case of philosophy, it can be argued, philosophical theories and philosophical convictions are of such a *general* character that it is impossible to deduce clear and specific practical expected results from them which could be tested by equally specific observations.

### 'EDUCATIONAL THEORY'

I cannot hope, in the course of a short article, to deal adequately with all of these objections, though I hope to deal generally with some of them. To begin with, I want to discuss the use of the term 'educational *theory*'. In the last paragraph the obvious distinction between scientific theory and philosophical theory has been assumed. But 'educational theory' is in common, and commonly vague, use, and it seems to include much more than strict science or strict philosophy. In order to say anything sensible of philosophy of education and its place in educational theory, I must first look at the term 'educational theory' itself.

Let us consider this term in the widest and most inclusive sense, without any special technical meaning at all. We can think of it as a large bag, a rag-bag if you like, containing all reflection and all talk about education, of whatever kind and at all levels. Educational theory will include, for instance, all discussion about the curriculum and content of education, of good and bad teaching, teaching methods, specialization in relation to general education, of structure and administration and law; questions of parent-teacher relations; coeducation; and psychological, sociological, and philosophical questions that underlie these.

This notion of education theory does not imply that there is any single coherent body of knowledge—comparable, say, to the theory of relativity or even to Kant's ethics—called 'educational theory' or 'the' theory of education. I shall return later to the question of whether there is such a thing. All that I am saying at the moment is something descriptive, or if you like, permissive. There are *theorizings* about education of all kinds, and at all levels, taken part in by the many sorts of people interested, in different ways, in education. It may help if I illustrate some of the different levels by reference to the kind of thing which happens within any centre for the training and education of teachers.

Suppose we begin at the most practical end—the actual work of teaching in a classroom. Here things are being done and decided all the time. This is practice, not theory. On the other hand, when human beings, including teachers, do things, they do them with some purpose, with ideas in their heads, making all kinds of assumptions, many of which they are certainly not thinking about at the time. Into what the teacher does there clearly enters much knowledge, for example, of the subject, of the children he is teaching, of their background, of the system in which he is working, etc. Again, his action may imply or assume some knowledge of, say, theories of psychology. Nevertheless, the focus is upon action. The teacher is *doing*, and if he is thinking, he is chiefly thinking about what he is doing. Conscious 'theorizing' may be entirely absent. This is intelligent action, not theory.

Suppose, however, the teacher is also a student and is working under the supervision of a tutor; after the lesson perhaps he will discuss it with the tutor and they will have a conversation about what was right or wrong with the teaching. They are theorizing, at a very practical level, and with a view to improving teaching. Or, a little later on, the student may discuss the 'practical problems' of the aims and methods of teaching a subject which may lead, in a quite smooth transition, to a discussion of the nature of the subject and perhaps of some of the general aims of education. Or some question may arise about difficulties which the teacher experienced during the lesson through some inadequacy of social or psychological understanding. This might easily lead to some development of social or psychological ideas. It can be seen at once that a good deal of this talk, this theorizing, will be immediately and directly practical, concerned with how to do something and how to alter things in the future.

These practical theorizings with the tutor are very much *ad hoc*. Only those parts of theory which are immediately useful are, so far, being discussed. All this may be interesting, but it is scrappy. Yet such discussions inevitably open up the way for more detached, general and systematic study of various theoretical aspects of education: scientific (such as the psychological and sociological), philosophical and perhaps historical. These can be interesting as studies in themselves and can all be included in the omnibus term, 'theory of education'. 'Theory of education' is then, so far, like Joseph's coat, of many colours.

How these various studies are related to one another is a knotty question, and an interesting one. Is there just a number of studies, related somehow? Is the 'theory of education' just the sum of these? Or is there something more, 'the' theory of education? Is the right question, 'Who *are* the educational theorists?' or, 'Who *is* the educational theorist?' These are intriguing questions. Let me postpone them for the time being, and return for a moment to the problems of the student teacher, exploring theory of education.

Suppose the student of teaching to be detaching himself sufficiently from the immediate needs of active teaching to study different theoretic studies of education more systematically. There will arise, before long, a fresh challenge to understand, theoretically and intellectually, the relationship back to practical teaching. The first rather scrappy reflections which I mentioned, arising out of the practice of teaching, are so intimately related to the practice from which they arose that their application back to practice is obvious. But, if one goes far in trying systematically to study philosophy, or psychology, of education, one may get such a long way from immediate practical necessities that some quite conscious thinking back about the relation to practice may have to be done. This raises interesting and difficult questions to which I shall return. In the meantime, we should look a bit more carefully at the problems at the root of the very idea of 'educational theory'. What does the term mean?

Is 'educational theory' just a plurality of theorizings related to educational needs, or is there some synthesis of them, called 'educational theory'? If there is simply a plurality of theorizings, then there will be a plurality of educational theorists: the psychological educational theorist, the sociological, and so on. If there is one, synthetic discipline called 'educational theory', then there is a special kind of animal, the 'educational theorist' who takes all he can get from the others and puts them together as far as he can in a single system. If there is *not* one synthetic theory, there will be psychologists with an educational theory, sociologists with another, and so on: and they may, if in compartments like this, contradict or in other ways conflict with one another. This will hardly do, it seems. Yet, if there is the other animal, the educational theorist in general, he will have a very broad and difficult job to do. It will be very difficult to be sufficiently competent all-round, and we shall be apt to hear all the usual criticisms of educational theory being an amateurish rigmarole. Either way there are difficulties, either of limited specialist-theories of education, perhaps conflicting, or of amateurism.

It may be said that there is another answer: that 'educational theory' is not the prerogative of any one person, specialist or generalist, but that it is a social phenomenon. The unity of educational theory, it may be said, is not the possession of one individual mind but is something which—at least in some degree—comes into being only through the conversation together of the different experts who have the care for education as a common concern. It is the social product of conference—not necessarily *a* conference—of the meeting of minds. I believe this to be of central importance, and to be a vital part of the truth. Yet although it is a part of the truth, it does not solve the problem, since there is (or so I should say) no group mind apart from or over and above the distinct minds in concourse. What happens through the conversations and conferences must be embodied in the enriched individual minds who have participated in the conversations.

If this is granted, does one then delegate the development of educational theory to the now socially fed and enriched individual minds of the psychologist, sociologist, the more practically oriented tutor, the reflecting teacher? I think that up to a point one must: the psychologist (for instance) who has listened to and learnt from conversations with the sociologist, the tutor of the teacher in the classroom, the practical teacher himself—will far better be able to think and say his say about educational theory than without it, and will tend to say it in a more guarded, wiser, catholic way. Indeed, without this he will be speaking as specialist only. This is 'educational theory' in the sense of inter-disciplinary thinking.

But there is 'educational theory' in another sense: philosophical theory of education. I believe that it is above all upon the philosopher of education that the special responsibility of thinking critically and 'globally' about theory of education must rest. Let us call this global thinking '*general* theory of education'. Assuming, as I am, that the philosopher has taken the fullest opportunities for learning from the special contributions to education of the experts in theory and in practical teaching, he can, by reason of his vocation, training and outlook, make contributions of a special philosophical sort to educational theory, 'general theory of education'.

So (summing this part up), I would say that better 'educational theory', in its *interdisciplinary* aspect, can only emerge through real communication between experts in the different parts of the educational field; and that all the experts will learn from this, and will teach the better. And it is no contradiction to say further that the philosopher's training in general thinking, in the critical examination of assumptions, in the thinking together of different modes of understanding, gives him a special qualification to think relatedly about the field of education, to construct all-over *general* theory of education.

This bears on the question: 'Is the study of education a "discipline"?' I have in mind that the allegation that it is *not* a discipline is sometimes used as an attack on education as a proper subject of academic study.

What is a 'discipline'? A systematic *body* of knowledge? Mathematics and science are bodies of knowledge; so, perhaps, with reservations, is history. But is the study of literature a body of knowledge? Is philosophy itself? It is doubtful, or more than doubtful. Yet these are all acknowledged disciplines. So a 'discipline' cannot be defined as a body of knowledge, since there are acknowledged disciplines which are not bodies of knowledge.

## Philosophy and the Theory and Practice of Education

Perhaps a 'discipline' is a discipline of *thinking*, or of *experience*? This may be true, but it is not always easy to define or to agree about. There are many obscurities about the nature of the 'discipline' of scientific enquiry, as there are, too, of historical enquiry. Each employs a number of thinking activities—observation (or, in the case of history, investigation of documents), analysis, inference, synthesis, imagination. 'The' disciplines of thinking are complex, often obscurely understood compounds. This is even more true of the study of literature, and it is certainly true of philosophy.

Nor, again, can it be said that a discipline applies to a *single* field of enquiry—for we know that there are a number of compound disciplines in science, bio-chemistry for example.

Theory of education, therefore, cannot be condemned outright because it is not a systematic *body* of knowledge nor a *simple* recognizable discipline of thinking, or because it has no *single* field. But we have seen that 'theory' is ambiguous. If we mean 'interdisciplinary' thinking, then its status *vis-à-vis* discipline is self-evident: it is interdisciplinary. If we are thinking of the *general* theory of education, I have suggested that this thinking is, admittedly, 'a' discipline, a philosophical one. Philosophical theory is varied enough, but it certainly *has* a discipline of its own.

### 'PHILOSOPHY'

Perhaps, now, it would be well, since the term 'philosophy' is being used, to say what I mean by it—not that I pretend that I have anything whatever original to say, but because contemporary philosophers do make varying assumptions about its nature and functions, and it is desirable to avoid misunderstanding.

Philosophy includes digging up and criticizing one's assumptions, one's experiences and one's judgments in all the main fields of human enterprise. Traditionally, for example, philosophy has examined the assumptions underlying the sciences, assumptions which are not in themselves the subject of scientific scrutiny. All this involves an examination of ideas and of the language (and languages) in which they are expressed, scrutinizing for ambiguity, exploring meanings. These things are included, broadly speaking, in the work of critical *analysis*. This analysis, we all know, has been greatly stressed in recent times. Now analysis (as I have been saying) is a fascinating occupation for the individual and a necessary and legitimate part of philosophical culture. But it is a part only. It is not an adequate lifetime occupation, and a culture wholly devoted to analysis would be decadent. The proper function of analysis is the better understanding of the wholes which are analysed; it is servant and not master. And analysis itself is strictly impossible without implicit relating: if it entirely loses the sense of the whole it ceases even to be intelligent analysis. Analysis is, in fact, one moment, one emphasis, in the strictly indivisible life of philosophy; synthesis is the other moment. Some philosophers are, legitimately, more interested in one side than the other, but each is a member of the other for the benefit of the whole 'organism' of philosophy. If synthesis without analysis is empty, or at least muddled, so analysis without synthesis is blind, or at least pointless or feckless.

Synthesis, construction, speculation, have, we know, been much played down of late. Metaphysics in particular was loudly pronounced to be dead, though it wouldn't lie down. It cannot be denied that some of the metaphysics attacked deserved it, though a good deal of criticism published did not reveal evidence of the careful study in depth of the subject-matter which good criticism presupposes. However that may be, it has always been, and remains (or so it seems to me), a major obligation of philosophy to try to relate; to attempt, however imperfectly and partially, to think together as systematically as possible the carefully analysed contributions from different fields of knowledge and experience—including experience of value as well as of fact—in their bearing upon the understanding of common experience. Philosophy, although of course it uses abstractions, is, and should remain, *concrete* in the etymological sense of thinking things together. This is a traditional view of philosophy, which I hold to be true. It is very difficult to do philosophy in this way—much more difficult than simply to analyse, and more frustrating, because the task is too large for human beings ever to accomplish with any high degree of accuracy, clarity or completeness. Unity is an impossible ideal. And yet the philosopher has to grope towards it as well as he can.

Two observations may be made in the light of this account of philosophy:

(1) Partly because of the tremendous developments of science, some philosophers deny that it is any longer the place of philosophy to make statements about the world. Truths about the world are a matter for empirical science; the job of philosophy (as in part we

have been saying) is the analysis of the meaning of statements. But why should it be assumed that 'statements about the world' must be of one kind only—the scientific kind? If the 'thinking together' account of philosophy is at all true, there is no reason why philosophy should not help to build up fresh perspectives of relationships within the world, fresh understanding of the connections between things not discerned by unreflective common sense. To the degree in which they were true, statements expressing such perspectives and connections would be 'statements about the world', though not of a scientific kind. We all know, of course, that the question of the verification of such statements is much in question. But we surely equally know nowadays that it is naïve to think that the scientific is the only sort of testing of statements.

(All this could have a bearing upon the possible function of philosophy of education in giving fresh perspectives about 'the world' of education.)

(2) In the realm of ethics too, though not wholly for the same reasons, it is frequently denied that the philosopher as such can have anything particular to say about the 'world' of moral conduct, with its values. The philosopher, it is said, has no special competence in his opinions or judgments about what is morally good and bad, right and wrong. His business, *qua* moral philosopher, is not to state moral truths, but to analyse the meaning of moral statements.

As before, we can agree entirely that analysis of the meaning of statements is part of his job, and a central part. Yet the negativism, the separation, is completely artificial and untenable, and if pursued consistently would reduce ethics to a trifling game which would scarcely even be ethics. For, however important the analysis of ethical statements, genuine ethical statements express moral judgments, and moral judgments in turn arise out of, and are only meaningful in relation to, moral experience. This, in a way, is quite trite and obvious. It may be said that the moral philosopher can be assumed, like everybody else, to be involved in moral relationships and in the making of moral judgments in his everyday life, and that this can be taken for granted when he is devoting himself, as philosopher, to the analysis of moral statements. This may appear to be true, but it is very superficial. It appears to be true in the very obvious cases of moral statements such as those about telling the truth, keeping promises, etc., where moral validity is simple and familiar, taken for granted, and of minimum philosophical interest.

But even here, of course, the moral statements are meaningless except in relation to the familiar concrete human situations out of which the judgments arise.

But where the human relations are complex and subtle, or where there are deep and perplexing conflicts—such as those which are familiar in great drama, or in the painful dilemmas of life—the moral judgments and statements which arise out of them cannot be intelligently analysed without deep, sensitive participation, actual and imaginative, in the concrete situations out of which the judgments arise. No philosopher could competently analyse moral statements, say, about mercy killing (what, for instance, it might be right to do about an unborn baby whose mother had taken the drug thalidomide), without a sympathetic, imaginative entry into the whole agonising situation. If the philosopher did not, at least vicariously, feel the conflict and devote every ounce of his imaginative thinking to the understanding of it, his analysis would be worthless and incompetent; he would not *know* what he was talking about.

Contrariwise, if he does know what he is talking about, and as a human being has a concern for it, his 'second order' critical anlysis of 'first order' moral judgments may well affect the structure of those judgments, and compel a revision of them. The philosopher as a man can have something to contribute to moral understanding which the less reflective man has not. He can have something to say about the 'world' of moral conduct.

(This could have an important bearing on the function of philosophy of education. Significant thinking about educational values (*a*) is dependent upon concrete educational experience, and (*b*) such thinking can throw light upon educational practice.)

### 'PHILOSOPHY OF EDUCATION'

So much for philosophy as such. Now let us turn to 'philosophy of education'. Philosophy of education will be the use of philosophical instruments, the application of philosophical methods, to questions of education, as well as the relation to education of the relevant results of philosophical thinking. In this statement I am, of course, including both the more analytic emphases of philosophy (with linguistics) and the synthetic ones. This is 'philosophy of education'. '*A* philosophy of education' will be a more worked out, systematic philosophical treatment of those aspects of educational theory which are susceptible to philosophical treatment.

How is philosophy of education related to other parts of theory of education, and to practice of education?

We have to emphasize in the first place that philosophy is an intellectual, theoretic activity, following its own disciplinary rules, and not in itself a practical, and in particular, a reforming one. This is true also of philosophy of education as a form of philosophy. It can and must be pursued for its own intrinsic intellectual interest, and not because one is thinking always of the reform of education. On the other hand, it is not only natural, but I think essential, that the *man* who philosophizes about education should be a person who cares intensely about the practice and improvement of education. *Qua* one part of himself, he has got to be in a sense detached and contemplative; *qua* another part of himself he ought, I am quite certain, to be a man with a passionate concern for education. If he does not possess the passionate concern, he is unlikely to be interested enough to be informed from the inside to know what teachers who do care are doing and thinking about; he is unlikely to understand what the living problems of education are. He is, therefore, the less likely to think and talk to the educational point. The good philosopher of education isn't just 'applying' patterns of philosophy (idealism, realism and so forth) to education. Nor is he just playing an interesting intellectual game; he is thinking of matters of great human importance, and if his thoughts are to have any influence at all upon teaching, he must have first-hand knowledge and experience, supplemented by sympathetic, imaginative entry into others' experience, of what he is talking about. I repeat that philosophy is, in the end, about life, and not only about reported statements concerning life, and that one must live richly in order to think and talk sense. This applies, *a fortiori*, to philosophy of education.

It is not, admittedly, an easy balance to keep. The passionate reformers are often so near to the immediate that their thought lacks clarity and balance, and they are often insufficiently trained to think philosophically. (This is true of many historical writers on education.) On the other hand, the great danger of importing pure philosophers into education is that they may be so very pure that they don't know what are the important things to talk about. My point is quite simple; I am urging that the man who is the philosopher of education must give himself, must submit, to everything he can learn from educationists of every kind, theoretical and practical. He must possess humility; he must be ready to open his preconceived ideas to the impact of educational experience and ideas at every level. If he does not, he may talk cleverly, but not to the point.

I have been stressing, in recent pages, the need for the good philosopher, and hence the philosopher of education, to be sensitively and constantly aware of the complexity of the concrete human *experience* which is (I think) the prime material out of which the important questions arise. If I have laboured the point it is because I think that the quite valid contention that philosophy is nowadays a highly professional business sometimes obscures the dependence of at least some parts of philosophy upon refined human sympathy and understanding. But I have also stressed, at the beginning of this paper, the inseparability, particularly in educational matters, of theory at all levels from experience. So the need for the philosopher of education to be in touch with experience includes the need to be aware of educational theory of different kinds.

## PHILOSOPHY OF EDUCATION AND EDUCATIONAL PRACTICE

Having said something about the place of philosophy of education in educational theory, I now turn to some questions of the relation of philosophy of education to the practice of education.

First, a word about the place, and limits, of deduction in educational thinking. Sometimes it is said that normative principles in educational theory can be deduced from normative principles which emerge from a general philosophy. Thus, from a Neo-Thomist position like Maritain's, which affirms certain views about the nature of knowledge, of man, of the hierarchy of values, it is said that we can deduce rules for a policy of education. (I may observe here that I do not think that Maritain himself would put it in this simple way.) Exactly the same could be said of deduction from other philosophical positions.

Now deduction may sometimes be an element in a total pattern of thinking, and there is no reason why it should not—though the deductive form does not seem to me to matter very much here. If a general philosophical position affirms that religion is important (or unimportant, perhaps superstitious), one can make deductions that it should play such and such a part in education. This is in one way legitimate, but it is in another way dangerous. It is legitimate and right in that, if anyone holds fundamental beliefs of whatever kind, which are in any way relevant to education, integrity demands that his beliefs should enter in an important way into his educational thinking.

But the operative phrase is 'enter in an important way'. We do not (or should not) deduce *a priori* from philosophy, exact and adequate rules for a policy of education. Belief (sometimes grounded in philosophy) *enters* in an important way into the whole complexity of educational thought and experience, and it gives some general maxims. But what comes out at the other end in a particular practical policy is not just a logical deduction (though it may contain some passages of deduction) but an educational *judgment*, a principled decision, made in the light of the fullest possible consideration of all the relevant factors in the individual educational situation.

The whole business of educational judgment can indeed be distorted by the logician's obsession with deduction. The psychology of 'sets' and 'dispositions' can here be much more relevant than logic. We come to educational thinking and action with beliefs which (*inter alia*) are dispositions to pay more attention to some things—to what is believed to be important—than to others. Thought is shaped, and grows, in a living context of value-feelings and judgments; and the end-product, the educational judgment, is really much more the outcome of what I may perhaps be allowed to call 'sensitive principled global thinking' than of cold logic. I am not being in the least anti-rational or irrationalist in saying this. But the best educational judgments come, I think, when a person of principle can keep his principles and can come to the educational field (if I may repeat) ready to learn from the ripest educational wisdom, both theoretic and practical, of all the others. He lets his own principled, structured mind ruminate, and so discovers his own answer.

There is a good deal of confusion about the application of educational theory to practice.

It is quite clear that in one sense theories can be put into practice, or can be 'applied'; rules can be derived from theories which guide action. Psychological knowledge about memory can yield rules about how to space learning; knowledge of the mental development of children can guide us to giving them the help they need at different ages, or as to the presenting to them of abstract ideas. Or philosophical distinctions, say about freedom and discipline, can help us to avoid confusion of purpose in the classroom and to clarify our purposes. All this and other understanding can be built into habits which become part of the daily routine of an experienced teacher.

But when all this is said, the phrase 'application of theory to practice' (or the application of rules derived from theory, to practice) can be very misleading if it is thought that intelligently learning how to teach is simply identical with applying theory to practice, or with applying rules intelligently. (And some philosophers do talk as if this were all there is to it.) Apart from many routine actions, there are daily arising new and individual situations which require decisions, and decisions which are more than the application of rules. To talk too much of the 'application of rules' is to be too intellectual about it. Teaching, although not to be simply identified with art, is a kind of art, and its relation to theory and rules are somewhat similar to those in art. The artist who has gone through a systematic art training has plenty of theory and plenty of rules at his disposal, and has probably done plenty of exercises. All of them, when he is trained, have, so to speak, 'got into his system', so that in a sense he is 'applying' them all the time. Yet (supposing he is a painter) it is not true to say when he is working creatively on a fresh picture that his action *is* rule-behaviour, behaviour which is adequate because conforming to rules. Rules are admittedly being to some extent carried out; but his painting is not good, as art, merely because it conforms to rules; rather the rule-conforming, in so far as it takes place, is assimilated into a different kind of action, his artistic construction of *this* individual picture, which is quite new, and does not derive its artistic merit from its conformity to any rules whatever (though, I repeat, it may conform to some rules). In a somewhat similar way, the good teacher, with all his theory and training (so necessary and important), has to do more than 'apply', through the use of rules, his general theory to his practice. He has to come, with his assimilated rules, to individual classroom situations, and take decisions which are fresh and individual, practical and not applied-theoretical, more like artistic intuition than rule-behaviour. He can only discover how to do this by doing it. And, if this is true of the 'application' of scientific (e.g. psychological) theory to education, it is more deeply true of the 'application' of philosophical beliefs to the work of teaching and education. Because of all this, one can't automatically blame—as is often done—theoretical training of teachers as useless or irrelevant because some theoretically instructed teachers are bad teachers. It may not be the 'theory' which is wrong, but the failure to assimilate it personally into artistry.

This is one aspect of the problem of 'putting theory into practice'. I have been saying that if you want to put a theory 'into practice' as we often do in education, it is not enough to deduce rules and act on them; practice involves a fresh and quite often an original sort of decision.

But there are special difficulties in putting the theory which is philosophy (as opposed to the theory which is science) into practice. There may seem to be a very wide chasm between philosophy and practice, and for a number of reasons:

(1) Philosophy does not appear to have, in any convincing way, the clear relation to the everyday world of common experience which even the purest science seems to possess. Though some part of theoretical physics, for instance, are remote indeed from the understanding of common sense, science is always ultimately related to the common world through observation and experiment. But there is no experimental philosophy (in the non-archaic sense of the word 'philosophy'). Still less is there anything analogous to scientific technology; there is no philosophical technology.

(2) Again, questions of philosophy, although they can and must to some extent be isolated and dealt with one at a time, tend to become entangled with one another in a disconcerting way. Thus philosophical discussion of questions seemingly relevant to education —such as those of values in education, freedom, discipline, the kinds of knowledge one wants to impart—quickly leads us into many difficult theoretical problems all mixed up with one another. A student of education may quite naturally say, 'What's this all about? Where is it leading?' Furthermore, even if the diffuseness be accepted and the entangling enquiries be pursued, the tentative answers (if any) possess a systematic complexity which is in very sharp contrast to, say, some of the findings of scientific psychology relevant to education. And the more fundamental the general philosophical questions are, the more tenuous their relation to particular practice may seem.

Some philosophical questions there are which are certainly not of interest to teachers or educationists as such, and they need not be discussed. However, all questions which seem to be remote at first sight are not necessarily irrelevant. For example, the problem of the relativity of morals, discussed at any deep level, takes us far into difficult ethics. Yet it has important practical bearings. Unreflective assumptions (met with every day) that 'all morals are relative' directly involve the view that practical moral education is induction into social morals. A critical intellectual revision of 'relativity' can radically affect a policy of educational practice. The same could be said of theories of knowledge, of freedom, of discipline. Philosophical discussions of these can lead us into problems, some of which seem to have no direct relationship to practice; yet deeper understanding can be importantly relevant, potentially transforming the practice of education from a confused and complacent muddle to intelligent and enlightened action. It is important that the student of education should be made aware of all this, seeing and thinking it for himself, not simply learning and repeating it from books and lectures. His thinking will not give him all the answers; it may drive him into greater puzzlement. But he is at least alive and ongoing and, other things being equal, is more likely to be a stimulating teacher.

All this assumes that the teacher really does want, and will, his theory to affect his practice for the better. Very often this assumption is well justified, particularly when the 'theory' is scientific. A good, keen, intelligent teacher both wants to understand more about learning and motivation and the mental development of children, and to translate it into practice, just as a lively intelligent doctor wants to understand the scientific basis of his art in order to help his treatment of patients. His learning, his feeling, and his will all point in the same direction. There is no conflict of will or feeling, no yawning chasm between theory and practice—provided the teacher or doctor are reasonably intelligent and of good will.

(3) But between convictions philosophically grounded and relevant to education, and the practice of education, there may be a gap or an obstacle, of an emotional and dispositional kind. It is very familiar.

The teacher, after philosophical study, may have acquired clear and mature ideas of the nature of discipline, freedom, knowledge, the nature of teaching. Yet there may be blocks in himself which impede his ability to express them in his practice as a teacher. Because of personal insecurity, he may over-assert his authority; this will conflict with the freedom and growth of his pupils, the importance of which (we are assuming) is well understood by him. Or he may be simply selfish, or lazy, yielding to the temptation not to do what he perfectly well knows he ought. Or through fear he may do far too much for his pupils, not allowing them to make their own mistakes. He may keep them immature by over-insisting on rules instead of helping them to discover their own reasons for their decisions.

The general bearing of all this is that such benefits as the study of philosophy may bring to the teacher in practice must depend upon its being a part of his total growth, its being assimilated into his character and personality. I cannot at this stage possibly develop this idea; it is discussed at some length in my book *Philosophy and Education.*[1] Such typical critical comments as 'The notion that the resolution of educational problems depends upon one's theory of reality is largely academic' or that 'an appeal to everyday purposes and facts is usually sufficient and where it is not it is highly doubtful whether philosophical considerations will have much effect'—such comments beg an important question by simply assuming that philosophical thinking is being done in a compartment, is a function of a fragmented something called the intellect. We all know that it can be so; but if it is we can only expect that practical effects will be at a minimum, though it would be rash to assert that they must be *nil*. If the thinking is to be of this fragmented kind, certainly the study of philosophy of education should be cut out of a crowded course of teacher 'training' as almost useless lumber.

But a less unenlightened view of a professional course is that it is a special kind of personal *education*, and not merely a training in performance (as though student teachers were superior rats, cats or dogs). If the aim of a professional course is indeed a total reorientation of the person of the student towards education and teaching, with adequate emphasis on serious commitment, moral responsibility, development of the 'art' of teaching, as well as the development of scientific and philosophical understanding, and if this last is really integral to all the rest, then there is good reason for saying that better intellectual (and in particular, philosophical) understanding can, and will, so alter a person's perspective that as a teacher he will act with more insight and more intelligence. It does not (once again) mean that, philosophically, he will come with any blueprint for action. Indeed, it may be freely admitted that depth of thinking may sometimes increase his perplexities. He will certainly be less cocksure than his colleagues, the insistence of whose claim to be practical sometimes seems to be proportional to their contempt for reflective thinking. Yet will not the teacher whose thinking is vital and ongoing, who himself has some sense of life's depths and continuing complexities, be a more stimulating and a wiser guide to pupils who are growing up in a difficult world where ready made answers are of less and less use?

### THE ASSESSMENT OF THE BENEFITS OF PHILOSOPHY OF EDUCATION

I return now to an earlier objection: that the claim that the study of philosophy of education is of benefit to practical teachers cannot be proved scientifically. Philosophical ideas, it was suggested, are not always easily related to specific practice. This is perfectly true; it can now better be assessed in the context of what has been said.

Claimed benefits could not be scientifically assessed—though scientific methods might have some minor part to play in an investigation into them. The assessment could not be finally scientific, because any generalization (say) that study of philosophy of education is in a significant number of cases practically beneficial to the teacher would have to be based on a number of highly individual investigations, each shot through and through with value-judgments. Before he could make any statement in any case about whether 'philosophy' had been beneficial, the investigator would have to know the person who taught it, what was taught, and how, the extent and depth of reading, the amount and kind of discussion, the pupil's fellow-students and their influence, how the pupil himself had studied and assimilated it, how intelligent and thorough he had been. Without all this—and a good deal more—any statement about the impact of 'philosophy' would be quite meaningless. (It would just be making verbal 'bah' noises to assert that study of philosophy has NO beneficial practical results if the speaker did not know what 'study' meant in this or that case.) In addition to all this, there would have to be an equally exhaustive analysis of the 'benefits' (again involving value judgments at every point and a complete systematic view of 'good education'), as well as of their causal connection with the study of philosophy. And since if I am right any beneficial effects would be integral with the impact of the teacher as a whole person upon his pupils, the judgment of benefit would be inseparable from a global or total one, as opposed to the highly specific, abstracted, partial, observable data of science. 'Benefits' could not be isolable observed items related deductively to specific parts of a course in training. And if all this is true of individual cases, it means that general statements of benefit or otherwise are so vague as to be worse than useless. You simply cannot say generally, in any scientific way, 'Study of philosophy has such and such specific effects upon teaching', still less, 'Philosophy is good (or no good) for teachers.'

Does this prove too much? Does it imply that nothing responsible, particular or general, can ever be said of the effects of benefits or otherwise of philosophical study for the teacher? It does not. The logic of reputable statements in this field is a fascinating and complex one, and I can only touch upon it in my concluding paragraphs.[2]

I am certainly not saying that nothing sensible can be said about the claimed effects and benefits of the study of philosophy of education for the teacher, though what is said is not of a 'scientific' character. What I am affirming is that the bases of any generalisation are radically individual, total judgments, made in a manner which is not scientific. This implies that if one were to say of a group of teachers who had studied philosophy of education that (say) 'they teach the better for it', one would be talking about a number of individual cases, each individually 'case-studied' intensively and extensively in the way described above. The general statement would be about a group of individuals each complex and individually different (and not instances of a universal with simple common characteristics).

The statement 'They have all studied philosophy of education and teach the better for it' is of course thoroughly vague. It makes a *propter hoc* claim; but even the *post hoc* element is undefined; *what* is 'better'? Again, better than what? Better than the teaching *those* teachers would have done if they had not studied philosophy? Or better than *other* teachers who have not so studied? And how do we know that the claimed betterness is *due* to the study of philosophy, or that less good teaching is due to the lack of the previous study of philosophy?

None of these questions can be answered with the kind of precision which science claims and demands. Nevertheless, one may investigate them, and tentatively answer them, in ways which are both reputable and rational, though not scientific. (And why should

35

we so often assume that the scientific method is the only model of rational enquiry? Aristotle long ago saw through that.) These ways are the ways of questioning and self-questioning, by honest, critical, intelligent experienced teachers and other educationists, carried out always within the framework of a system of sound educational values. 'Sound educational values' may seem to beg the question, but does not, since any rational testing and revision of values must start from *within* a system of beliefs about values. We graduate to more objective thinking about values but never to a completely impersonal and detached knowledge of them. There are no wholly impersonal judgments of value, however objective.[3]

From within this framework there can be rational judgments as to *what* is the 'betterment' claimed for the influence of philosophical study. Experienced teachers who have studied philosophy in their maturer professional years can to some extent assess changes in their own teaching and relate it to their philosophical development —perhaps aided in their assessment by an experienced interviewer. (One may say, 'I used to think of "discipline" in such and such a muddled way which I now see to be wrong; my actions have changed accordingly.') Comparisons between teachers with, and without, 'philosophy' are more difficult, but not impossible in some degree—provided the investigation is individual, analytic, and honestly and carefully carried out. Finally, the question whether any improvement is or is not *propter hoc* is not insusceptible of being explored in the same careful, individual analytic way.

The results of such careful investigations, though not complete or scientific, are certainly not to be dismissed as mere 'hunches'. They are in their own way reasoned. Value-judgments of this kind—call them 'critically intuitive' if you like—are, I believe, and will continue to be, of major importance in matters of education. The enormous and important development of scientific methods in educational research should not allow us to depreciate them. At their best, they are, or so I should say, more trustworthy than *some* of the research results which are given scientific *cachet*.

I need hardly add, in conclusion, that I do believe that the study of philosophy of education can be, when truly integrated into a teacher's total professional education, of great value to him as a teacher; I believe that there is 'evidence' (of the appropriate sort) which does indicate it, and I know of none against it. I believe this, and have reasons for believing it, though I cannot 'prove' it.

## NOTES

1. L. A. Reid, *Philosophy and Education* (London: Heinemann, 1962), Chap. 6.
2. I have written something bearing on it in the chapter of *Philosophy of Education* [*op. cit.*] entitled 'The justification of judgments of value'.
3. 'Sound educational values' are those for which philosophical reflection could find better rational grounds than for any others—though this does not, of course, imply that they are discovered in the first place by philosophical reflection. (See *op. cit.*, especially pp. 45–49 and pp. 57–65.)

# COMMON CONFUSIONS IN
# EDUCATIONAL THEORY

## Edward Best

STUDENTS in university departments of education study such topics as educational psychology, educational statistics, the history of education, comparative education, educational hygiene, etc., and for understandable economy of speech people have thrown a cordon around the lot and called it 'education'. Perhaps because this name is too vague, experts in England and elsewhere have devised the term 'educational theory' to distinguish those studies which have a more obvious bearing on the actual practice of teaching children.

Along with the growth of these special studies that form the core of teacher-training has spread the illusion that they comprise a unified body of expert knowledge by means of which problems of education can be appropriately tackled and solved. This illusion has been cherished most, perhaps, among those school teachers who so often tell us that the skill of teaching rests upon a precise and expert knowledge akin to that of the dentist, and that without this knowledge one cannot teach properly. In fact, the untrained teacher—that is, someone who lacks this knowledge—is to be compared with a quack, except that whereas the one merely causes physical mishap, the other plays havoc more seriously with the child's mind.

Many examples can be cited to show that the word 'theory' is used in several different ways. Perhaps the widest difference in the use of the word is seen when we contrast the terms 'physical theory' and 'educational theory'. The problem of the status of any theory is one that can hardly be treated competently in a few lines. It can be shown fairly easily, however, that the presentation of an *educational* theory must necessarily use a kind of language which would be quite out of place in any presentation of the other.

We can make this clearer by saying something first about a physical theory. A simple example will suffice. By the middle of the last century it was universally accepted that the behaviour of gases was to be accounted for by the existence of molecules. It was put forward by Clausius, therefore, that owing to chance collisions which are occurring with perfect elasticity at any instant, the molecules of a gas are moving with all velocities in all directions. From these premises it was deduced mathematically that the pressure of a gas is equal to one third of the average value of the square of the speed of the molecules multiplied by the density of the gas. The elementary theory of gases thus described may be expressed by a mathematical formula, from which the observable facts witnessed in the behaviour of gases may be deduced. Such a theory, as an empirically testable hypothesis, must stand or fall on whether statements which we deduce from it are true.

Now a mere glance at any of the historically famous educational theories will convince the reader that in certain critical respects the mode of address is quite different from anything to be found in text-books of physical science. For whatever linguistic subtleties lie hidden in the statement of a scientific theory it is obvious that its purpose can never be to advise or commend a course of action. On the other hand, it would be wholly impossible to give a faithful version of one of the well-known educational theories without implying advice or, in more general terms, a prescription. For instance, in writing *Some Thoughts Concerning Education* John Locke had as his aim the production of the Christian squire, the prototype of England's late 17th century gentry, and, however one appraises the logic involved, it was from this that he reached such prescriptive conclusions as these:

> The great thing to be minded about Education is what Habits you settle.
> Playing and childish actions are to be left perfectly free and unrestrained.

Now although lack of rigour may occur within an educational theory—as when, for instance, the writer invites us to infer a duty to act in a certain way from apparently descriptive premises, there is no lack of agreement that educational theories are meant to guide and advise teachers in their educational activities, and this is true whatever explanation we give of the language of advice. Unhappily, however, the educational theories whose language is obviously advisory and prescriptive can be contrasted with educational theories in which the advice mingles with the statements and even the theories of the particular sciences. Thus an educational writer in advocating a new method of teaching may account for the supposed result of his method by the psychological explanation known as the 'gestalt theory', so that he gives within one and the same account two disparate theories: a scientific theory, which we may assume to be empirically verifiable, and an educational theory, of which it makes no sense to talk of verifiability. One source of confusion to which we refer lies in the failure to disentangle these two senses of the word 'theory'.

### THE LANGUAGE OF EDUCATIONAL PSYCHOLOGY

Such confusion can be seen in the various attempts to define the purpose of educational psychology. For example, Charles E. Skinner maintains that the methods of this study are those of a science which investigates human behaviour under the social process of education; it 'centres' in the 'fundamental problem' of 'continuous growth and wholesome personality development'. We are told that the educational psychologist seeks to understand 'learning' (as a process?) and 'teaching' (as an activity?); he 'aims to aid the teacher' so that he may 'more effectively motivate and direct the learning and growth of children'; he aims to give 'guidance' in teaching. Yet its purpose must be contrasted with that of such speculations as the aim of education.[1] J. M. Stephens describes educational psychology as that which aims at understanding the phenomena of educational growth, just as social psychology aims at an understanding of social phenomena. But, again, its purpose is to help the teacher to 'discharge his responsibilities'. Even after the most exhaustive scientific scrutiny, however, there is much in education which is concerned with 'rights and values'.[2] G. M. Blair also speaks of educational psychology as helping the teacher to fulfil his 'obligations and tasks'.[3] The educational psychologist's task, writes R. S. Ellis, is like that of the engineer who merely indicates how we can get certain desired results; questions of what is worthwhile or what should be done are 'practical objectives' beyond the scope of educational psychology.[4] Yet, he maintains, psychological principles do have an important bearing on the objectives of teaching, since they indicate that some aims are practicable, or that 'certain aims are suitable for some age groups and not for others'. Thus, quoting from G. S. Counts he affirms the view that:[5]

> Democratic faith is sustained ... by the discipline of free men ... our goal in the disciplinary training of children is the development of socialised self-control by the individual.

And this in a handbook on a supposed science which is not concerned with educational aims!

W. W. Charters and H. L. Hollingworth are also amongst those who compare the educational psychologist to the engineer who seeks to produce results with maximum efficiency.[6] The aims of education are not the direct concern of the educational psychologist, yet, in speaking of the curriculum and of the 'principles of selection' involved, Hollingworth maintains that these decisions 'ought to be established on adequate psychological grounds'.[7] J. B. Stroud explains that the function of the educational psychologist is to supply theories of learning. Because he is familiar with 'genetic psychology and with classroom conditions' he is 'expected to acquaint the teacher with the facts of learning' and to give *advice concerning effective teaching and learning situations*.[8]

Perhaps one can discern the same underlying confusion of purpose in the perplexity which people display over the evident failure of educational psychologists to construct a stable syllabus. N. B. Cuff and others, raising the question of what should be included in educational psychology, have remarked that among the texts consulted two books only had as much as one third of their subject matter in common.[9] 'It is somewhat remarkable', writes one, 'that we never know when we open a book on educational psychology, what subject matter it is likely to contain'. Such a diversity of topics is 'entirely opposed to the uniformity that we have learned to expect in text-books in the physical sciences'.[10] Thus, if we extract a passage from a random selection of books on educational psychology, we might encounter such a sentence as this: 'The method by which skill of various kinds is attained will now claim our attention'.[11] Who made the momentous decision to include 'skill'?

W. A. Brownell, complaining that teaching and its results are no better after thirty years of educational psychology, suggests that teachers are not being taught from the right kind of syllabus. Accordingly he suggests a new approach: that the educational psychologist, instead of anticipating what the teacher wants, should enquire what the problems of teaching really are so that he can devise a procedure to suit this limited purpose.[12] R. S. Ellis, mentioned above, wrote his own educational psychology in compliance with this scheme. Presumably, therefore, he set out to describe a psychological theory that would explain how 'socialised self-control' develops. Hence, we may assume, he was satisfied that the criterion of such a theory is whether in fact a certain teaching method will bring about the development of socialised self-control. In short, he invites the reader to consider whether the sentence 'This method will bring about the development of self-control' is *true or false*.

The fact is that the vocabulary of such studies is systematically misleading since it leaves the reader ambiguously placed between an assent to what may or may not be true and an assent to what should or should not be done. We will now examine some of this vocabulary in greater detail. P. Sandford maintained that educational psychology depends upon the researches of those whose sole wish is to understand. The applied psychologist, he tells us, is interested in such topics as the 'avoidance of waste', etc., and the educational psychologist in such topics as the 'permanence of learning', and the 'best methods of bringing (emotional and instinctive responses) under social control'.[13] Such a word as 'interested' is used here to prescribe an attitude towards certain situations—one, for instance, in which there is no 'waste'. Superficially, of course, this use of 'interested' is the same as the use of 'interest' in the following passage taken from Sandford's book:

> The inheritance of these traits, their variability etc., are topics of interest to the experimental psychologist.

There is one important difference, however. Whereas one cannot but accept certain natural phenomena, one chooses to avoid waste, to make learning permanent, and to bring certain emotional and instinctive responses under social control. If we say that someone is interested in the avoidance of waste, we imply that he has made up his mind that the avoidance of waste is desirable, and that he is casting about for a means of achieving this end. On the other hand, if we say that someone is interested in the origin of a trait, we more usually imply that he has that sort of attraction towards a study which accounts for his taking it up rather than, say, conchology.

43

Modern usuage lends a slightly pejorative sense to 'trait', though the word normally denotes features of a kind which people are not called upon to change, and this seems to be the sense in the quotation. At least, there seems to be no significant difference in the meaning of 'interest' in these two sentences:

Smith is interested in the inheritance and variability of these traits;

and

Smith is interested in the formation and variability of proteins.

Smith's interest in birth-control, however, does not necessarily imply the same attitude as an interest in inherited traits or in the formation of proteins. There would be no waste if there were no users. What constitutes the difference then in the interest concerning waste and that concerning traits is the linguistic sense of guiding our actions, which is present in one case, but absent (or only ambiguously present) in the other. Whatever the word 'waste' may refer to materially, we recognise a linguistic use which tells us that it is something to be avoided. Also, whatever describable result is denoted by the phrase 'social control' we accept that it may be used to commend this state of affairs. One can often get the right sense merely by considering the people to whom a sentence containing the word is addressed. If we say to a teacher 'This method will bring emotional and instinctive responses of children under social control', then, unless he doubts our sincerity, he will probably assume that we are putting forward 'social control' as a teaching aim, whatever else we may say about method.

The teacher will understand such phrases as 'economy of learning', 'permanence of learning' and 'social control' not as descriptions but as prescriptions of educational aims. The 'social control' which the educational psychologist predicts as the result of some practical, classroom procedure is no less an aim for the teacher who assents to use such a method than the aim which was openly prescribed by such a writer as Quintilian. Once the educational psychologist offers the findings of research as reasons why the teacher should do his job in one way rather than in some other, then it is assumed that there are certain aims. This is not to deny that one can study the way in which children learn, for instance, with no other object in view than the enlargement of our knowledge on such matters. Clearly one can study the process of learning with the same objectivity that one would study a sequence of chemical actions. Much research has been done on the process of learning, and for obvious reasons much of this information has been derived from the classroom. It is not difficult to conceive these and similar pieces of research as belonging to the field of some special science, and in this case no confusion is likely to arise through a request for verifiability. On the other hand (and for the same reasons that I. M. D. Little[14] gives in explaining why welfare economics cannot be developed without such terms as 'human happiness' among its presuppositions) it is logically impossible for educational psychology to develop without certain value-terms. For however much we deplore the presence of value-terms in any account that is meant only to describe, be it economics or psychology, we are bound to accept their presence in speech or writing the very purpose of which is to tell people what to do.

Before concluding this section let us look at two examples in one of which misunderstanding could arise through a confusion of two uses of speech. The following quotation occurs as an exercise in a well-known text-book on educational psychology:[15]

> Discuss the implications of Piaget's views on the development of reasoning in children for the teaching of arithmetic....

Now here the emphasis is almost entirely on this theory of the development of reasoning in children. If this theory is tenable then it may be shown to follow that, although young children readily learn the *names* of numbers, it is only by concrete manipulation that they grasp the more formal relationships. It may even follow that older methods of teaching will produce no results in children below a certain age. Let us assume that the statement deduced from the theory—the statement that 'method X produces result Y'—can be empirically verified. Allowing that some version of this is the implication of Piaget's views, we should hardly fail to understand the import of the quotation. And we should betray no misunderstanding even if we gave this as our response:

> One of the implications of Piaget's views...is that we should use method X for teaching arithmetic to children.

Generally, this use of '*should*' is confusedly ambiguous. In answer to the question, 'Why should I?', one might have been told, 'So that you will save time, a good thing'; and whether one should or shouldn't save time certainly could not be determined by any experimental procedure. Indeed, it would be meaningless to ask for verification. As it happens, however, the desirability of saving time can be taken for granted, so that we read 'should' in another sense. 'We should use method X...' is read as an idiom which simply informs us that method X produces result Y. Imperatives, for example, are often used in this way. 'To stop the train pull the chain' may mean no more than, 'Tension in the chain stops the train', which is prescriptively neutral.[16] But in what way are we to understand this statement?:

> One of the implications of the differentiation of abilities is that there should be a tripartite system of secondary education.

The last sentence could mean that since 'there is overwhelming evidence' (in children over eleven) 'for various specialised intellectual factors', then these factors can be made to develop by selective education. And this is empirically testable. It could also mean, however, that for reasons which lie outside the empirically verifiable sequence, such tripartite separation is desirable. The implication of differentiation of abilities is now that we should (i.e., ought to) have three kinds of schools for pupils over eleven. If these reasons are not given, however, the use of 'should' is incorrigibly ambiguous. As we have seen the expected role of educational theory is to prescribe what is desirable, but what is desirable cannot be tested by any kind of experimental investigation. This prescriptive rôle has been frequently attracted into that part of educational psychology which is concerned with the verification (or falsification) of a special range of theories, and the confusion which results is manifest in those linguistic forms whose use is ambiguous.

### THE LANGUAGE OF PHILOSOPHY OF EDUCATION

It may be said at once that the phrase 'philosophy of education' would be considered by most contemporary English-speaking philosophers to be very ill-chosen. This would hardly matter, of course, if it could be shown that a number of responsible people had agreed to use such a phrase in a technical sense of their own. One can only decide this by reading samples of writing called philosophy of education. If it should happen that the authors are trying to give answers to certain factual questions that cannot be answered by the other empirical methods of education, then one should be able to identify their methodological procedure. If, however, it would appear that they are asking such questions as 'What are the aims of education?', as though the answer can be given by some methodological procedure, then the reader can quite fairly ask whether any meaning can be ascribed to their professed claims. Thus, if the reader finds that these writers are purporting to supply a means of answering the second kind of question as though it were of the same *genre* as the first, then he can consider whether they are not confusing two different uses of language.

Educational writings abound in references to the use of philosophy to the teacher. Fichte once said that the art of education can never attain clarity without philosophy. Herbert Spencer maintained that true education is practicable only to a true philosopher; Giovanni Gentile, that the precise nature of education can be understood only by those acquainted with the subtle problems of philosophy; and lesser writers like B. H. Bode, that without some guiding philosophy in the determination of objectives, we get nowhere at all in education. Robert R. Rusk wrote:[17]

> There is...no worker whose practice is more affected by his philosophy than the teacher's; it behoves him, as he cannot avoid it, to secure as adequate a philosophy as he can command.
>
> The welcome interest recently manifested in the problem of the curriculum is at present arrested for want of a philosophical criterion. (Abridged.)

Now a careful perusal of modern texts in which the words 'philosophy' and 'education' are conjoined in the title will show that they nearly all make the same assumption, namely that the aims or purpose of education can be supplied by some sort of philosophical enquiry. J. S. Brubacher writes that the overall purpose of education, a synthesis of data from various sources, is the quest of educational philosophy; or, again, wholeness or unity of outlook is its legitimate aim:[18]

> Perhaps the faculty is in doubt whether to introduce some new... technique or cling to traditional procedures...philosophy considers its function to clarify various factors of experience involved, to reduce conflicts...by finding some larger common denominator of their differences.

Where educators are in doubt as to what course they should follow, the philosopher of education intervenes to put them on the right road:

(Educational philosophy) restores the continuity of the educative process by continuing the former process of education with a re-adaption.

How, then, is educational philosophy to set about this task? We read that some educationists have tried to determine aims from a historical analysis of social institutions, or from an analysis of contemporary life. Individuals in this group have made records of the errors and mistakes which the schools should aim to correct in their pupils. Others have tried to postulate educational aims from a psychological study of the original nature of man. But these, according to the author, are merely the normal procedures of social science, and are not what he has in mind. They describe what values are current in society, but they do not say what values should be preserved or changed; they say what is desired, but not what is desirable. It is only through philosophy, he writes, that one can determine the ends of education.[19] Accordingly he proposes a study of those educational philosophers who have claimed to be able to arrange educational values in some definite order.

In writing his very long book Professor Brubacher is by no means devoid of good, sound advice to the teacher, but however tolerant one's approach may be, and however painstakingly one reads through the relevant sections, there is no indication as to how these philosophers have arrived at such maxims as those mentioned by the author. In one case, the ultimate aim of education is said to be the pursuit of intellectual experience for its own sake; or, in another, the aims of education are said to be discernible in the results of the educative process itself. Yet, no matter how these aims are expressed —and many are, indeed, overt prescriptions[20]—it is obvious that they are *all* prescriptive forms of speech, even though this may be concealed by the grammatical idiom.

S. J. Curtis who is known chiefly for his excellent writing on the history of educational theories talks in much the same vein in *An Introduction to the Philosophy of Education*. If ever there was a time for a 'philosophy of education', he tells us, it is the present. One looks to philosophy to provide the teacher with the principles which will enable him to put his work on a sound basis.[21] True, there are differences in philosophy, but perhaps some synthesis may 'transcend' them. Could not this synthesis be the final purpose of education? Throughout the book are long digressions on various educational views characterised by such names as 'realism', 'idealism', 'pragmatism', etc., but for himself the author prefers an eclectic approach which he describes by the unusual simile of a tripod in which each leg represents one of the 'isms'. The careful reader may perhaps discover precisely what steps led the great philosophers of educational thought to those general conclusions which Dr. Curtis mentions as representing their schools. Without exception, however, their conclusions are all prescriptions, even though they are each prescribing a different thing. The ultimate aim is perfect organisation of life under one great purpose whose meaning is one great idea; we must deeply respect the pupil's personality; the teacher's task is to 'direct the pupil to foregather with himself and, in the chambers of his mind, find the truth which is there'; the fundamental 'factors' of education are freedom and authority; a point of fundamental importance is the function of the teacher in the matter of adjustment, the 'end and essence' of education; the part of the teacher is to furnish the environment which stimulates those responses which lead to desirable dispositions. Apart from such obviously prescriptive forms as 'we must...' and 'the teacher's task...', the prescriptive sense of each of these paraphrased conclusions is conveyed adequately by such phrases as 'the great purpose', 'adjustment' and 'desirable dispositions'. Even apparently indicative sentences, whose overt prescriptions are hidden by the author's intention to mention rather than to use, can be shown to have the same hortative sense:[22]

> ...in a personalist in distinction from a pragmatic philosophy of education, the teacher not only supplies the environment but is environment, not only modifies stimuli but is a stimulus...

It is evident from the subject-matter and treatment of topics in such books as these, that 'philosophy of education' shows no discernible difference from what others call 'educational theory'. A *philosophy* of education is only a theory of education masquerading under a fancy name, and one cannot but suspect that many of those who freely use this phrase mean only the educational theories of people with a historical reputation as philosophers. Thus whereas Plato, Aristotle, St. Augustine, St. Thomas Aquinas, Locke, Rousseau, Kant and Dewey wrote 'philosophies of education', lesser people like Vittorino, Vives, Sturm, Hartlib and Froebel were more inclined to write theories. Perhaps it is an unfair question to ask of such an author as L. A. Reid, who apparently sets out to give another interpretation to 'philosophy of education', what precisely he considers his rôle to be in such passages as this:[23]

> My plea in these chapters has been in effect that teachers ... should above all set themselves to discover for themselves a sense of the depth of living, which is the attaining of education. In so doing they may be able to open up the way for others to live, in place of the living death ... which seems ... the awful prospect for some. ...

He is dismayed by the mass conformity, the sense of futility, the boredom, the expressionless faces of the young, and he concludes by prescribing as above. But in what sense is this an *introduction* (or part of an introduction) to a philosophy of education?

Professor Reid tells us that philosophy of education is an application of the methods of philosophy to the problems of education;[24] which itself is highly ambiguous. For in what sense does this differ from the statement (expressed by C. L. Hull) that psychology is the application of the methods of statistical science to human behaviour? We know roughly what the methods of statistics are, but what are the *methods* of philosophy? Quoting with evident approval from the late Oxford philosopher, F. Waismann, the author disclaims that philosophy can yield proof in any demonstrative sense; but instead of considering the word *problem* as it pertains to educational theory, a course that might very well have produced some interesting results, he writes a charming mélange of ethical theory, practical advice, and sporadic allusions to education.

He asks whether there is one dominant 'principle' by which we can justify our educational acts as 'appropriate and right'. In saying that the recognition of 'ought to be', 'ought to do' and 'good' is that of adopting an attitude towards some action, and that the sense of judgments containing these words shows that they are not susceptible of proof as factual statements are, he skirts very near to saying something that ought to be said in education. Yet he returns to the worn-out phrases about the transformation of educational practice by philosophical thinking. One might expect, then, that the section entitled 'The Application of Philosophy to Education' would surely be the core of the book.

It is not enough, he writes, merely to voice the phrases and slogans of educational theory. The teacher must 'sweat them out for himself'. Philosophical thinking, we read, must be 'hard thinking', but more than that, it must be the activity of the *person*.

This is said to be the 'key of everything'. Thinking is that of a person who feels, values, and acts in every kind of way. Hard thinking makes the teacher what he would otherwise never become, for it subtly affects what he does for 'better or worse'. To think these educational ideas, without at the same time taking up one of those moral attitudes towards them, is impossible. But getting the disposition is not philosophy. Philosophy is all the hard thinking that jockeys the teacher into the appropriate attitude. Roughly stated, Professor Reid's point seems to be that by reflecting on the possible meaning of, say, equality of educational opportunity the teacher will eventually get an urge to do something about it.

The view that philosophy of education is the elucidation of, and, presumably, the defence of educational aims seems also to be the expressed opinion of those who prepare typewritten digests for university departmental courses. The course, writes one, 'rests on the assumption that any understanding of human beings and . . . of their education . . . must be in essence philosophical'. But even without much probing it is clear that the meaning of 'understanding' in this context, especially when its object is the training of human beings, is ambiguous. A physiologist may be said to understand the organic structure of human beings, and a psychologist their behaviour; similarly, an observer may be said to understand a system of education, in the sense that he knows why the teacher is using this or that particular method, or that he knows what descriptive qualities the teacher is trying to produce in his pupils. There is another obvious sense, however, in which the words 'to understand' form part of a judgment of approval. Thus to understand teenagers, for example, would generally mean to approve in a certain way of what these people were doing, and a similar evaluation is almost certainly the intended sense in the above quotation. To understand the education of children would generally mean to discern values which are among our reasons for educating them in one way rather than in some other. 'Understanding their education' could even mean the approval of the grounds for a unique system of education. The point would seem to be that these grounds can only be revealed through a special insight given by philosophy. This interpretation is borne out by those who say more explicitly that their course in the philosophy of education is to help students to use philosophical works as a means of extending and deepening their insights into people and of making their educational perceptions more subtle. But what meaning can be given to such a phrase as 'educational perception' except some kind of recognition of how people ought to be educated?

What seems to be a matter of importance is that the discernment should be of the right kind. Thus the promoters of this course of 'philosophy of education' would avoid lecturers with 'strong behaviouristic and positivist leanings', because this would oppose the 'essential purpose which dignifies all true education'—the purpose of 'transforming circumstances by free and rational choice'.

It would appear then that 'the prime purpose of the study of (the philosophy) of education . . . is to enlighten students in the ways in which free, rational and responsible choices are made . . . to encourage awareness of this essentially human power'? The student, it is said, will thereby increase his 'capacity' for 'rational and discerning interpretation' of such words as humanity and freedom as they are used by the greatest minds. Here, we are told, philosophy of education, if 'properly conducted' will have its 'most immediately and profoundly practical' effect. Professor L. A. Reid writes virtually the same thing when he assures us that Departments of Education and Training Colleges (in capitals) would not appoint people to teach the philosophy of education if they did not hold the accepted values of British education. Of course the departments and colleges have the right to appoint only those they want as *persons*, but what relevance can this have to the function of the philosopher whose job is no more to insinuate educational aims than the chemist's?

The elucidation of educational aims is not, and never has been, the appointed task of the philosopher. That such aims have been voiced by philosophers from time to time is purely accidental. The most influential educational aims have been put forward by all sorts and conditions of men, Colet and Rosmini were clerics; Francis Bacon was a statesman; Cassiodorus, first an official of the Gothic régime, was finally a monk; Quintilian, Vittorino, and Pestalozzi were, each in his own way, famous teachers. Some were indeed philosophers too, but it would be absurd to suppose that their educational aims derived from a special philosophical expertise of which they were masters.

The educational writings of John Locke, for instance, were quite independent of what he said in his famous philosophical essay, and this is what one would expect. Locke's aim in the *Essay Concerning Human Understanding* was to put order into the confused state of contemporary philosophical writing, to remove 'some of the rubbish that lies in the way to knowledge', and his method was analytical. In *Some Thoughts Concerning Education* he was telling Edward Clarke how to educate his boy as a Christian magnate.

This is not said to disparage the educational writings of philosophers as mere *obiter dicta*. Locke was a man of wide experience, considerable intelligence and some wisdom, with a flair for writing; he had lived abroad for several years, he was sometimes near to the centre of political events, and he had suffered a mild persecution; he was a friend of Shaftesbury, Cudworth and Newton. Of course his views on education were worthy of attention, but not simply because he was the doyen of British philosophy in the later years of his life.

The philosopher, as philosopher, is no more concerned with the utterance of educational aims than he is with the purely technical problem of teaching purblind children to read. An educational aim can be put forward by anybody, but whether it is good or bad, foolish or wise, is something on which each of us must make up his own mind. Philosophy cannot help here. The ordinary problems of education are of method, and these are properly left to the educational psychologist or statistician who is entrusted to 'solve' them in accordance with the rules of procedure of one of the special sciences. If one may be excused for distorting somewhat the original meaning of the word, these experts may be said to give an *apodeixis*, a demonstration, of how a certain result can be achieved, and in this sense they give a solution of the problem. If the philosopher has a rôle in education it is with another kind of problem, an *aporia* or difficulty, which cannot be met by any of the rules appropriate to the special sciences. Perhaps it may be shown that his business is with a class of problems for which there is no solution, in the sense of demonstration.

This does not mean that such difficulties are unreal; indeed an educational difficulty that cannot be met by any of the methods of the special sciences is a very real one. If, however, someone can show that such a difficulty has its origin in the language of educational theory; if he can give, not a demonstration—for it would be nonsense to ask for this, but a *lusis*, a dissolution of the difficulty, so that where there was formerly a difficulty there is now none, it may be assumed, perhaps, that a useful service has been done for education. Educational theory is choked with such difficulties, but a random one which occurs in J. S. Brubacher's book discussed above is this:

> ... the philosopher is interested in the personal attitudes of superiority or inferiority that children learn when homogeneously grouped ... and the impact of these groups on the democratic outlook. ...

The occurrence of this implied question in such a book suggests that it is one of the problems which educationists who use experimental procedures would abandon as insoluble; that it is one of those problems which must be handled by the philosopher with his own special techniques. But what sort of answer is he to give? The answer, for Professor Brubacher, is apparently an *apodeixis*, though of a more subtle kind than the scientist's, that certain attitudes are (or are not) deleterious to the democratic society. His answer would take the form: 'Yes, these attitudes are deleterious, *etc.*'

Inspection of the way in which they are commonly used, will show that such simpler questions as, 'What is homogeneous grouping'? and 'What are the several attitudes learned by these groups'? permit the widest range of descriptions, and these are punctuated throughout by choice. Answers to these questions cannot be given by empirical enquiry. Yet such questions as that implied in the above quotation *are* asked as though they can be answered by some kind of procedure, and we can only assume that they constitute real difficulties. Could one of the tasks of the philosopher be to analyse such sentences and show that they are not real problems? And lest this should read like a request for a plethora of new books on the philosophy of education, let it be said at once that the task envisaged could be done quite well in essays, critical notes and even reviews.

Perhaps it may be said that by making flank-attacks on the language of the educational writer, one is avoiding the topics of education. Now it must be frankly conceded that the philosopher can never construct educational systems as part of his job. At the same time it must not be overlooked that through analytical techniques philosophers have had the indirect effect of bringing about improvement in the special sciences. An instance that springs readily to one's mind is Berkeley's criticism of Newtonian mathematics. This was directed mainly at the verbal contradictions in the concept of fluxions and in the method known as the compensation of errors. The issues that were traversed and retraversed in the several pamphlets that passed between Berkeley and others seemed detached from the leading part that mathematicians were playing in the development of 18th century physical science. Yet Berkeley's criticisms were sound and as a result of the controversy, which was an early application of philosophical analysis, the worthless terminology of fluxions and compensation of errors was expunged, and the calculus was subsequently developed on the method of limiting ratios.

Analysis might well lead to the erasure of a systematically confusing vocabulary in educational theory.

## NOTES

1. C. E. Skinner, *Educational Psychology* (Englewood Cliffs, New Jersey: Prentice Hall, 1959), p. 11 and p. 1ff.

2. J. M. Stephens, *Educational Psychology* (New York: Holt, Rinehart and Winston, 1957), pp. 6–10 and p. 16.

3. G. M. Blair, quoted by R. S. Ellis, *Educational Psychology* (Princeton, New Jersey: Van Nostrand, 1951), p. 6.

4. R. S. Ellis, *op. cit.*, p. 12.

5. *Ibid.*, p. 489ff.

6. W. W. Charters, 'Is There a Field of Educational Engineering?', *Educ. Research Bulletin*, 24, (Ohio State Univ., 1945), p. 29ff.; H. L. Hollingworth, *Educational Psychology* (New York: Appleton-Century, 1933), p. 3f.

7. *Ibid.*, p. 521f.

8. J. B. Stroud, *Psychology in Education* (New York: McKay, 1956), p. 393 (italics added).

9. N. B. Cuff, 'What Should be Included in Educational Psychology?', *Journal of Educational Psychology* (1935, 26), p. 689f.

10. R. L. Archer, 'Educational Psychology, American and British: Some Points of Comparison', *British Journal of Educational Psychology*, 11 (1941), p. 128.

11. C. Fox, *Educational Psychology*, 1925 (New York: Harcourt, Brace and World, 1926), p. 111.

12. W. A. Brownell, 'Learning Theory and Educational Practice', *Journal of Educational Reserach*, 41 (1948), p. 481ff.

13. P. Sandford, *Foundations of Educational Psychology* (New York: Longmans, 1938), p. 32ff.

14. I. M. D. Little, *A Critique of Welfare Economics* (New York: Oxford University Press, 1957), pp. 82 and 267f.

15. E. A. Peel, *The Psychological Basis of Education* (Philosophical Library, 1956), p. 84.

16. See R. M. Hare, *The Language of Morals* (New York: Oxford University Press, 1952), p. 35.

17. R. R. Rusk, *The Philosophical Bases of Education* (Boston: Houghton Mifflin, 1928), pp. 23 and 15.

18. J. S. Brubacher, *Modern Philosophies of Education* (New York: McGraw Hill, 1950), p. 5ff.

19. *Ibid.*, p. 105ff.

20. *Ibid.*, p. 331f.

21. S. J. Curtis, *An Introduction to the Philosophy of Education* (London: University Tutorial Press, 1958), p. 7.

22. *Ibid.*, p. 108.

23. L. A. Reid, *Philosophy and Education, An Introduction* (London: Heinemann, 1962), p. 182.

24. *Ibid.*, p. 17.

# THE CONTEXT OF
# EDUCATIONAL DISCUSSION

THE three essays that make up this section are concerned with an examination of how to proceed to *talk about* education. The points of view are fresh ones. Professor Perry's paper considers what an educational situation is by looking at two ideal versions of what it ought to be: the traditional and the progressive. He then looks at the actual structure of a typical practical educational situation, and concludes that fruitful directions for improvement in education must stem from analyses of real situations rather than those ideal ones which are constructed on assumptions that may be irrelevant to practical contexts. By so doing, his essay is emblematic of recent trends in philosophical analysis, and consistent with the views of several of the other contributors to this volume.

Professor Peters' concerns relate to Perry's, but are broader in scope. He rejects many conventional ways of describing or characterizing education: education as 'growth', as controlled by ultimate 'ends', as 'experience', as 'acculturation', as 'training'. He concludes that education is a process aimed at the development of motivation of a certain kind, and of cognitive structure. It is properly concerned with the *initiation* of the young into activities, modes of conduct, and thought, which have public standards written into them. Education has no ends beyond itself, and what is perhaps most significant, its aims should be stated in terms of the explicit manner of teaching. Again we note the choice of a clear and tangible context for the investigation of problems.

Professor Hirst turns to a definition of *liberal* education, proceeding through an examination of traditional notions on the one hand, and a famous contemporary statement on the other. He begins by analysing the structure of knowledge that seems intrinsic to both of these ideas, an approach which is frankly epistemological and consequently relatively abstract; yet a major portion of his paper is concerned with the applications of the principles thus derived to the practical educational context. He concludes by examining such commonplace problems as teaching for critical appreciation, selecting content within the disciplines, and organizing the school curriculum.

# WHAT IS AN EDUCATIONAL SITUATION?

## Leslie R. Perry

COMMON CAUSES OF CONFUSION

WHATEVER may be the task of philosophers of education, the typical task of the teacher is a practical one: that is, he is constantly preoccupied with what to do in a situation requiring him to do something. This does not at all mean that thinking and reflecting is a less important part of his business, for, as the old controversy aroused by pragmatism showed,[1] theory is not opposed to practice but essential to it. The teacher, however, needs a type of thinking particularly suited to practical problems—it might be called practical thinking, in contrast to that which arose without a practical end in view. Without it, the way a teacher acts can be inconsistent, indecisive, or mechanical and rigid. Nor is it likely that he can free himself from these hindrances to effective work unless he forms, in the course of his practical thinking, what may be called a 'concept' of education—that is to say, a set of ideas, characterized by their common capacity to contribute to his practical work. These may be combined in various ways according to the practical problem concerned, and they consist of a number of procedures appropriate to the carrying out of the teacher's work, plus a number of aims in pursuit of which those procedures are operated. This 'concept', then, would provide him with some basic notion of his role as a teacher and how to carry it out. Such a concept need not arise—a teacher may continue indefinitely doing his work in an inferior way—but it *can* arise out of an intelligent and observant assessment of the results of daily practice, an awareness of the convictions that one is using as aims, and a constant attempt at improvement. This demand is at present commonly met by the recourse to technical knowledge of one sort or another. But it need not mean this. It can mean what is meant here by formulating a concept; namely, the attempt to obtain insight into one's aims and purposes in grappling with practice (which is not purely a matter of method) as well as reflection upon questions of method.

I am suggesting then that teachers often work less effectively than they might because of lack of a clear concept of education. In other words, thinking that is antiquated, or not quite to the point, or in conflict with other thinking but not realised to be so, can obstruct the work of the teacher. More: this is, as a matter of fact, largely what happens. It is not my intention, though, to urge teachers to believe in some kind of faith—some scheme of systematic and inter-related beliefs. All I would suggest is that, without some purposes to co-ordinate action, and enable individual decisions to be consistent and reinforce each other, teachers will not attain the mastery of the practical situation which they want. A systematic faith, presented as a picture of what the educational situation might be if it were immaculate, does not seem indispensable to effective teaching. It is true that without purpose actions tend to become random, but whether all purposes need to be connected, and to be related to some general beliefs about the meaning of life, or something of the kind, is quite another question. Certainly the teacher can achieve consistent action without such general beliefs.

As a matter of history, and recent history included, instead of forming such clear, constructive concepts, teachers seem to have suffered from an obstruction of action occasioned by the prevalence of generalized models. These arise, apparently, from an unfortunate but well-established habit of thinking about the problems, that is, the habit of supposing, widespread among writers on education, that there are *particular places* in which they find it going on; and this has resulted in some versions becoming standard versions of *the* educational situation. But they differ a great deal and have given rise to a lot of confusion to the working teacher. And the first source of confusion is that these 'standard' educational situations serve two main purposes, not one, and these have been very mixed up.

The first is that of a concept for method purposes. The writer conceives teacher and pupil or pupils in certain specifiable circumstances. This initial conception is vague, and he explores it further by enriching its detail and by analysing the relationships involved to discover their implications. For example, he imagines a teacher and a pupil as a first step to giving some principles of history teaching method. His next step might be to ask:

(a) what age and sex is the pupil?
(b) is this taking place in a school or a home?
(c) is the teacher the father, a tutor, a paid state employee?
(d) are there other pupils present?
(e) are there other classes, with a head teacher?

and the like; and with the answers his first assumption becomes ever more detailed and specific. He forms then a concept of a *typical* educational situation, not a particular one; and it has to be changed to fit a particular case. What he in historical fact does, is to generalize from his own experience as a teacher. He thinks of a typical case based on his experience of a large number of particular cases, and works out principles of method from it. And he supposes that these principles can be used by *any* teacher in *any* teaching situation, because they seem to work well with those that he himself has experienced. These suppositions I propose to call into question.

The second purpose, however, is very different—it depicts the *ideal* situation towards which educators should work, and which teachers should try to emulate. It usually offers a vision of the 'perfect' teacher and the 'perfect' pupil in 'perfect' circumstances. The use of this type of situation is not specially to do with clarity and the analysing of ideas, although the earlier commentaries on methods developed under its aegis. Rather it is concerned with strengthening the belief and thereby heightening the motivation of people. Its function is that of a guide, a means by which teachers may control and direct their action, and to which they may refer whenever their course is not clear. The ultimate justification of any action a teacher takes is provided by this picture, which gives a norm by which the whole working life of the teacher may be judged. Trouble arises, however, when the two uses are mixed; for it is one thing to urge upon teachers practical recommendations which arise from analysing a model to see what it implies for practical teaching method, and quite another to urge people to act in such a way that they live up to an ideal. If a teacher ignores conclusions that have been arrived at after examining an educational situation to see how it may be organized to the best advantage, he may be accused of neglecting valuable information

## Leslie R. Perry

for his job. But if he fails to behave exactly like the ideal teacher, he is not necessarily failing to use valuable and relevant knowledge, whatever other censure he may be open to. He may indeed be guided by the model in one sense whilst not conforming to its use as an ideal picture. The confusion of the two uses has resulted in much unfair criticism of teachers. We may hope a man will become a saint, but hardly accuse him of *incompetence* if he fails.

A second cause of confusion is no less harmful in its consequences than the first. Standard versions, or models, of the educational situation, tend to be first thought of in a particular set of educational circumstances, say, from a certain age-range, or class of the community, and then generalized to cover all parts of the educational system. An attempt is made below, in the detailed account of the 'traditional' and 'child-centred' models, to show what has happened in these cases, for these, so widely taken to be general models, both turn out to be principally devised to meet particular needs, the 'child-centred' model being in this respect no improvement on its predecessor. But such a generalised use is also a source of confusion now, because, with the growth of technical information, new model situations have appeared, and they tend to offer themselves as *general* models on the assumption that the educational situation is solely a field of application of the particular technical discipline concerned. We may instance the therapeutic model:[2] this supposes that education is fundamentally an occasion for the skilled psychotherapist, acting as teacher, to modify the personality structure of pupils in an educational context. All questions of discipline become matters of adjustment, and an unsatisfactory educational product is thought to be the outcome of imbalance in either teacher or pupil. Another is the learning model. The educational situation is here equated (cogently enough) with an occasion for learning. But in practice the supposition is introduced that particular kinds of learning are the focal point of the business; this is particularly true of the emphasis, powerfully backed by research, on intellectual learning. As soon as this basis is introduced, learning loses its general character and the learning model becomes a technical model posing as a general one; for the educational situation is clearly wider than an occasion for intellectual learning, with other kinds playing a subsidiary role.[3] Similarly for the sociological model; education in school is one of many occasions in which behaviour towards others, and the accompanying mental attitudes, may be learnt. The reader will readily multiply instances for himself—the economic model, the statistical model, and those models vague and unsatisfactory to a degree, customarily used by architects, administrators and medical personnel.

Let us turn now to examine the matter more closely, as exemplified in what may be called the 'traditional' and the 'child-centred' models. The title 'child-centred' will be self-explanatory; but the word 'traditional' is intended to indicate the earlier model, the one reacted against, something which the successor wanted to jettison because of its uselessness. Its historical background is particularly England of the nineteenth and into the twentieth century, but its features are widely recognizable elsewhere.

### THE STANDARD EDUCATIONAL SITUATION

The framework of the model or standard educational situation is simple enough. Its components are a teacher, a pupil or pupils, a class, a school. These elements can obviously compose more than one situation; we could have one teacher and one pupil (Rousseau), a teacher and a small informal group (Socrates), a teacher and a class (Montessori), a teacher and classes in a school (probably Quintilian) and still other combinations. Many have been tried. Both schools and tutors flourished in the ancient world. But of the two models above-mentioned one appears to start thinking from a teacher and a pupil, and the other from a community, though both are concerned with teacher and class—a point commented upon later.

The pictures drawn will look exaggerated and extreme, and it would be easy to choose passages from books in which their cases were more moderately and guardedly presented. But here, as said above, we are trying to deal with theory as modified by practice; and whereas the theorist may present his views in a cautiously argued way, his practical disciples tend to apply those views with less circumspection, as with Dewey, bringing out in an extreme way both the strengths and weaknesses of the theoretical position. And so I have looked to the practical situation, rather than to its theoretical begetters, to summarise the views here given.

These, mainly ideal pictures, are to be found to some extent in the literature and manuals of teaching method.[4] It will be objected that these are the very books that would provide rather the analysis of a concept for practical purposes than the picture of an ideal; surely the ideal picture should be looked for in books on philosophy of education? Certainly one would think so; but in the literature of the nineteenth and earlier twentieth centuries in England, such an opinion would be disappointed; for, owing to the confusion of the two uses of the model situation, such manuals are full of pictures of the model teacher and pupil. In fact, it seems to have been thought a principal point of insistence for *method* that teacher and pupil try to be perfect in character and conduct; as if, owing to paucity of research and poverty of new ideas on technique, the writers assumed that the thing to do was make their readers vividly aware of the ideal picture, and then the reader would be able to devise for himself a sound practical educational method. Hence we are a mixture in which the ideal picture predominates.

The side which exhorts the teacher to live up to the ideal may be called the positive side of the matter. But from the history, and from the implications of the advice on method given to teachers, we get a glimpse of the negative side, namely the 'expense of spirit in a waste of shame' that the educational situation actually prevailing too often was.[5] This is merely hinted at, often in a rather furtive and guilty tone, as if such things ought never to happen. What is rejected by the ideal is denigrated and nowhere really examined; and the discussion is carried on with a strongly religious air, as if sin and salvation were the subject-matter. Neither for that matter is this note an unfamiliar one now. So problems were neglected, and had to await a different attitude, in which moral judgment was suspended, whilst investigation of the causes of the actual situation proceeded. And this marks the point of breakaway of the child-centred from the traditional model, for whilst the dominant emphasis of the latter was religious, that of the former was mainly scientific. The result was that the child-centred model was a much better informed and more ample and detailed account of the educational situation.

## THE TRADITIONAL MODEL

To the question, what is an educational situation? the traditional answer is, roughly, that it is a completely dominant teacher instructing a completely submissive pupil in a place set apart for the purpose. The word 'instructing' is used to imply that the teacher is already educated (a completed process), and he gives education to the pupil. 'A place set apart' is used to mean that the school does not intentionally in any way resemble the environment, and no comparison was felt necessary between its proceedings and those of everyday life. Moreover, no emphasis was laid upon the immediate connection between what was done at school and how such skills would be used afterwards, although this was the ostensible reason for much that was done. The exact connection remained vague and at times it is difficult to see that any was intended at all. A school was withdrawn from society; it was a specialised place as a hospital, a workhouse, or a factory (and often enough in buildings of a similar plan).

The traditional educational situation was conceived of as static. The same model served throughout schooldays. No growth in attitude of the pupil was allowed for, and no profit of an educational kind accrued to anyone but the pupil, since the teacher was already educated. The teacher did not change; the pupil changed only because he learnt certain specific things taking a certain time, and when he left, no basic matter of importance remained to be done. This view of education contains elements of very long ancestry and wide influence; behind it we see that the old are wise and they display their wisdom to the young and thereby instruct them. Only the young change; the old traverse the known ground. Great teachers are very frequently (and incorrectly) thus pictured. The corollary of this way of looking at a model educational situation is, that very special kinds of personality and characteristics are attributed to both teacher and pupil. To these we now turn.

First, as to the teacher's knowledge: he knew everything that was necessary for the education of the pupil. This knowledge was subject-matter, the transferring of which to the pupils was the ostensible purpose of lessons. This subject-matter was not all there was to be known about a subject, but all that a teacher needed to know; and this he knew with complete mastery. It was highly selected, and what had been selected was deemed absolutely essential. So, certain parts of the Bible and not others; certain Latin authors and not others; certain arithmetical processes and not others. Curricular subjects were in a strict hierarchical order; Latin and religion headed the list for the leisured classes, whilst arithmetic and English took that place for working class pupils. Being judged the most important, they received a certain kind of detailed elaboration from the teacher; he told the pupils the facts to understand and how to understand them. And if they did not, he repeated the process. Understanding the knowledge was of less importance than learning it (by which was meant committing it to memory). The teacher knew the subject-matter and the reasons for it. His image to the pupil was of a person knowing everything.

To this perfect mastery of the appropriate subject-matter he added responsibility for character, insofar as this meant the habit of behaving in certain ways acceptable to society, and the disposition to entertain certain approved beliefs. To undertake this part of his work, the teacher was thought of as completely at one with those ways of behaviour, and completely convinced of the truth of the beliefs. He was, so to speak, the perfect representative of adult society in the school situation, and was pictured as entirely competent to mediate its beliefs, values, and ways of behaviour to the pupils. His job, in this respect, was not to present conduct and action as problematic or contentious, but to exhibit it as the field of established and agreed ways of behaviour, and to use all occasions to indicate which agreed way was appropriate. Particularly this was so with morality; he indicated at all times the morally right attitude and conduct in particular cases, as well as announcing the principles governing them. His ideal image was, then, that of a person to whom all problems of conduct were solved, who did not work by reflection upon them, and did not teach them by tracing the course of reflections. He taught by giving a rule and applying it.

Very characteristic of this 'traditional' picture of the ideal educational situation in some ways, is its view of discipline. For this, the teacher bore the sole responsibility. He organised it, laid it down and imposed it. The waiting pupil was told by the teacher what to do, what to say, what to think, and this disciplinary control was actively maintained throughout the schooldays of a pupil. Initiative, authority, planning of a school day, were part of the dictatorial powers of the teacher; such powers were not shared. Discipline meant making the pupil do what the teacher decided was good for him to do. This implied that the teacher was perfectly disciplined himself; he was in authority but his ideal image was not authoritarian. He directed the helpless without taking advantage of their helplessness. Any frustration arising from this way of viewing the educational situation was borne by the teacher, because only he was mature; and only the mature can wield discipline and accept frustration, because they discipline themselves.

## What Is an Educational Situation?

This formidable array of teacherly qualities required of course a very special type of person. Here we find that throughout a vocational, as contrasted with a professional, attitude is assumed. Teachers were supposed to be drawn to their work by an exalted sense of duty, a selfless regard for the welfare of others, a zeal for true religion and the ideal of immaculate conduct, care for the young, and so on. Here is a major point of confusion between the ideal situation and the real one; for, in effect, all teachers were assumed to be like the Great Teacher so far as their attitude was concerned. They were thought of as following a call to teach, like Socrates and Christ; and too often through failing to conform to this expectation were thought to be scoundrelly and incompetent pedants. What one might call the 'professional' attitude, that of a man working conscientiously and with technical skill in order to do a sound and efficient job of work and earn money for himself and his family, was not allowed for. This is all the more surprising in that the vocational man, whether saint or zealot of any other kind, is everywhere admired but not expected to appear in large numbers. And whilst Great Teachers in very exceptional circumstances may exhibit to the full some of the qualities mentioned, one is at a loss to see how whole education systems can be founded on the assumption that numbers of such people will be found. This is in fact one side of the model situation's neglect of the teacher's personal life and its problems. Such a viewpoint is still present and active: students entering training are too frequently thought of as vocational; 'professional' ones tend to be rated as inferior: with the result that the training problem of creation of interest is burked.

The attitude to training, in the traditional model, is not unrelated to all this. Some training of course took place, but the belief was common then, and not unknown now, that training was not all that essential. As mentioned above, the right belief, the right attitude, the requisite knowledge, would themselves guide one to the mastery of effective teaching. Certainly sufficient intensity of belief may, in the case of the Great Teacher, lead to a self-education amounting to a thorough training. Similarly, it was argued that complete mastery of the subject-matter was really the only indispensable thing, a belief not unpopular in our own time. In both cases, the fundamental notion is that the possession of certain information would carry with it the capacity to teach that information to others: an interesting, but hardly a verified, supposition.

## Leslie R. Perry

Naturally, if we think of the teacher as a Great Teacher, he does not change, because he is perfect. Change of character was not therefore allowed for in the model. The teaching process, so far as the teacher was concerned, was repetition of the learnt. At best it might be a reasoning through of what was already thought out: the reasoning became part of the facts to be memorised. Change of viewpoint, growth, further movement to maturity when the teacher was already mature, was unthinkable. The teacher was complete: he functioned as an example of what could be done. Thus the teacher in the model role meted out to him, was completely static. Behind all this is the view that education is a process that comes to an end, and the end is the perfect memorisation of a mass of selected fact. Since memorisation and repetition is the daily procedure, a static situation adequately enough represents the educational process.

We turn to the model role of the pupil. Parts of the picture worth mention are these. The personality attributed to the pupil is an entirely passive one. He initiates nothing in the educational situation, but is thought of as utterly receptive. The well-worn metaphors of a substance to be moulded, or a blank tablet on which anything can be written, betoken well enough a personality capable of impress but not of impressing itself. This follows from the fact that if the teacher is to provide all the character, all the knowledge, all the discipline, he must have a clear and blank beginning for his efforts. The pupil has no history, no other environment which has the slightest relevance to the educational situation, and no one else can make a significant contribution; the teacher bears the responsibility for all. The notion that the pupil has relationships with other adults which he has to relate to what the teacher does, has not dawned in this model.

Discipline could not be acquired by the pupil as a progressing feature of school education. All that was assumed here was that the pupil would gradually acquire the meaning and application of moral injunctions and exhortations for future use, without having any present use for them. Nevertheless, the pupil had a basic personality; it was assumed to consist of wild and untrammelled impulses, which would make bedlam and chaos out of school life, were it not for the iron hand of the teacher. So that this perfectly passive attitude was the result of strict control of a primitive and wild person, always ready to burst through to expression. This wild nature could not be used, was irrelevant to the teacher's purposes: it had, in school as elsewhere, to be suppressed, since it was no use for schooling or other civilized purposes. In place of this wild energy, a waiting and receptive pupil attitude was the only one capable of responding to the educational situation. Presumably the education of character consisted in bringing these wild impulses completely under the ultimate control of the pupil himself; but no training for this was given, and no responsibility was at any time granted to the pupil.

The perfectly passive and receptive attitude was taken to be the necessary condition for learning; learning, that is to say, firstly of knowledge, and secondly, to a lesser extent, of character. This type of learning, taken in the traditional model situation to be what was meant by education, presupposed great activity in the teacher and a passiveness in the pupil which consisted in his doing nothing but listen for long periods of time. The teacher was not teaching unless he was speaking, lecturing, instructing, demonstrating; and the pupil was not learning unless he was silent, observant, attentive and concentrating—a view of the educational Arcadia in which some even now would be at ease. Some discussion was allowed for in the model situation, but only of a question-and-answer type, to check that what was to be learnt had been correctly memorised by the pupils: the teacher was given of his own again, and was satisfied. Learning was thus judged effective if the instruction could be repeated by the pupil. Thinking was the teacher's business, and he supplied to the pupil a standard way of connecting the facts. Behind this is the assumption vaguely that the pupil possessed a mental apparatus for grasping thought, and even for thinking over and understanding later what he memorised now. But no training for thinking came into the picture. No real theory of learning (and much less a theory of thinking) was present: memorisation of a lesson, probably the crudest and most approximate check that the pupil was not totally inattentive, was thought, in the absence of knowledge of learning processes, to be an adequate one. In this picture the views of men like Pestalozzi and Froebel counted for nothing.

The 'traditional' educational situation was a preparatory one. The pupil was not living life, but getting ready to do so. The school situation was harmless practice, of no immediate import, but indirectly for use later. The purposes of all this were thought to be inscrutable to the pupil; he would not only learn now and realise

## Leslie R. Perry

its importance later, but would be quite satisfied that his activity
was worthwhile if it was justified to his elders and betters. No justification was offered to the pupil; indeed, questions as to the usefulness of what was done were unwelcome. The pupil's only reward
was the approval of the teacher, couched for the most part in moral
terms. No development of this situation occurred for the pupil during schooldays; attention and concentration were thought to be the
same at eight years as at fourteen years, and the manner of presentation of the material was unvarying except for slightly greater
intellectual complexity of what was to be grasped. Practically no
concession was made to the inability of young children to grasp
complex thinking processes; they were provided with memories to
store these unintelligible things. As the pupil was not thought to
develop, ideas of varying the presentation of the material were
largely absent.

The 'traditional' model was worked out in terms of one teacher
and one pupil: it was supposed that whatever appeared to be valid
of that picture would remain unmodified if one had a number of
pupils instead of one, and if the surrounding environment varied.
Moreover, the circumstance, for instance, that a number of pupils,
or a classroom, brought other educational factors into view, was for
purposes of a model situation ignored. The relationship of each
pupil, for example, was to the teacher alone: pupils had no relationship to each other save of an indisciplinary kind. No such relation
could add to their education, except a kind of competition, rigidly
organised by the teacher. Pupils were all roughly of the same ability
for purposes of working out the model; those who were simply
incapable of fulfilling their rôle were either left out of discussion, or
were failing in moral endeavour. Which is to say, that to lack of
learning theory we must add lack of developmental theory, social
theory, and theory of intellectual development.

The answer returned from what may be called a 'child-centred'[6]
viewpoint to the question, 'What is an educational situation?' is,
crudely expressed, one in which a psychologically skilled teacher
attended educationally to the developmental needs of the child.

This model makes, on comparison, two principal criticisms of the
previous one: first, its lack of a theory of psychological development,
second in importance, its lack of a theory of learning. Discoveries
in both of these fields stimulated great interest in the *pupil* and the
object of the research utilised by educationists was to find out more

about him: the results were over a long period virtually not applied to the teacher. This brought about a striking change in emphasis in the educational situation: for in the traditional picture, the teacher was very much the dominant partner and all initiative lay with him, whereas now the pupil and his *needs* took the dominant role, whilst the teacher had to adjust his work to those needs, and minister to them. The main emphasis was a developmental one, but the model situation here also makes use of a psychology of learning. Its currency arises out of its ability to point to research backing: all of its conclusions, with few exceptions, were anticipated by the pioneer educational thinkers, but the ideas did not gain currency until the late nineteenth and early twentieth centuries, and that only very gradually.

### THE CHILD-CENTRED MODEL

The child-centred educational model did not, however, make the mistake of thinking in terms of a pupil and teacher and generalizing to pupils and teacher. It was realised that a different relationship was introduced by teaching a number of pupils together. It generalised instead from a community situation to a classroom one. True, the model had not yet available any sociological research, so that the developmental and learning sides of it stand on a different basis. But it foreshadowed, by its picture of the changed school and classroom, problems which have provided starting points for writing on the social psychology of education. The model acknowledged that experience was a continuum for the pupil, that is, that learning and development were going on all the time; this led to criticism of the older model's rigid classroom and subject divisions and its neglect of the learning opportunities provided by other aspects of the school situation. Instead, the view of the school as a single community, with all its potentialities for a wide concept of educational development, came forward. None of this was new, much of it was very old. The school came now to be considered as a miniature society, not in the sense of a simplified adult one, but as the society possible among children in the presence of a few trained adults. It was assumed that this version of the school had the closest connection with the adult society for entry to which it was working. So, where the older model never compares school with the life outside in any significant way, the newer model is dominated, on this side, by its possible developmental similarity with adult society. But neither model could be said to have conducted an enquiry into the question, 'How is the education of children best furthered: by a school of a different type, of a closely similar type, or neither?'

To follow the previous order of discussion: the first thing we note about the teacher is that his mastery of subject-matter was no longer so important. The subject-matter became now rather the ostensible occasion of an educational activity deeper and richer than itself; and insistence upon facts, and upon rote learning, retired before the demand that what mattered most was the development of appropriate knowledgeable behaviour in a social context, rather than the equipping of persons with knowledge for possible future use. With the decline in emphasis on subject-matter went the decline of the view that the mastery of certain knowledge was the sign of a completed education. Skills, and the knowledge that went with them, basic to social behaviour, came nearest to this in the child-centred model. But there was also present the opinion that this knowledge arose naturally in a healthy social situation in form of answers to problems and enquiries presenting themselves; pupils would therefore look after the knowledge aspect for themselves, and it was not necessary for the teacher to emphasise it as well. The fact that curricula abridge and compress knowledge was neglected. The practical result of this, over a period, was the tendency to accept standards of attainment in which less than the minimum knowledge was present.

The teacher no longer undertook to inculcate a standard pattern of character. Rather he was concerned to provide fitting circumstances for the development of very various personalities (rather than character), dependent upon the pupil's natural development. 'Personality', a more neutral word from the viewpoint of teacher involvement than its predecessor, was shaped out of the reactions of pupils to their environment; the best the teacher could do was aid in the unfolding of this natural potential. He did not, on this side of his work, advocate solutions to problems supplied by social living, but commented upon and interpreted the daily growth experience of the pupil. Here is to be found the assumption that such commentary could be free of pressure on the pupil to grow in one way rather than another—certainly a point of the model requiring further scrutiny. The idea of a specific adult rôle for the pupil was not overthrown, it was the process by which the pupil was to be brought to play it that was so different; he was to arrive there by unobtrusive guidance in grappling with his problems, until, in an unbroken developmental sequence, they became adult problems. The question here not really faced by this model is, what is the best preparation for adult life?—the learning of knowledge known to be useful by adults plus training in behaviour, or training in behaviour plus an incidental introduction of the necessary knowledge?

In this as in the previous model it appears to be assumed that the teacher would be satisfied by current beliefs, and perfectly fitted to mediate them to his pupils. He does not specifically instruct pupils in these beliefs, but concentrates on thoughtful discussion of them, attempting however to lead his pupils in the direction of accepted convictions about the rights and duties of the adult citizen. He is not expected to instruct in what to believe, since this would exert pressure on the free development of the pupil; but his example is taken to recommend, without verbal persuasion, the worthiness of the beliefs he represents. And with this uneasy solution, the child-centred model seeks to avoid the taint of indoctrination. But it does not really face the question of how developing pupils need to accept belief, nor how the developed capacity to criticise can cohabit in one mind with the acceptance of beliefs. The model assumes that the pupil will be reasonable, thoughtful, critical, but finally accepting: the problems of other types of personality are hardly given a full treatment.

The disciplinary sides of this model are in startling contrast to those of the previous one. The teacher, fallen from his high estate as mentor of the minds and spirits of his pupils, now becomes basically a child psychologist working in the educational field. The child-centred model is a psychological one. The teacher guides and helps the pupils where possible, quietly and subtly, observing them ceaselessly and in a scientific manner, deducing his conclusions, and remaining passive where in any particular case he feels his help useless. His business is to study a situation and to remain on the periphery of it except where he can enter without arousing a situation obstructive to development and learning. It is assumed that he is trained to observe and assess the suitability of action, and that psychological training is the one that gives him this capacity. The same kind of guidance that equips the child psychologist will be effective in the teacher-pupil model. With his pupils he attempts to cultivate a friendly relationship on a basis of mutual acceptance, where his predecessor made no such attempt. In that friendly relationship, with its atmosphere of mutual respect, he guides pupils to self-discipline. The pupil was expected to refrain from unruly behaviour because (a) he did not wish to interrupt the harmonious co-operative activity of the class, and (b) he understood the teacher and his rôle as guide, not as imposer and controller. The child-centred teacher has a bad conscience about acting authoritatively, which for him tends to be identified with an authoritarian attitude. The disciplinary consequence of this, for pupils who do not accept their rôle, are by now well known. Disciplinary difficulties, to the child-centred teacher, were essentially problems of personality, which he could enquire into and diagnose and solve, whereas the traditional teacher knew only of laziness, ineptitude, moral dereliction, and the like, in those who would not (rarely could not) learn. The order that discipline implies was then, in the child-centred model, an order built by pupils, and teachers could not make it, but only assist in its construction.

It follows that the pupil now bore full responsibility for his actions and was encouraged to do so. The teacher was for the most part divested of responsibility, which belonged by right, almost by nature, to the pupil. In this model then, functions thought previously to be beyond the pupil's capacity were handed over to him. But the model further implies that all responsibilities can ideally be handed over, even those for conducting a mature relationship with adults. Yet if adult responsibility is something reached after developing through stages only, for many of the school years it must rest with the teacher. The assumption of the child-centred model here was that, broadly, pupils in ideal conditions would exhibit a maturity beyond their years, and behave rather like adults. Not the least of the pits dug for itself by the child-centred viewpoint arises from this assumption in the model.

The teacher of this model was assumed to be as vocational as his predecessor: the demand that he should be a kind of saint was still there—but a different kind of saint. For the whole educational model here outlined devotes no thought to the needs and the fulfilment of the teacher: he was apparently thought to obtain all the fulfilment necessary from the selfless delight of being present at the spectacle of the unfolding pupil, and of aiding that process. No matter how many times over how many years he ministered to how many pupils, it was assumed that the delight would never pall. And so the model never looked into the frustration that an adult can incur from being perpetually present at a banquet where he was forbidden to eat; that is, from watching growth, development, fulfilment, the expression of a self, without ever being allowed to be more than a watcher. Behind this we see the view that the teacher is already fulfilled, as in the older model; he tastes again, it is thought, the delights of his own self-realisation in the involvement with those of others. Unbroached for this model is the question, is there any further new fulfilment for the teacher himself in the educational situation? a place where bearing the frustration will give place to some personal fulfilment within the situation? The teachers of both models bore frustration, but perhaps the child-centred teacher is the more burdened. It would be interesting, if figures had been available, to compare the breakdown rates of the two kinds of teacher. Suffice it here to say that the child-centred model is nowhere more defective than in its neglect of the teacher and his problems within the educational situation.

Perhaps from the pupil's aspect, the strongest emphasis of the child-centred view has been the persistent tendency to think of children as growing according to the laws of their own nature, which seems to have been thought of as largely hereditary, and to work out in a different way for each individual. Such a pupil is never thought of as passive, and never susceptible to moulding; he is growing, solving his own problems, developing quite apart from the teacher's efforts. Where the traditional view thinks in terms of a pupil on whom the system is impressed, the child-centred view thinks of a dynamic and vital type of pupil, critically aware of and capable of sensible comment upon the teacher's activity. Despite therefore the variety of development allowed for, there is some supposition of standard personal attributes in the model: indeed, without a vital and outgoing personality, the model would fall. If there are a minority of personality types not conforming to this expectation, we hear markedly less of them; just as we hear less of the non-passive character in the traditional view. This vital personality is required if the teacher is to be only a guide, and also the teacher must be a guide in order to allow this vital development. Growth also is never thought of as passive and recessive, but as positive, concerned with action, intelligently willing to accept help, and appearing in well-balanced personalities. If others are present, with skilled treatment from the teacher they will become like this.

As well as a much more specific awareness of development, this model had a much more ample view of learning to back it. The rôle of the pupil as a positive factor is fully recognised; his interest, his effort, his attention, are essential: learning cannot go on without the presence of these things and all of them. The most favourable conditions for learning require not only the retirement of the teacher from dominance but the advance of the pupil into the continual maintenance of the right attitude because of his own development.

Not only this: we find it also assumed that learning goes on best in a spontaneous environment, freely chosen by the pupil, who sets his own goals, and that the school should imitate these optimum circumstances in order to achieve the best results. The fundamental alteration involved in setting goals for a pupil, and having an adult constantly present whose business it is to ensure, however warily and quietly, the pursuit of them, is not examined in its implications: it is supposed that people who set their own goals will maximise their interest and choose the most effective means, whilst learning at the behest of others will obstruct this. But whether these suppositions are valid in all circumstances arising in the school is another matter.

In this version of a learning situation, the relation of pupil to pupil is very close, with pupils teaching other pupils frequently and freely, and the teacher more in the position of head of group of teachers—a kind of first among equals. The object is to assimilate the teacher as much as possible to the community of pupils in class and school: furthermore, it is thought that he may have learning to do himself, he may learn from his pupils, he is a pupil himself. This is the beginning of the view that teaching and learning may be aspects of one process. But it is not carried far; what learning exactly the teacher is to do, what teaching the pupils do and how the teacher's teaching is related to these, receive no detailed attention. They serve as part of the argument for presenting the teacher as a mature and advanced *pupil*, the best and most skilled of a community in which all members teach all others, and in which the real importance is to be a pupil, not a teacher. The learning-teaching situation of the teacher is in particular neglected.

Certainly the second model made considerable headway in pointing to the defects of the first, and just as certainly it is not without its own. It is, as we have seen, very difficult with this model in mind to give to the factual side of knowledge the importance which many think it has. If education compresses into a short period of life the collected results of long years of sustained enquiry through the ages, how is the child to experience all this afresh for himself? At most his experience will be a token as far as information is concerned, though it may well teach him the principles of methods of enquiry. This problem the model did not in practice solve. A related point of criticism concerns frustration. Can the model freely assume that all learning is capable of being interesting if only the teacher tries? Perhaps, when much is to be learnt in the short period of schooling, and a great deal of it represents discoveries by adults, the teacher can never do more than make it as interesting as possible. Beyond that, frustration will appear and the pupil is obliged to bear it. And voices are not lacking to urge that this can be a salutary experience; for the teacher to acknowledge it and guide his pupils through is a true preparation for a frequent experience of adult life. Possibly then the teacher should encourage pertinacity as well as interest.

Again, the working day of co-operative harmony has all the aura of the ideal about it. The supposition that citizenship of adult society is best furthered by types of immature 'citizenship' of an immature miniature society or community, needs further examination. The idea suffers from its lack of sociological basis; children were expected to exhibit a social maturity frequently beyond their years. The model further assumed that the more ideal the community of the pupils, the more quickly they would learn a co-operative rôle, which is a view ignoring how much social behaviour is learnt by suffering the consequences of incorrect action. But all of this social side of the child-centred model was bound to be marked by a lack of technical knowledge; and analysis of the school, the class in relation to it, and of the relations between school and home, was present only in a rather primitive form. The idea of Pestalozzi, that the school should be modelled on a family, may after all be no less true than likening the school to a community or society; and it has different consequences for educational practice.

But for all this, the rise of the model to currency was little short of a revolution in educational practice; it was a great advance to gain what enlightened educationists had struggled for so long: greater attention to the child's capacities and needs.[7]

### DEFECTS IN THE MODELS

Both models have their defects; the second, whilst serving as a corrective to the first, throws out, as reforms tend to do, some good with the bad. A conspicuous defect of both is that they start from particular ages—the traditional one from late childhood and early adolescence, and the child-centred one from early childhood—and generalise outwards to cover other pupils. Consequently, the traditional model is nothing like so sure about early childhood, whilst the child-centred model has real difficulty in generalising its conclusions to late adolescence. It is proper to younger children to emphasise the exploration side and under-emphasise the factual side of knowledge, for instance; but the attitudes and needs of late adolescence have little in common, surely, with such a simple distribution of emphasis.

The greatest single common defect of the models, however, lies in their wholesale neglect of the teacher. If it is true, as Adams has held, that education is a bi-polar process,[8] then this process requires the fullest investigation of which we are capable of what happens at both poles. The first model, it is true, led us to see the dominant position of the teacher in all respects. The teacher however was a mere symbol, an idealised image, and the ideal was conspicuously out of touch with human beings as they are. Consequently, demands are made upon the teacher's time and energy and tolerance that are impossible. The second model directed, as we have seen, a much more searching enquiry to the pupil. But it is remarkable that with the research means now at our disposal so little has been accumulated on the problems of the teacher. The mere entry into an educational relationship involves frustration for both teacher and pupil; the interaction involves learning for both, and teaching for both; the continual variation in age, not to mention experience, for both, must make their relationship always a sensitive one, requiring frequent scrutiny and adjustment. Habit-forming, routinising of the work, occurs in both parties and is the undying enemy of fruitful educational work. The child-centred model has shown us the pupil as a human being with problems of growth and maturity; it remains to see the teacher in precisely those terms but in a different phase. Moreover, we know nothing systematically of how the school surroundings, the pressure of other responsibilities, the additional duties, the expectations of parents and of the local community, facilitate or obstruct the work of the teacher. We have not enough research in detail to support the common observation that the indifference or hostility of parents and communities can bring the work of the teacher almost to nothing on some sides. The problems of the teacher are various and important; we may instance the effect of his educational rôle on his learning processes; how his teaching is affected by continuing in the same work for a large number of years; how new learning affects the learning he already has; exactly how obstructive habits and attitudes grow; causes of resistance to change; the effect of certain varieties of frustration (e.g. the insistent splitting of his attention by pupils) upon him; and the like. The adjustment problems, incidence of neurosis, rate of breakdown in the profession,[9] incidence and intensity of mental fatigue, are as yet only glimpsed. So long as the teacher is assumed to be vocational, and therefore capable of making a superhuman effort at self-denying adjustment, these problems could be conveniently shelved by both models.

However, the lot of the teacher has been made difficult for another reason as well as the neglect of his problems. The use of the models is itself an obstruction. I tried to suggest above that models arise from a habit of thinking. The writer (or advocate of them) has experienced innumerable instances of the educational situation, as a teacher. He generalises these into a 'typical' instance, from which he derives certain convictions about aims and principles of method as 'averagely' used. Then he assumes that these aims and principles can be applied to *any* particular case of the educational situation. But can they? Let us concentrate first on method models. The crucial question is how to modify the principles recommended to deal with the particular case being considered, for the particular case is the real practical problem of the teacher. How does the model help? Suppose the teacher adopts it to try to help solve his practical problem (and teachers are prone to use a ready-made model because of the complexity of the type of problem they face). He can make one of two assumptions:

(a) this model is the real way to look at this particular situation (i.e. the model is generally applicable to it)
(b) this model applies to one aspect of the particular situation (i.e. it is partially applicable to it).

Take the first: for example, the teacher says, 'All educational situations are child-centred and this one therefore is.' So it will be tackled as the model prescribes. So he attempts, say, to organise the class as a harmonious self-disciplined community, and, owing to the presence of a high proportion of maladjusted children, it fails. The model led him to assume things about a community of children of a kind that are common to all communities—it led him to think of ways in which this particular community, where his problem is, resembled others. It does not lead him to study the differences between this one and the average, and that is what he really has to take into account. He can look again at the general model and try to change it somewhat to fit his needs. Or he can say, this model really only supplies one aspect of my problem, it is not the basic framework of it; then he has changed to assumption (b) above. He may then suppose that the model is basically sound—that a community of children should be as the model says, and the model is right, for the social aspect. But here there is a therapeutic aspect of importance. Here (i) some children must be taught separately; or (ii) the community in this case must tolerate anti-social behaviour of an extreme and disruptive kind; or (iii) he must himself intervene to limit the behaviour of the maladjusted children. So the child-centred model is partially right, but requirements of a therapeutic model must supervene here.

In what sense now is it true that the child-centred model is partially right? Has it contributed anything of value to the analysis of the situation? Can the teacher allow himself the modifications mentioned, in the interest of the maladjusted children, and claim that the child-centred model is *valid* for this particular community? Besides, the normal children have their own demands to make; are they then getting the communal training said to be necessary? The teacher imposes in his practice some modifications on the child-centred model for therapeutic reasons; but one could as well argue from the child-centred standpoint that he should impose some limitations on the therapeutic side in the interest of the normal children. All this, as is obvious, is simplified; in actual problems the teacher has to face still further partial models, such as that of parents, of administrators, and so on, which would affect the example given above. The procedure however seems to be that the teacher, to use a partial model, supposes it to be correct and then modifies it. So he works at the model to make it fit the particular situation. Surely a direct analysis of the situation would be a more effective way of going about it, using technical knowledge as required, without apology or remorse. A model may make sense of a limited range of problems, as the child-centred one does with younger children. But when we apply such a model as a partial model outside its chosen area of reference, it requires so much time and attention to modify that it is more of a hindrance than a help. I conclude that partial method models, like general ones, are not a helpful way of tackling particular problems.

### THE USE OF THE MODEL OR AN IDEAL

At the beginning, however, two *uses* of models were distinguished —the method use and the ideal use. We now turn to the use of the model as an ideal picture, meant to cater for the convictions of teacher, that is, to provide him with aims, purposes and beliefs in facing the educational situation. This distinction between the two kinds of model has become more sharp as questions of method, at one time developed in this field solely under the aegis of belief, have been recognized as separate questions. It seems to have been thought until recently that a teacher needed to have intense convictions in order to do his work well. The ideal picture was described and recommended to teachers in such a manner, that clearly they were expected to believe in it with great fervour. No doubt, for believers in some faith, and for those with a strong call to teach, such an expectation will be found acceptable. Most people entering teaching nowadays are not, and in the foreseeable future are not likely to be so. What is the use of an ideal model to them? If we wish to recommend an ideal model, presumably we do so on the following suppositions:

(1) An element of conviction is present in all practical teaching.
(2) Problems of practical teaching cannot be solved unless we are consciously aware of this element and its rôle.
(3) This element must be consistently related to all other elements in practical teaching situations in a systematic way.
(4) Only systematic belief can ensure effective teaching.

We may grant without comment the first two suppositions, for they denote no more than the presence of conscious purposes in the work of a teacher. Supposition (3) however, though strongly held by many, is a stipulation pure and simple. Suppose it is not observed; does the effort of the teacher to deal with educational problems fall into un-avoidable chaos? By no means. The kind of problem he faces may be, for example, 'What shall I do to get this form of thirteen-year-olds interested in English literature'? His purpose then is to rouse interest in this experience. If he forms an ideal picture at all, it will be of this class engaged, to their own satisfaction, in literary studies. What has that to do with an ideal picture of the perfect educational situation? It may be replied that, insofar as the teacher solves his problem, the children will exhibit features of a wider ideal picture—the harmonious self-disciplined community for instance. Further, the purpose above mentioned is in a setting of wider purposes. So if the teacher says, I want to arouse interest in English literature among these pupils, he will say, if asked why, I want to improve the knowledge of children generally. But such wider purposes are of the same kind as his first one—they are not related specifically enough to be in an ideal picture. If they were, he would reply for example, I want to improve the knowledge of children generally, so I shall instruct them in what they are to know and providing the children listen quite passively I will improve them—an answer on the lines of the traditional model. The ideal picture gives rise to very specific convictions in the teacher about the rôle and importance and relationship of elements in the educational situation. He cannot accept some and reject others, for this would involve detaching himself from subscribing to the ideal picture. But why should the non-believer among teachers not be free to study his educational problem and adopt the purposes that seem appropriate for bringing some order into his work? His problem is this class now: to say, I want to interest them in English literature because I want to improve the knowledge of children generally may well be an adequate expression of purpose for tackling the problem. If, on further study of his solution of a number of problems, one seemed inconsistent with another, he could amend his general purposes, but would not necessarily need to accept a whole ideal end-picture of the educational process. I conclude that supposition (3) can be resisted. Supposition (4) appears true on the above showing if we interpret 'systematic belief' as meaning that we must have general purposes as well as specific ones. But if it means that we ought to have an ideal model, the answer must be that effective teaching does not depend on this—effective teaching can and does go on without it. Moreover, intense conviction that a certain ideal model is the right one can result, as said at the beginning, in great neglect of the ways in which the actual situation falls short of it. Educational history is full of the most profoundly anti-educational practice carried out in the presence of an ideal model. I conclude then that though for many they appear necessary, ideal models are not indispensable, and may well be a hindrance, to the practical educational problem of the teacher.

CONCLUSION

In summary: our enquiry into what is an educational situation? has led us to the following answers:

A. It is a model situation showing, for method, how things would be if it worked perfectly.

B. It is a model situation showing, for convictions, how things would be if the teacher believed with sufficient intensity of conviction.

Of these, we have rejected (A) as obstructive to educational work, and have suggested that (B) though it may be used by some teachers, can be dispensed with without detriment to the work of a teacher, and possibly with benefit to it. So we are led to answer:

C. It is the situation the teacher is facing at the moment, dealt with by such technical commentary as he decides to bring in, and such purposes, whether wider or narrower in range, as he chooses to use.

In reaching this conclusion we have cast doubt on the use of a habit of mind customarily used by many teachers. It seems necessary therefore to add a few words on what the alternative is. It was suggested at the beginning that a 'concept' of education, a set of ideas about methods and aims, was necessary in any case. But the use of a model amounts to assuming a fixed relationship of aims and methods which is applicable to all circumstances without basic change. Of course a model provides a concept of education of a kind; but this kind of concept of education, whilst it appears to be useful in a certain restricted area, acts as an impediment to understanding and taking the right action elsewhere. The 'concept of education' referred to at the beginning was a looser and more flexible affair altogether; and the way it is likely to work is this:

(1) The teacher is confronted with a practical problem.
(2) He makes himself aware of his precise aims in this particular situation.

(3) He scrutinises the relationship between these and any general aims he has, modifying either general or particular aims where his analysis of the situation leads to it.

(4) He considers the methods by which he can attain these aims, reviewing whatever technical commentaries he knows.

(5) He will utilise this technical knowledge not in some order of preference but in a combination of any kind that best furthers his efforts at solution, adjusting the combination if necessary.

Example: let us say his problem is an attitude hostile to school learning in a class of fifteen-year-old boys in a secondary grammar school. His precise aims are: to teach them nineteenth century European political history, to produce in them a favourable attitude to learning it, and to get them through an examination. His general aims are: (a) to produce a generally favourable attitude to learning; (b) to attend to their developmental needs without repressive discipline of any kind; (c) to treat them as equals in all respects. He decides to change to an alternative syllabus because he judges that will promote the first two of his general aims. He modifies the third general aim because he feels this kind of behaviour will perpetuate rather than change the hostile attitude in question. (He adopts say a more directive attitude himself with a resolution to bring back the equality aim as soon as the situation allows it.) He reviews technical knowledge available, and decides to investigate the learning history of this class, discovering that a bad relationship to a particular teacher is partly responsible. From the therapeutic side he tries to analyse what caused it and avoids certain behaviour himself as a consequence—for example, misdirected punishment. On the other hand he discovers that some active disruptive influences are present; a large and well-led group in the class does not favour a co-operative attitude and will not allow it under threat of sanctions. His own adjustment from the therapeutic side produces no effect; he does not alter it but proceeds vigorously against the group, risking misdirected punishment rather than refrain from measures. For example he defends non-members under threat of punishment; though at the same time he attacks by making his teaching situation as unlike as possible to the one associated with the teacher in bad relationship. He may select favourable occasions to clash directly with the leader in order to weaken the leader's power if he can. A third influence will be the type of learning techniques he actually uses meanwhile, and how they modify the therapeutic and social ones. For example, he may abandon direct addressing of the whole class altogether for a period and resort to group teaching and individual work. According to the results he is achieving, he may give temporary prominence to one or other of the technical commentaries. And, as the solution of the problem progresses he may modify his general or particular aims.

Such a teacher's 'concept' of education is surely a very useful instrument to him. His behaviour is highly purposive but not in the sense of consistently following the same purposes at every moment. Many aims can be present, and one can drop some, modify others, make some more prominent, and still be well within the framework of educational purposes. The same applies to methods; their degree of relevance and their relationship cannot be known ahead of the problem, because these factors must be adjusted as its solution matures. Such a 'concept' then has not the apparent clarity of a model; but I suggest it is likely to be more effective in practice.

## NOTES

1. See, for example, J. Dewey, *Logic* (New York: Holt, Rinehart and Winston, 1938), Pt. I, Chap. II, III, IV, and F. H. Bradley, *Essays on Truth and Reality* (New York: Oxford University Press, 1914).

2. P. Halmos, 'Personal Involvement in Learning About Personality', *Sociological Review Monograph No. 1* (Keele, Un. College of N. Staffordshire, 1958).

3. See, for example, C. M. Fleming, *Teaching: a Psychological Analysis* (London: Wiley, 1958); J. S. Bruner, *A Study of Thinking* (New York: Christopher, 1956); R. L. Munroe, *Teaching the Individual* (New York: Columbia University Press, 1942), Chap. I; and I. Scheffler, *The Language of Education* (Springfield, Illinois: C. C. Thomas, 1960), for some discussion of models and concepts.

4. See, for example, A. H. Garlick, *A New Manual of Method* (New York: Longmans, 1901); National Society, *An Advanced Manual of Teaching* (London, 1880); J. R. Blakiston, *The Teacher: Hints on School Management* (London: Macmillan, 1883); A. Tomkins, *The Philosophy of School Management* (Boston: Finn, 1901); E. Holmes, *What Is and What Might Be* (New York: Dutton, 1912).

5. See, for example, C. Birchenough, *History of Elementary Education* (London: University Tutorial Press, 1938); E. B. Castle, *Moral Education*

*in Christian Times* (London: Allen and Unwin, 1958); R. L. Archer, *Secondary Education in the Nineteenth Century* (New York: Macmillan, 1921).

6. See J. Dewey, *The Child and the Curriculum and The School and Society* (Chicago: University of Chicago Press, 1956), and *Experience and Education* (New York: Macmillan, 1938); also E. Thring, *Theory and Practice of Teaching* (New York: Macmillan, 1899).

7. E. Holmes, *op. cit.*

8. J. Adams, *The Evolution of Educational Theory* (New York: Macmillan, 1921).

9. See the *Registrar-General's Statistical Review of England and Wales* (London: H.M. Stationery Office), periodically: 'Mental Health Supplement'.

# EDUCATION AS INITIATION[1]

## R. S. Peters

### INTRODUCTORY

A NOVEL feature of the 1960's is the extent to which education has become a subject for public debate and theoretical speculation. Previously it had been something that was prized or taken for granted by those few who had it, but not widely discussed. Of course there were plenty of school-day reminiscences; but these were indicative more of narcissistic self-absorption than of a passionate interest in education.

All this is now changed. Some politicians whose noses quiver at the scent of any sort of under-privilege, have found in education a quarry that they think they may more safely run to earth than the ferocious old foxes of private ownership and disparity of income. Others, with nervous eyes on the technical achievements of the U.S.A. and U.S.S.R., gladly listen to economists who assure them that education is a commodity in which it is profitable for a community to invest. Sociologists assure teachers that they have a role of acting as a socialising agency in the community.

Teachers tend to be either bitter or gratified at this growing grasp of the obvious. Here are they, quiet men working at the job at which they have always worked—underpaid, unappreciated, under-staffed. And now all this. Confronted with such a welter of chatter by people, many of whom have no inside experience of the object of their theorising, it would be human, in one sense, for the teacher to turn a deaf ear. But in another sense it would not be human. For one of the distinguishing features of man is that he alone of all creatures has a variable conceptual framework which determines the aspects under which he acts. A man can conceive of his task as a teacher in many different ways. To shut his ears arbitrarily to such different accounts is to limit his view of the world—to take refuge in a kind of monadic myopia.

87

It may well be, however, that some of the descriptions given of what he is doing *qua* teacher seriously misrepresent what is distinctive of his calling by the generality of the description or by assimilating it to something else. Suppose, to take a parallel case, kissing were to be described as a movement of the lips that has the function of stimulating the organism. The generality of this description would omit some essential features of kissing; furthermore, by describing it as a mere bodily movement it would be assimilated to salivation or to a knee-jerk which is, I think, dangerously misleading. Indeed I often think that a conceptual scheme such as that employed by behaviourists is not simply intellectually mistaken; it is also morally dangerous. For such men may habitually come to think of their fellows in such attenuated terms which they regard as scientifically sterile. Luckily most behaviourists to date have been humane men who have talked like kings in their laboratories but have preserved the common touch of ordinary discourse when they emerge. But succeeding generations may be more consistent.

Teachers may be afflicted by a similar conceptual blight if they think too much in terms of their socialising role, or pay too much attention to the notion that education is a commodity in which the nation should invest, or to the suggestion that their main concern should be for the mental health of children. Education is different from social work, psychiatry, and real estate. Everything is what it is and not some other thing. In all the hubbub about plant, supply of teachers, shortage of provision, streaming, and selection, too little attention is being paid to what it is that so many are deemed to be without. Education has become rather like the Kingdom of Heaven in former times. It is both within us and amongst us, yet it also lies ahead. The elect possess it, and hope to gather in those who are not yet saved. But what on earth it is is seldom made clear.

### 'EDUCATION' AND EXTRINSIC ENDS

To get clearer about the concept of 'education', then, is an urgent necessity at the present time. Such conceptual clarification is pre-eminently the task of a philosopher of education. But is a philosopher who embarks on such a task committed to the suspect conviction shared by Socrates that there is some 'essence' of education which conceptual analysis can explicate? In suggesting that teachers may be affected by a conceptual blight if they pay too much attention to economists, sociologists and psychologists, have I already put my foot on the primrose path that leads to essentialism?

Frankly I do not much mind if I have. What would be objectionable would be to suppose that certain characteristics could be regarded as essential irrespective of context and of the questions under discussion. In the context of the planning of resources it may be unobjectionable to think of education as something in which a community can invest; in the context of a theory of social cohesion education may be harmlessly described as a socialising process. But if one is considering it from the point of view of the teacher's task in the class-room these descriptions are both too general and too embedded in a dangerous dimension; for they encourage a conformist or instrumental way of looking at education.

Perhaps one of the reasons why these economic and sociological descriptions of education can be misleading, if taken out of context, is that they are made from the point of view of a spectator pointing to the 'function' or effects of education in a social or economic system. They are not descriptions of it from the point of view of someone engaged in the enterprise. In a similar way one might say that the function of the medical art is to provide employment for the makers of medicine bottles or to increase the population. But this is not what the doctor conceives of himself as doing *qua* doctor, and it would be regrettable if he came to view what he should be doing *qua* doctor in terms of such remoter effects of his art. Furthermore a description of what he is doing in terms of these effects does little to distinguish his art from that of the chemist. What is essential to education must involve an aspect under which things are done which is both intentional and reasonably specific. Things like increasing the suicide rate or providing employment for printers should not be built into the concept of 'education'.

There are, of course, some intentional and specific activities falling under moral education and sex education which are forms of socialisation in an obvious sense. The teacher has to decide on the extent to which he is to concentrate more on these types of education than on the development of other forms of awareness—e.g. scientific, mathematical. Such decisions about the content of education are usually decisions about priorities. Also, as I shall argue later, all education can be regarded as a form of 'socialisation' in so far as it involves initiation into public traditions which are articulated in language and forms of thought. But this description is too general in that it fails to mark out the difference between education and other forms of socialisation. In the context in which the sociologist is speaking it may be quite clear what specific aspect of the teacher's role is being picked out. But the fact is that when these notions get noised abroad they are not always understood in the specific sense in which the sociologist may be using them. The teacher who hears that he is an agent of socialisation may come to think of himself as a sort of social worker striving in a very *general* sort of way to help children to fit into society. He may get the impression that the teacher's task is not to educate children, in the sense in which I will later define it, but to concentrate on helping them to get on with others and to settle down contentedly to a simple job, healthy hobbies, and a happy home life. It may well be the case that for some children, whose plight in our status-ridden society is spotlighted by the Newsom Report *Half Our Future*,[2] there is not much more that can be done. But so little is known about the conditions which are necessary for that cognitive development which education requires that it would be rash and dangerous to come to such a conclusion too soon. Such research as has been done[3] suggests that a great number of children, because of their early schooling and home life, are grossly deprived in this respect. It would be disastrous to say too soon that a large percentage of children are not capable of education before a serious and sustained attempt has been made to provide the necessary conditions without which talk of education is a pious hope. My fear is that teachers will be led by too undiscriminating talk of their socialising role to conceive of their task in terms of 'gentling the masses'. Clearer and more specific concepts both of 'education' and of 'socialisation' should help to avert this danger.

The other danger, which is encouraged more perhaps by the way in which economists rather than sociologists speak of 'education' lies in the widespread tendency to assimilate it to some sort of instrumental process. It is actually easy to see how such an assimilation can be encouraged by rather cavalier handling of the concept. To bring this out I must now make the first of three conceptual points about 'education' which are necessary for the explication of its essence.

'Education'[4] relates to some sorts of processes in which a desirable state of mind develops. It would be as much of a logical contradiction to say that a person had been educated and yet the change was in no way desirable as it would be to say that he had been reformed and yet had made no change for the better. Education, of course, is different from reform in that it does not suggest that a man has been lifted out of a state of turpitude into which he has lapsed. But it is similar in that it implies some change for the better. Furthermore education is usually thought of as intentional. We put ourselves or others in the relevant situations, knowing what we are doing. I know that Rousseau claimed that 'education comes to us from nature, from men, and from things'. There is this derivative sense of 'education' in which almost anything can be regarded as part of it—visiting a brothel, perhaps. But the central uses of the term are confined to situations where we deliberately put ourselves or others in the way of something that is thought to be conducive to valuable states of mind.

Given, then, that 'education' implies the intentional bringing about of a desirable state of mind, it is only too easy to assimilate it to the most familiar cases of bringing about what is desirable. First of all, there are cases where something is done of a neutral sort for the sake of something else that is thought to be worth-while. Buses are boarded in order to listen to a concert; stamps are licked in order to communicate with a friend. So education, from the point of view of those being educated, often appears as something which has to be gone through, in order that some desirable outcome will ensue, like a well-paid job or a position of prestige in the community. If, on the other hand, it is viewed from the point of view of the teacher, a second type of model crops up—that of the useful arts where neutral materials are fashioned into something that is valuable. Just as clay is made into pots or rubber into golf-balls, so minds are moulded into some desirable end-product, or topped up with something desirable like beer-mugs. When education is viewed in either of these two ways the question 'What is the use of it?' has pointed application—especially if a lot of money has to be spent on it.

There is, however, a fundamental confusion involved in these ways of thinking. This is due to applying these banal ways of conceiving of the promotion of what is valuable to education itself rather than to the processes or activities involved in it. Obviously enough activities which can form part of the content of education can be viewed as being either instrumentally or intrinsically valuable. It is possible to think of science or of carpentry, for instance, as being both valuable in themselves and valuable as means to increasing production or the provision of houses. Thus it is reasonable to ask what the purpose of instructing or of training someone in such activities might be. But it is as absurd to ask what the aim of education is as it is to ask what the aim of morality is, if what is required is something extrinsic to education. The only answer that can be given is to point to something intrinsic to education that is regarded as valuable such as the training of intellect or character. For to call something 'educational' is to intimate that the processes and activities themselves contribute to or involve something that is worth-while. Talk about 'the aims of education' depends to a large extent on a misunderstanding about the sort of concept that 'education' is.

To enlarge upon this point which is crucial for my thesis: 'Education' is not a concept that marks out any particular type of process such as training, or activity such as lecturing; rather it suggests criteria to which processes such as training must conform. One of these is that something of value should be passed on. Thus we may be educating someone while we are training him; but we need not be. For we may be training him in the art of torture. The demand, however, that there should be something of value in what is being transmitted cannot be construed as meaning that education itself should lead on to or produce something of value. This is like saying, to revert to my previous parallel, that reform must lead up to a man being better. The point is that making a man better is not an aim extrinsic to reform; it is a criterion which anything must satisfy which is to be called 'reform'. In the same way a necessary feature of education is often extracted as an extrinsic end. People thus think that education must be for the sake of something extrinsic that is worthwhile, whereas the truth is that being worth-while is part of what is meant by calling it 'education'. The instrumental and moulding models of education provide a caricature of this necessary feature of desirability by conceiving of what is worth-while as an end brought about by the process or as a pattern imposed on the child's mind.

Confirmation of this thesis about 'education' can be obtained by a brief examination of the concept of 'aim'. This term has its natural home in the context of activities like shooting and throwing. 'Aiming' is associated with the concentration of attention on some object which must be hit or pierced. When the term is used more figuratively it has the same suggestion of the concentration on something within the field of an activity. It is odd to use it, like the term 'purpose' or 'motive', to suggest some end extrinsic to the activity. We ask people what they are aiming at when they seem rather confused about their purposes, or when they seem to be threshing around in rather an aimless way, or when they are drawing up their plan of campaign and have to formulate what they intend in a coherent way. Asking a person what he is aiming at is a way of getting him to concentrate or clear his mind about what he is trying to do. It is obvious enough, therefore, why the term 'aim' is used so frequently in the context of education. For this is a sphere where people engage with great seriousness in activities without always being very clear about what they are trying to achieve. To ask questions about the aims of education is therefore a way of getting people to get clear about and focus their attention on what is worthwhile achieving. It is not to ask for the production of ends extrinsic to education.

Of course moral policies cannot be derived from definitions. A man who has been brought to see these conceptual points about 'the aims of education' could reasonably reply 'Well, I am against education then. I prefer to train people in science simply in order to increase productivity in the community, or to get them well-paid jobs. I cannot see any point in teaching science unless it can be shown to be obviously useful in these ways'. This is an arguable position. But it should not masquerade as a view about the aims of *education*.

### 'EDUCATION' AND 'GROWTH'

Historically speaking, when the utilitarian or the moulding models of education have been challenged, others were substituted which likened education to a natural process in which the individual develops or 'grows' like a plant towards something that is presumed to be desirable. Gradually, a positive child-centred ideology emerged which was passionately embraced by those in revolt against traditional methods still prevalent in the schools.

The word 'ideology' is used advisedly to draw attention to a loose assembly of beliefs whose origin in an indeterminate matrix of psychological preoccupation is more obvious than their validity. The ideology of the 'progressive' child-centred educator, who believes in 'growth', cannot be attributed to any one central thinker. He or, more likely, she, tends to believe that education consists in the development from within of potentialities rather than 'moulding' from without, that the curriculum should arise from the needs and interests of the child rather than from the demands of the teacher, that self-expression is more important than the discipline of 'subject-matter', that children should not be coerced or punished, that children should be allowed to 'learn from experience' rather than be told things. The difficulty is to pin down such views to any one important educational theorist. Froebel certainly stressed the importance of studying the child at his various stages and adapting what was provided to the child's interests and stage of development. But he believed very definitely in structuring the environment along desirable lines (witness his 'gifts') and his conception of education was dominated by the mystical demand that in the individual that unity should be experienced which permeated the whole of Nature. Dewey, with whose name concepts such as 'growth' and 'experience' are closely associated, had to write a book[5] in order to disclaim responsibility for some of the doctrines and practices of the Progressive Education Movement and to rectify misunderstandings of his more moderate position. Even Rousseau himself, so some interpreters argue, did not believe that education consisted purely in aiding the enfoldment of 'natural' propensities, but in guiding the boy, stage by stage, towards 'moral freedom', self-reliance and self-control, and a love of truth and justice.

It would require the erudition of a historian of educational thought and practice to trace the development of the child-centred, Progressive ideology in England and the U.S.A. This would be beyond the scope of this paper and the competence of its author. But what emerged as associated with this ideology was a model of the educational situation in which the teacher was regarded as one who has studied the laws of development, and who has to provide appropriate conditions by arranging the 'environment' so that the child can 'realise himself' to the full or 'grow' without becoming stunted or arrested. This model avoids the illiberal and instrumental intimations of the other models; but, like Icarus, it cannot remain for long romantically aloft once the glare of philosophical analysis is turned upon it. For concepts such as 'self-realisation' and 'growth' presuppose standards of value which determine both the sort of 'self' which is worth realising and the direction of growth. Human beings are not like flowers in having a predetermined end which serves as a final cause of their development. 'Growing' or 'realising oneself' implies doing things which are thought to be worth-while rather than others. The standards by reference to which they are judged to be worth-while are grasped by men and handed on from generation to generation. The moulding model of the educator at least brings out this inescapable fact that the teacher has to choose what is worth-while encouraging in children; but it does so, as I have already argued, by using too brutal a metaphor.[6]

In spite, however, of the lack of determinateness about standards which unanalysed uplift about 'growth' and 'self-realisation' often encourages, such caricatures of an educational situation are morally important in another way; for they suggest another dimension in which value-judgments can enter into education, which relate to the *manner* rather than to the matter of education. They emphasise the place of *procedural* principles. By this I mean that they stress the importance of letting individuals choose for themselves, learn by experience, and direct their own lives. The importance of such principles, which all stress the self-direction of the individual, was often overlooked by traditional teachers. They represent value judgments not so much about the matter of what is taught, nor about some illusory 'end' for which things are taught, but about the manner in which children are to be treated. This is salutary not simply from a general moral standpoint but more specifically because it picks out one sort of way in which values can be conceived of as being intrinsic to education, rather than as extrinsic ends. Indeed I have argued elsewhere that much of the controversy about 'aims' of education is in reality concerned with disagreements about such principles of procedure.[7] The problem for those who emphasise 'growth' is to do this in a way which does justice to the fact that no educator can be indifferent to the way in which an individual grows. Dewey's treatment of the case of the burglar who might grow in stature as a burglar is one of the most unsatisfactory passages in his argument.[8]

Conceptually speaking, however, the 'growth' model of education, like the instrumental or moulding model, is a caricature; though like all effective caricatures, it distorts a face by emphasising some of its salient features. For just as the instrumental and moulding models erect the necessary moral feature of 'education' into an extrinsic end, so also the growth model converts a necessary feature of educational processes into a procedural principle. Evidence of this is provided by the tendency of its adherents to stress the connection between 'education' and 'educere' rather than 'educare', thereby moulding the concept towards 'leading out' rather than 'stamping in'. This emerges as a persuasive definition of 'education' which intimates that nothing is to be counted as 'education' in which such procedural principles to do with 'leading out' are ignored. The rationale underlying this transition from a conceptual point about 'education' to specific moral principles needs further elucidation, which is my second main conceptual point about 'education'.

It comes about as follows: although 'education' picks out no specific processes it does imply criteria which processes involved must satisfy in addition to the demand that something valuable must be passed on. It implies, first of all, that the individual who is educated shall come to care about the valuable things involved, that he shall want to achieve the relevant standards. We would not call a man 'educated' who knew about science but cared nothing for truth or who regarded it merely as a means to getting hot water and hot dogs. Furthermore it implies that he is initiated into the content of the activity or forms of knowledge in a meaningful way, so that he knows what he is doing. A man might be conditioned to avoid dogs or induced to do something by hypnotic suggestion. But we could not describe this as 'education' if he did not know what he was learning while he learnt it. Some forms of drill might also be ruled out on these grounds, if the individual was made to repeat mindlessly a series of narrowly conceived stereotyped acts. For something to count as education a minimum of comprehension must be involved. This is quite compatible with children being told to do things in the early stages. For they do, in an embryonic way, know what they are meant to be doing and understand the standards which they are expected to attain. Furthermore there is a minimal sense in which they act as voluntary agents; for they can rebel and refuse to do what is required of them. These conditions do not apply to what has been induced by hypnosis, drugs, or brutal forms of brain-washing.

Those who believe in such authoritarian methods of education assume that, though children may not care about these performances in the early stages, once they get started on them they will eventually come to care. They will thus emerge as educated men. Growth-theorists, on the other hand, grasping that being educated implies interest in and care for what is worth-while, assumed that this could only develop if the worth-while things are always presented in a way which attracts the child. On psychological grounds they held that coercion and command are ineffective methods for getting children to care about what is worth-while. Furthermore they had moral scruples about treating children in this way, which emerged as procedural principles demanding that children should be allowed to learn by experience and choose for themselves. Their concept of 'education' was moulded by their consciences.

In brief my second conceptual point is that to be 'educated' implies (a) caring about what is worth-while and (b) being brought to care about it and to possess the relevant knowledge or skill in a way that involves at least a minimum of understanding and voluntariness. This point has been blown up by 'growth' theorists into a persuasive definition of 'education' in which 'education' is equated with the observance of procedural principles to do with self-determination. The main defect of their view, however, is not that they were induced by psychological speculation and moral demands to puff up conceptual points about 'education' into procedural principles. Rather it is that they evaded the other feature stressed by traditional teachers that education involves the intentional transmission of worth-while content.

Plato's image of education as turning the eye of the soul outwards towards the light is, in these respects at least, much more apposite than either of the two models so far considered. For though he was convinced that there are truths to be grasped and standards to be achieved, which are public objects of desire, he claimed that coercing people into seeing them or trying to imprint them on wax-like minds was both psychologically unsound and morally base. Plato emphasised, quite rightly, what growth theorists evaded, the necessity for objective standards being written into the content of education. But he was not unmindful of the procedural principles stressed by 'growth' theorists.

### 'EDUCATION' AND COGNITION

The emphasis on 'seeing' and 'grasping' for oneself which is to be found both in Plato and in the 'growth' theorists suggests a third conceptual point about 'education' in addition to those already made about the value of what is passed on and the manner in which it is to be assimilated. This concerns the cognitive aspect of the content of education.

We often say of a man that he is highly trained, but not educated.

What lies behind this condemnation? It is not that the man has mastered a skill of which we disapprove. For we could say this of a doctor or even of a philosopher who had mastered certain ploys or moves in argument; and we might very much approve of their expertise. It is not that he goes through the moves like a mindless robot. For he may be passionately committed to the skill in question and may exercise it with intelligence and determination. It is rather that he has a very limited conception of what he is doing. He does not see its connection with anything else, its place in a coherent pattern of life. It is, for him, an activity which is cognitively adrift. The slogans of the educationalist such as 'education is of the whole man' bear witness not simply to a protest against too much specialised training, but also to the conceptual connection between 'education' and seeing what is being done in a perspective that is not too limited. We talk about a person as being trained as a philosopher, scientist, or cook, when we wish to draw attention to his acquired competence in a specific discipline of thought or art which has its own intrinsic standards; we do not use the phrase 'education *as* a philosopher, scientist, or cook'. We can, however, ask the further question whether such people are educated *men*. To ask this question is at least to probe the limitations of their professional vision.

Confirmation of this conceptual connection between 'education' and cognitive perspective is provided by considering what we say about less specialised matters. We talk more naturally of 'educating the emotions', than we do of training them. This is surely because the distinct emotions are differentiated by their cognitive core, by the different beliefs that go with them. The fundamental difference, for instance, between what is meant by 'anger' as distinct from 'jealousy' can only be brought out by reference to the different sorts of beliefs that the individual has about the people and situations with which he is confronted. A man who is jealous must think that someone else has something to which he is entitled; what comes over him when he is subject to a fit of jealousy is intimately connected with this belief. But a man who is angry need have no belief as specific as this; he may just regard someone as frustrating one of his purposes. If, therefore, we are contemplating bringing about changes in people's emotional attitudes or reactions, our main task consists in trying to get them to see the world differently in relation to themselves. The eye of the jealous man must be made less jaundiced by altering his concept of what has a right to, or by getting him to see the actions of others in another light. We speak of 'education' because of the work that has to be done on his beliefs.

If, on the other hand, we speak, as we sometimes do, of *training* the emotions, the implications are different. We think of standard situations such as those of the fighter pilot or the gentleman in the drawing room. Such moral heroes have to acquire by training or by drill a pattern of habits which will not be disrupted in emergencies; they will not be paralysed by fear or overcome by grief or jealousy in a public place. 'Training' suggests the acquisition of appropriate habits of response in a limited situation. It lacks the wider cognitive implications of 'education'. We talk naturally of 'the training of character' when we wish to ensure reliability of response in accordance with a code; for 'character' is exhibited in the things which people can decide to do and can manifest itself in a very rigid and unadaptive form of behaviour.[9] But when we speak of 'moral education' we immediately envisage addressing ourselves to the matter of what people believe, and to questions of justification and questions of fact connected with such beliefs. To make my point even more sharply: 'sex education' is given by doctors, schoolmasters, and others who are capable of working information and value judgments about sexual matters into a complicated system of beliefs about the functioning of the body, personal relationships, and social institutions. If these oracles proceeded to try a bit of 'sex-training' with their pupils no class-room could contain their activities.

I have often wondered what converted physical training into physical education. No doubt, historically speaking, this came about, as do most changes in educational institutions, through pressures of a militant group requiring fuller recognition. But the underlying rationale of the change was surely the conviction on the part of some that exercising the body must not be seen merely as a skilful and disciplined business related to a specific end such as physical fitness; rather it is to be seen as related to and contributing to other worth-while things in life. To be asked to imagine that one is a leaf is to be given an unusual way of conceiving of what one is doing in the gym. But at least it conveys the impression that one is not just being trained in circumscribed skills.

This connection between 'education' and cognitive content explains why it is that some activities rather than others seem so obviously to be of educational importance. Few skills have a wide-ranging cognitive content. There is very little to know about riding bicycles, swimming, or golf. It is largely a matter of 'knowing how' rather than of 'knowing that',[10] of knack rather than of understanding. Furthermore what there is to know throws very little light on much else. In history, science, or literature, on the other hand, there is an immense amount to know, and, if it is properly assimilated, it constantly throws light on, widens, and deepens one's view of countless other things. Similarly games are of limited educational value. For, even if a game requires great skill and has considerable cognitive content internal to it (e.g., bridge), part of what is meant by calling it a 'game' is that it is set apart from the main business of living, complete in itself, and limited to particular times and places.[11] Games can be conceived of as being of educational importance only in so far as they provide opportunities for acquiring knowledge, qualities of mind and character, and skills that have application in a wider area of life. Hence their accepted importance for moral education. That *many* games have these features in a pre-eminent degree is a myth perpetuated by schoolmasters who convert esoteric enthusiasms into educational panaceas.

It might be objected that in drawing attention to the cognitive content implied by 'education' I am in danger of degrading it to the level of mere instruction. To suggest this would be to misunderstand the main lines of the analysis which is being proposed. My thesis is not that 'education' refers to any special sort of process which might be equated with instruction, training, or drill; rather that it encapsulates three basic criteria which such processes must satisfy. Neither instruction alone, nor training alone, could properly be so described. For both training and instruction might be in futile things like opium-taking, thus failing to satisfy the first criterion of being worth-while. Furthermore instruction might consist in presenting inert ideas which are incomprehensible to children, whilst training might approximate to mindless drill, thus failing to satisfy the second criterion of 'education' already picked out.

Those, however, who have been hostile to mere instruction with its suggestion of 'inert ideas' have been too prone to conceive of education as if it were merely a matter of acquiring skills. This is, perhaps, because the tendency of American pragmatism and behaviourism is to assimilate thinking to doing, to regard it as 'surrogate behaviour'. But an 'educated' man is distinguished not so much by what he does as by what he 'sees' or 'grasps'. If he does something very well, in which he has been trained, he must see this in perspective, as related to other things. It is difficult to conceive of a training that would result in an 'educated' man in which a modicum of instruction has no place. For being educated involves 'knowing that' as well as 'knowing how'.

It might also be objected that I am equating the concept of 'education' with that of 'liberal education'. This is not my intention. The demand that education should be 'liberal' has usually been put forward as a protest against confining what goes on to the service of some extrinsic end such as the production of material goods or the promotion of health or empire. The mind, it is argued, should be allowed to pursue its own bent untrammelled by such restrictions. Allegiance should be given only to standards such as those connected with truth which are intrinsic to the mind's functioning. This interpretation of 'liberal' raises different issues about education which are more relevant to the first point I made about it when I stressed its necessary connection with the promotion of what is desirable. There is, however, another interpretation of 'liberal' which is closer to the point I have just been making about cognitive perspective. This is the plea that education should not be confined to specialist training. The individual, it is argued, should be trained in more than one form of knowledge. This requires more than what is written into the concept of 'education'. For whereas an 'educated' man can be trained in one sphere—e.g. science, and yet be sufficiently cognizant of other ways of looking at the world, so that he can grasp the historical perspective, social significance, or stylistic merit of his work and of much else besides, 'liberal' education requires that he should also be *trained*, to some degree at least, in such other ways of thinking. This is a much stronger requirement than that which is implied by anything that I have said about 'education', though it is obviously a development of what is intimated by it.

But I must digress no further on this point. The discussion has been sufficient, I think, to exhibit the importance both of training and of instruction in education and to safeguard my thesis against the misinterpretation that I am equating education with either of these processes.

EDUCATION AS INITIATION

I now propose to put forward a more positive account of education which is constructed, in a truly dialectic manner, out of considerations brought forward in criticism of the discarded models, and which is consistent with the three criteria of 'education' that I have made explicit. Of course this account will not itself present yet another model; for to produce such a model would be to sin against the glimmerings of light that may have so far flickered over my treatment of the concept of 'education'. For, I have claimed, 'education' marks out no particular type of transaction between teachers and learners; it states criteria to which such transactions have to conform.

'Education' involves essentially processes which intentionally transmit what is valuable in an intelligible and voluntary manner and which create in the learner a desire to achieve it, this being seen to have its place along with other things in life. Terms like 'training' and 'instruction'—perhaps even 'teaching'—are too specific. Education can occur without these specific transactions and they can take place in ways which fail to satisfy all the criteria implied by 'education'. The term 'initiation', on the other hand, is general enough to cover these different types of transaction if it is also stipulated that initiation must be into worth-while activities and modes of conduct.

No man is born with a mind; for the development of mind marks a series of individual and racial achievements. A child is born with an awareness not as yet differentiated into beliefs, wants, and feelings. All such specific modes of consciousness, which are internally related to types of object in a public world, develop later *pari passu* with the pointing out of paradigm objects. Gradually the child comes to want things which there are means of obtaining instead of threshing round beset by unruly and unrealistic wishes; he comes to fear things that may hurt him, and to believe that things will come to pass which have come to pass. He learns to name objects, to locate his experience in a spatio-temporal framework, and to impose causal and means-to-end categories to make sense of events and actions. He creates pools of predictability by making promises and stating his intentions. In the beginning it was not at all like this. Such an embryonic mind is the product of initiation into public traditions enshrined in a public language, which it took our remote ancestors centuries to develop.

With the mastery of basic skills the door is opened to a vaster and more variegated inheritance. Further differentiation develops as the boy becomes initiated more deeply into distinctive forms of knowledge such as science, history, mathematics, religious and aesthetic appreciation, and into the practical types of knowledge involved in moral, prudential, and technical forms of thought and action. Such differentiations are alien to the mind of a child and primitive man —indeed to that of a pre-seventeenth-century man. To have a mind is not to enjoy a private picture-show or to exercise some inner diaphanous organ; it is to have an awareness differentiated in accordance with the canons implicit in all these inherited traditions. 'Education' marks out the processes by means of which the individual is initiated into them.

Why do I start off my positive account of 'education' with this selective thumb-nail sketch of the social history of mind? Partly because I want to establish the notion of initiation in the centre of my account, and partly because I want to draw attention to the enormous importance of the *impersonal content and procedures* which are enshrined in public traditions. Initiation is always into some body of knowledge and mode of conduct which it takes time and determination to master. This association with activities which have what I called 'cognitive content' satisfies the third of the three essential criteria of education that I dwelt on in my earlier discussion of inadequate models. But there are additional points to stress about the importance in education of impersonal content and procedures.

There have been many like Dewey who have attacked the notion that education consists in the transmission of a body of knowledge. Stress is placed instead on critical thinking, individual experimentation and problem-solving. I have witnessed lessons in American schools where this view was slavishly applied: the teacher used poems purely to encourage 'critical thinking'; history was used, as it were, to provide riders for problem-solving. The notion that poetry should be listened to, or that one has to be, to a certain extent, a historian in order to understand a historical problem, was an alien one. The emphasis on 'critical thinking' was salutary enough, perhaps, when bodies of knowledge were handed on without any attempt being made to hand on also the public procedures by means of which they had been accumulated, criticised, and revised. But it is equally absurd to foster an abstract skill called 'critical thinking' without handing on anything concrete to be critical about. For there are as many brands of 'critical thinking' as there are disciplines, and in the various disciplines such as history, science, and philosophy, there is a great deal to be known before the peculiar nature of the problem is grasped.

It is of course important that people should be initiated gradually into the procedures defining a discipline as well as into mastery of the established content, that people should learn to think historically for instance, not just know some history. But the only way to learn to think historically is to probe the past with someone who has mastered this form of thought. The procedures of a discipline can only be mastered by an exploration of its established content under the guidance of one who has already been initiated. Whitehead said that a merely well-informed man is the most useless bore on God's earth. I do not entirely agree. I always find encyclopaedias interesting. Equally boring, in my view, are those for whom being critical is a substitute for being well informed about anything. To parody Kant: content without criticism is blind, but criticism without content is empty.

The further point needs also to be made that the critical procedures by means of which established content is assessed, revised, and adapted to new discoveries, have public criteria written into them that stand as impersonal standards to which both teacher and learner must give their allegiance. The trouble with the models of education that I considered is that they fail to do justice to this essential inter-subjectivity of education which D. H. Lawrence referred to as 'the holy ground'. To liken education to therapy, to conceive of it as imposing a pattern on another person or as fixing the environment so that he 'grows', fails to do justice to the shared impersonality both of the content that is handed on and of the criteria by reference to which it is criticized and revised. The teacher is not a detached operator who is bringing about some kind of result in another person which is external to him. His task is to try to get others on the inside of a public form of life that he shares and considers to be worth-while. In science it is truth that matters, not what any individual believes to be true; in morals it is justice, not the pronouncements of any individual.

At the culminating stages of education there is little distinction between teacher and taught; they are both participating in the shared experience of exploring a common world. The teacher is simply more familiar with its contours and more skilled in handling the tools for laying bare its mysteries and appraising its nuances. Occasionally in a tutorial this exploration takes the form of a dialogue. But more usually it is a group experience. The great teachers are those who can conduct such a shared exploration in accordance with rigorous canons, and convey, at the same time, the contagion of a shared enterprise in which all are united by a common zeal. That is why humour is such a valuable aid to teachers; for if people can laugh together they step out of the shadows of self-reference cast by age, sex, and position. This creation of a shared experience can act as a catalyst which releases a class to unite in their common enterprise. This feeling of fraternity is part of the emotional underpinning for an enterprise conducted according to impersonal principles.

There has been too much loose talk about the dimension of the personal in teaching. Indeed one often fears that 'the enjoyment of good personal relationships' with pupils is in danger of becoming a substitute for teaching them something. What is required of the teacher, in addition to the feeling of fraternity already mentioned, is respect for persons, not intimate relations with his pupils. In a teaching situation love must be of a type that is appropriate to the special type of relationship in which the teacher is placed, to his concept of them as pupils rather than as sons or brothers. The teacher must always remember that he is dealing with others who are distinctive centres of consciousness, with peculiar idiosyncratic purposes and feelings that criss-cross their institutional roles. Each one is bound up with and takes pride of some sort in his own achievements; each one mirrors the world from a distinctive point of view. In the early stages of education the emphasis on individual differences must be more marked; for the enterprise is to present the basic skills, which are necessary for later explorations, in the manner which is most appropriate to minds comparatively unformed by public traditions. Hence the relevance of activity methods and of the model of individual growth; hence the appositeness of the slogan 'We teach children, not subjects'; hence the need for teachers to understand what psychologists have discovered about individual differences and child development. Such a 'child-centred' approach is as appropriate in dealing with the backward or difficult adolescent as it is at the infant stage. For the crucial difference is not one of age, but of the development of motivation and of cognitive structure, and of degrees of initiation into public and differentiated modes of thought.

At the other end of the enterprise of education, however, in universities, adult education classes, and the later stages of secondary education, the emphasis is more on the canons implicit in the forms of thought than on individual avenues of initiation. Respect for persons, enlivened by fraternity, here provides the warmth in which the teacher can perform his cardinal function of exhibiting the form of thought into which he is trying to initiate others. It is one thing to understand the canons of any discipline or mode of conduct; it is quite another to apply them with skill and judgment in particular circumstances. Judgment, said Quintilian, is the final flower of much experience. But such experience has to be acquired in the company of a man who already has judgment; it cannot be learnt from books or formal lectures alone. Oakeshott has written so tellingly on this aspect of the personal element in education that it would be otiose for me to labour this point any further.[12] Need I add that the notion of 'initiation' is a peculiarly apt description of this essential feature of education which consists in experienced persons turning the eye of others outwards to what is essentially independent of persons?

'Initiation' is an apt description, too, of that other aspect of education stressed by the 'growth' theorists, the requirement that those who are being educated should want to do or master the worthwhile things which are handed on to them. This must be done in such a way that the coercion of the old formal instructor is not replaced by the cajoling of the progressive child-watcher. I am inclined to think that the value of command and direction is underestimated by modern educational theory, especially perhaps with less intelligent children. At least it indicates clearly what the educator considers to be worth-while and is certainly preferable to bribery and the production of irrelevant incentives. At least it may awaken some rebellion in the child and generate a jet of desire in him to do what he thinks worth-while, if he can find an avenue. Where everything is only to be done if it can be seen by the child to relate to what he wants, the coinage of wanting becomes debased because there is too little with which he may contrast it.

This brings me to my final and perhaps most fundamental point about 'education'. I have remarked before that 'education' implies standards, not necessarily aims. It consists in initiating others into activities, modes of conduct and thought which have standards written into them by reference to which it is possible to act, think, and feel with varying degrees of skill, relevance and taste. If teachers are not convinced of this they should be otherwise employed. They may be a bit hazy about why these things are more valuable than others. This is not surprising; for the problem of justification in general is a very difficult problem with which moral philosophers since Socrates have been constantly wrestling. The relative weight to be given to these valuable things also presents acute problems; hence the importance of having a system which permits options. But *that* these things are valuable no dedicated teacher would dispute.

Now the teacher, having himself been initiated, is on the inside of these activities and modes of thought and conduct. He understands vividly, perhaps, that some created objects are beautiful and others not; he can recognise the elegance of a proof, or a paragraph, the cogency of an argument, the clarity of an exposition, the wit of a remark, the neatness of a plot and the justice and wisdom of a decision. He has perhaps a love of truth, a passion for justice, and a hatred of what is tasteless. To ask him what the aim or point of this form of life is, into which he has himself been initiated, seems an otiose question. For, like Socrates, he senses that really to understand what is good is, *ipso facto*, to be committed to its pursuit. How can a man who really understands what a cogent argument is, or a wise and just decision, settle for one that is slipshod, slovenly, or haphazard? This sort of question, he senses, can only be asked by barbarians outside the gates. Of course he realises that science, mathematics, and even history *can* be viewed in an instrumental way. They contribute to hospitals being built and staffed, wars being won, the cultivation of the land, and to communication across the face of the earth. And then what, he asks? What are men going to do, how are they going to think, what are they going to appreciate when their necessary appetites are satisfied? Are these hard men indifferent to all that constitutes being civilised?

Children, to a large extent, are. They start off in the position of the barbarian outside the gates. The problem is to get them inside the citadel of civilisation so that they will understand and love what they see when they get there. It is no use concealing the fact that the activities and modes of thought and conduct which define a civilised form of life are difficult to master. That is why the educator has such an uphill task in which there are no short cuts. The insistence, which one confronts in American schools, that children should be happy, ignores this brutal fact. People can be happy lying in the sun; but happiness such as this is not the concern of the educator. Most of our thinking about 'welfare' is bedevilled by the confusion of being happy with living a worth-while life.

It may well be asked: if this is what is meant by 'education', how many people are capable of it? This is not a philosophical question; for though a philosopher might concern himself with the general conditions necessary for the application of a concept, it is an empirical question to determine to what extent such conditions are actually realized. To take a parallel: a philosopher might map out what it means to be moral and what general conditions must be satisfied for the concept to have application—e.g. the possession of a central nervous system, the ability to feel sympathy for others. But it is not his business, *qua* philosopher, to speculate about how many people there may be in whom such conditions are satisfied.

It is clear, however, from this analysis of 'education' that there are necessary conditions to do with cognitive structure and motivation. Although it is not a philosopher's task to speculate about the empirical facts in this matter, it is not out of place for him to note that very little is known about them. As has been remarked before, such evidence as there is suggests that a great deal depends on early conditions in the home and school. Since a large proportion of the population in Great Britain suffers from an environment which militates against such motivation and cognitive development it would be unwise as well as unfair to conclude too soon that education can only be for the 'elite'.

Many educators, seeing both the indignity and the inefficacy of the traditional attempts to coerce children into doing difficult things for which they had no inclination, preached the doctrine of 'interest'. If these difficult things could be ingeniously harnessed to what children want, then, they said, the task and not the man will exert the discipline. Skill, judgment, and discrimination can be erected on a foundation of existing wants. There is much in this technique. In the Youth Service, for instance, we used a predictable interest in sex to develop manners, skill in dancing, and taste in clothes and personal adornment. The hope was that eventually the girls would come to value manners and skill in dancing for their own sake and not purely as a means to getting a boy, and would develop outwards from this solid centre. One technique of initiation is therefore to lure people inside the citadel by using their existing interests in the hope that, once inside, they will develop other interests which previously were never dreamed of. The danger of this technique is that, if used to the exclusion of others, it reinforces the instrumental attitude. It encourages people to think that things are only worth doing well if they are patently relevant to some extrinsic end.

This is, of course, a very limited conception of initiation. For it neglects the fluidity of wants. What people in fact want or are interested in is, to a large extent, a product of their previous initiation. The job of the educator is not simply to build on existing wants but to present what is worth wanting in such a way that it creates new wants and stimulates new interests. If teachers do not do this others will—advertisers, for instance, and other members of 'the peer group'. There are interesting studies emerging recently from the U.S.A. suggesting a connection between permissive methods in education and group conformity.[13] If teachers do not hold up standards of achievement to children in a way that gets them working, others will lure them along less exacting paths. Whitehead has much that it is wise to say here on the stage of 'romance' in education. Any method which can create interest in what is worth-while should not be debarred—even talk and chalk, if employed by a man who is good at it.[14] But the stage of romance must be followed by the stage of precision. The crunch of standards must come with all that it entails in blood, sweat, and tears. The 'playway' may open up a vista of a Promised Land; but of itself it may provide little of the precision, skill and judgment which may be necessary for getting there. The pupil has gradually to get the grammar of the activity into his guts so that he can eventually win through to the stage of autonomy. But he cannot do this unless he has mastered the moves made by his predecessors which are enshrined in living traditions. *How* he can come best to this is an empirical question; but talk of encouraging 'creativeness' is mischievous unless children are also equipped with competence; talk of 'problem-solving' is cant unless children are knowledgeable enough to recognize a real problem when they see one. The only way into mastering what Oakeshott calls the 'language' of any form of thought or activity is by first being initiated into its 'literature'.[15] This is an arduous business.

As a matter of fact there is evidence to suggest that the teacher may not have to rely purely on specific interests, or on the admiration which children have for him and their desire to please him, to provide incentives for precision. For there may well be a generalized interest in achievement and competence for its own sake.[16] To master some difficult task, to get things right, to do what is right, is a very powerful source of motivation. It can grip young children as well as absorbed adults. Perhaps it was one of the driving forces of the Puritan movement which once galvanised England into activity. It can, of course, degenerate into compulsiveness; it can be harnessed to things that are both futile and wicked. But when harnessed to things that are also worth-while, it is not to be despised. There is much to be said for the generalized Puritan virtues of enterprise, orderliness, thoroughness, and perseverance—especially in education.

Education, then, can have no ends beyond itself. Its value derives from principles and standards implicit in it. To be educated is not to have arrived at a destination; it is to travel with a different view. What is required is not feverish preparation for something that lies ahead, but to work with precision, passion and taste at worth-while things that lie to hand. These worth-while things cannot be forced on reluctant minds, neither are they flowers towards which the seeds of mentality develop in the sun of the teacher's smile. They are acquired by contact with those who have already acquired them and who have patience, zeal, and competence enough to initiate others into them.

'There is a quality of life which lies always beyond the mere fact of life'.[17] The great teacher is he who can convey this sense of quality to another, so that it haunts his every endeavour and makes him sweat and yearn to fix what he thinks and feels in a fitting form. For life has no one purpose; man imprints his purposes upon it. It presents few tidy problems; mainly predicaments that have to be endured or enjoyed. It is education that provides that touch of eternity under the aspect of which endurance can pass into dignified, wry acceptance, and animal enjoyment into a quality of living.

Education as Initiation

## NOTES

1. Another version of this paper was given as an Inaugural Lecture to the Chair of the Philosophy of Education at the University of London Institute of Education, delivered in December 1963.

2. *Half Our Future*. A report of the Central Advisory Council for Education (London: H.M. Stationery Office, 1963).

3. See, for instance, B. Bernstein, 'Social Class and Linguistic Development: A Theory of Social Learning' in *Education, Economy, and Society*, Ed. Halsey, Floud, and Anderson (New York: Free Press, 1961).

4. 'Education' is actually both what Ryle calls a 'task' term and an 'achievement' term (see G. Ryle, *The Concept of Mind* [London: Hutchinson, 1949] pp. 149–153). The complications introduced by this cannot be dealt with in a paper of this nature and do not affect the main lines of the analysis. They will be dealt with at more length in my forthcoming book on *Ethics and Education*.

5. J. Dewey, *Experience and Education* (New York: Macmillan, 1938).

6. For further comments on both 'moulding' and 'growth' metaphors see I. Scheffler, *The Language of Education* (Springfield, Illinois: Thomas, 1960), Chapter 3.

7. R. S. Peters, *Authority, Responsibility, and Education* (London: Allen and Unwin, 2nd edition, 1963), Chapter 7.

8. J. Dewey, *Experience and Education* (London: Constable, 1961), pp. 37–38.

9. For further complications in the concept of 'character' see R. S. Peters, 'Moral Education and the Psychology of Character' in *Philosophy*, January 1962.

10. See G. Ryle, *The Concept of Mind* (London: Hutchinson, 1949), Chapter 2.

11. See J. Huizinga, *Homo Ludens* (London: Kegan Paul, 1949), Chapter 1.

12. See M. Oakeshott, 'Political Education' in *Rationalism in Politics* (London: Methuen, 1962).

13. See, for example, F. Kerlinger, 'The Implications of the Permissiveness Doctrine in American Education' in H. Burns and C. Brauner, *Philosophy and Education* (New York: Ronald Press, 1962).

14. A. N. Whitehead, *The Aims of Education* (London: Williams and Norgate, 1962), Chapter 2.

15. See M. Oakeshott, 'The Teaching of Politics in a University' in *Rationalism in Politics* (London: Methuen, 1962).

16. See D. McClelland, *The Achievement Motive* (New York: Appleton-Century, 1953), and other more recent publications, as well as R. White, 'Competence and the Psycho-sexual Stages of Development' in M. R. Jones, ed., *Nebraska Symposium on Motivation* (Lincoln: Un. of Nebraska Press, 1960).

17. A. N. Whitehead, *Religion in the Making* (Cambridge University Press, 1926), p. 80.

# LIBERAL EDUCATION AND THE NATURE OF KNOWLEDGE

## Paul H. Hirst

THE phrase 'liberal education' has today become something of a slogan which takes on different meanings according to its immediate context. It usually labels a form of education of which the author approves, but beyond that its meaning is often entirely negatively derived. Whatever else a liberal education is, it is *not* a vocational education, *not* an exclusively scientific education, or *not* a specialist education in any sense. The frequency with which the term is employed in this way certainly highlights the inadequacies of these other concepts and the need for a wider and, in the long run, more worthwhile form of education. But as long as the concept is merely negative in what it intimates, it has little more than debating value. Only when it is given explicit positive content can it be of use in the serious business of educational planning. It is my contention in this paper that whatever vagaries there have been in the use of the term, it is the appropriate label for a positive concept, that of an education based fairly and squarely on the nature of knowledge itself, a concept central to the discussion of education at any level.

The fully developed Greek notion of liberal education was rooted in a number of related philosophical doctrines; first about the significance of knowledge for the mind, and secondly about the relationship between knowledge and reality. In the first category there was the doctrine that it is the peculiar and distinctive activity of the mind, because of its very nature, to pursue knowledge. The achievement of knowledge satisfies and fulfils the mind which thereby attains its own appropriate end. The pursuit of knowledge is thus the pursuit of the good of the mind and, therefore, an essential element in the good life. In addition, it was held that the achievement of knowledge is not only the attainment of the good of the mind itself, but also the chief means whereby the good life as a whole is to be found. Man is more than pure mind, yet mind is his essential distinguishing characteristic, and it is in terms of knowledge that his whole life is rightly directed.

That knowledge is equal to its task was guaranteed by the second group of doctrines. These asserted that the mind, in the right use of reason, comes to know the essential nature of things and can apprehend what is ultimately real and immutable. Consequently, man no longer needs to live in terms of deceptive appearances and doubtful opinions and beliefs. All his experiences, life and thought can be given shape and perspective by what is finally true, by knowledge that corresponds to what is ultimately real. Further, the particular way in which reason is here represented as attaining knowledge, results in a view of the whole of man's understanding as hierarchically structured in various levels. From the knowledge of mere particulars to that of pure being, all knowledge has its place in a comprehensive and harmonious scheme, the pattern of which is formed as knowledge is developed in apprehending reality in its many different manifestations.

From these doctrines there emerged the idea of liberal education as a process concerned simply and directly with the pursuit of knowledge. But the doctrines give to this general idea particular meaning and significance; for they lead to a clear definition of its scope and content, and to a clear justification for education in these terms. The definition is clear, because education is determined objectively in range, in structure and in content by the forms of knowledge itself and their harmonious, hierarchical interrelations. There is here no thought of defining education in terms of knowledge and skills that may be useful, or in terms of moral virtues and qualities of mind that may be considered desirable. The definition is stated strictly in terms of man's knowledge of what is the case. The development of the mind to which it leads, be it in skills, virtues or other characteristics, is thought to be necessarily its greatest good.

The justification that the doctrines lend to his concept of education is threefold. First, such an education is based on what is true and not on uncertain opinions and beliefs or temporary values. It therefore has a finality which no other form of education has. Secondly, knowledge itself being a distinctive human virtue, liberal education has a value for the person as the fulfilment of the mind, a value which has nothing to do with utilitarian or vocational considerations. Thirdly, because of the significance of knowledge in the determination of the good life as a whole, liberal education is essential to man's understanding of how he ought to live, both individually and socially.

Here, then, the Greeks attained the concept of an education that was 'liberal' not simply because it was the education of free men rather than slaves, but also because they saw it as freeing the mind to function according to its true nature, freeing reason from error and illusion and freeing man's conduct from wrong. And ever since Greek times this idea of education has had its place. Sometimes it has been modified or extended in detail to accommodate within its scheme new forms of knowledge: for instance Christian doctrines and the various branches of modern science. Sometimes the concept has been misinterpreted: as in Renaissance humanism when classical learning was equated with liberal education. Sometimes it has been strongly opposed on philosophical grounds: as by Dewey and the pragmatists. Yet at crucial points in the history of education the concept has constantly reappeared. It is not hard to understand why this should be so.

Education, being a deliberate, purposeful activity directed to the development of individuals, necessarily involves considerations of value. Where are these values to be found? What is to be their content? How are they to be justified? They can be, and often are, values that reflect the interests of a minority group in the society. They may be religious, political or utilitarian in character. They are always open to debate and detailed criticism, and are always in need of particular justification. Is there not perhaps a more ultimate basis for the values that should determine education, some more objective ground? That final ground has, ever since the Greeks, been repeatedly located in man's conception of the diverse forms of knowledge he has achieved. And there has thus arisen the demand for an education whose definition and justification are based on the nature and significance of knowledge itself, and not on the predilections of pupils, the demands of society, or the whims of politicians. Precisely this demand was behind the development by the Greeks of an education in the seven liberal arts, an introduction to and a pursuit of the forms of knowledge as they were then conceived. It was precisely this demand that prompted Newman and Arnold in the nineteenth century to call for an education that aimed at the cultivation and development of the mind in the full range of man's understanding. It is the same demand that today motivates such classical realists as Maritain and R. M. Hutchins.

## A TYPICAL MODERN STATEMENT: THE HARVARD REPORT

It may well be asked, however, whether those who do not hold the doctrines of metaphysical and epistemological realism can legitimately subscribe to a concept of education of this kind. Historically it seems to have had positive force only when presented in this particular philosophical framework. But historical association must be distinguished from logical connection and it is not by any means obvious that all the characteristic features of the concept are dependent on such philosophical realism. If the doctrines about mind, knowledge and reality mentioned at the beginning of this paper are regarded as at best too speculative a basis for educational planning, as well they may be, the possibility of an education defined and justified entirely in terms of the scope and character of knowledge needs re-examination. The significance of the concept originally came directly from the place the basic doctrines give to knowledge in a unified picture of the mind and its relation to reality. Knowledge is achieved when the mind attains its own satisfaction or good by corresponding to objective reality. A liberal education in the pursuit of knowledge is, therefore, seeking the development of the mind according to what is quite external to it, the structure and pattern of reality. But if once there is any serious questioning of this relationship between mind, knowledge and reality, the whole harmonious structure is liable to disintegrate. First there arise inevitably problems of definition. A liberal education defined in terms of knowledge alone is acceptable as long as knowledge is thought to be necessarily developing the mind in desirable ways, and hence promoting the good life. But if doubt is cast on these functions of knowledge, must not liberal education be redefined stating explicitly the qualities of mind and the moral virtues to which it is directed? And if knowledge is no longer seen as the understanding of reality but merely as the understanding of experience, what is to replace the harmonious, hierarchical scheme of knowledge that gave pattern and order to the education? Secondly there are equally serious problems of justification. For if knowledge is no longer thought to be rooted in some reality, or if its significance for the mind and the good life is questioned, what can be the justification for an education defined in terms of knowledge alone?

Difficulties of both kinds, but particularly those of definition, can be seen in the well-known Harvard Committee Report: *General Education in a Free Society*.[1] (In the Committee's terminology the aims of a 'liberal' and a 'general' education are identical.) Though certain of the doctrines that originally supported the concept of a liberal education are implicit in this work, the classical view of the significance of knowledge for the mind is considerably weakened, and the belief that in metaphysics man has knowledge of ultimate reality is ignored, if not rejected. The result is an ambiguous and unsatisfactory treatment of the problem of definition and a limited and debatable treatment of the question of justification. Some examination of the Report on both these scores, particularly the former, will serve to show that adequate definition and justification are not only not dependent on the classical doctrines, but can in fact be based directly on an explication of the concepts of 'mind' and 'knowledge' and their relationship.

The Report attempts the definition of a liberal education in two distinct ways: in terms of the qualities of mind it ought to produce and the forms of knowledge with which it ought to be concerned. What the precise relationship is between these two is not clear. It is asserted that they are 'images of each other', yet that there is no escape from 'describing general education at one time looking to the good man in society and at another time as dictated by the nature of knowledge itself'.[2] Which of the forms of description is to be given pride of place soon emerges, however. First, three areas of knowledge are distinguished, primarily by their distinctive methods: the natural sciences, the humanities and social studies. But it is made plain that 'the cultivation of certain aptitudes and attitudes of mind' is being aimed at, the elements of knowledge being the means for developing these. Liberal education is therefore best understood in terms of the characteristics of mind to which it leads. 'By characteristics we mean aims so important as to prescribe how general education should be carried out and which abilities ought to be sought above all others in every part of it. These abilities in our opinion are: to think effectively, to communicate thought, to make relevant judgments, to discriminate among values'.[3] The meaning of each of these four is elaborated at some length. Amongst the many things detailed of 'effective thinking' it is first said to be logical thinking of a kind that is applicable to such practical matters as deciding who to vote for and what wife to choose: it is the ability to extract universal truths from particular cases and to infer particulars from general laws: it is the ability to analyse a problem and to recombine the elements by the use of imagination. This thinking goes further than mere logic, however. It includes the relational thinking of everyday life, the ability to think at a level appropriate to a problem whatever its character. It includes too the imaginative thinking of the poet, the inventor, and the revolutionary. 'Communication', though 'obviously inseparable from effective thinking', is said to involve another group of skills, those of speaking and listening, writing and reading. It includes certain moral qualities such as candour, it covers certain vital aspects of social and political life and even the high art of conversation. 'The making of relevant value judgments' involves 'the ability of the student to bring to bear the whole range of ideas upon the area of experience', it is the art of effectively relating theory to practice, of abstractions to facts, of thought to action. Finally there is 'discrimination among values'. This includes the distinction of various kinds of value and their relative importance, an awareness of the values of character like fair play and self-control, intellectual values like the love of truth and aesthetic values like good taste, and, in addition, a commitment to such values in the conduct of life.[4]

As to how exactly these abilities come to be those developed by the three types of knowledge, little is said. It is noted that 'the three phases of effective thinking, logical, relational, and imaginative, correspond roughly to the three divisions of learning, the natural sciences, the social studies, and the humanities, respectively.'[5] The difficult connection between education in the making of value judgments and the formation of moral character is noted. Otherwise the remarks are of a general nature, emphasizing that these abilities must be consciously developed in all studies and generalized as far as possible.

This double, if one-sided, characterization of liberal education seems to me unsatisfactory and seriously misleading if what is said of the four abilities is examined more closely. In the first place, the notion that a liberal education can be directly characterized in terms of mental abilities and independently of fully specifying the forms of knowledge involved, is I think false. It is the result of a misunderstanding of the way in which mental abilities are in fact distinguishable. From what is said of 'effective thinking', it is perfectly plain that the phrase is being used as a label for mental activity which results in an achievement of some sort, an achievement that is, at least in principle, both publicly describable and publicly testable—the solving of a mathematical problem, responsibly deciding who to vote for, satisfactorily analysing a work of art. Indeed there can be effective thinking only when the outcome of mental activity can be recognised and judged by those who have the appropriate skills and knowledge, for otherwise the phrase has no significant application. Thus although the phrase labels a form of mental activity, and such mental processes may well be directly accessible only to the person whose processes they are, its description and evaluation must be in public terms occurring in public language. Terms which, like 'effective thinking', describe activities involving achievements of some sort, must have public criteria to mark them. But in that case, none of the four abilities can in fact be delineated except by means of their detailed public features. Such characterisation is in fact forced on the Committee when they come to amplify what they mean. But their approach is simply illustrative, as if the abilities are directly intelligible in themselves, and the items and features of knowledge they give merely examples of areas where the abilities can be seen. If the public terms and criteria are logically necessary to specifying what the abilities are, however, then no adequate account of liberal education in terms of these can be given without a full account in terms of the public features of the forms of knowledge with which it is concerned. Indeed the latter is logically prior and the former secondary and derivative.

In the second place, the use of broad, general terms for these abilities serves in fact to unify misleadingly quite disparate achievements. For the public criteria whereby the exercise of any one of these abilities is to be judged are not all of a piece. Those that under the banner of 'effective thinking' are appropriate in, say, aesthetic appreciation are, apart from certain very general considerations, inappropriate in, say, mathematical thinking. In each case the criteria are peculiar to the particular area of knowledge concerned. Similarly, for instance, 'communication' in the sciences has only certain very basic features in common with 'communication' in poetic terms. It is only when the abilities are fully divided out, as it were, into the various domains and we see what they refer to in public terms that it is at all clear what is involved in developing them. To talk of developing 'effective thinking' is like talking of developing 'successful games playing'. Plainly that unifying label is thoroughly misleading when what constitutes playing cricket has practically nothing in common with what constitutes playing tiddly-winks. The implications of the term are not at all appreciated until what is wanted is given detailed specification. It is vitally important to realize the very real objective differences that there are in forms of knowledge, and therefore in our understanding of mental processes that are related to these. Maybe this unfortunate desire to use unifying concepts is a relic of the time when all forms of knowledge were thought to be similar, if not identical in logical structure and that the 'laws of logic' reflected the precise psychological operations involved in valid thinking. Be that as it may, the general terms used in the Report are liable both to blur essential distinctions and to direct the attention of educational planners into unprofitable descriptions of what they are after.

Thirdly, in spite of any protestations to the contrary, the impression is created by this terminology that it is possible to develop general unitary abilities of the stated kind. The extent to which this is true is a matter for empirical investigation into the transfer of training. Nevertheless such abilities must necessarily be characterised in terms of the public features of knowledge, and whatever general abilities there may be, the particular criteria for their application in diverse fields are vital to their significance for liberal education. But to think in these terms is to be in danger of looking for transfer of skills where none is discernible. We must not assume that skill at tiddly-winks will get us very far at cricket, or that if the skills have much in common, as in say squash and tennis, then the rules for one activity will do as the rules for the other.

Failure to appreciate these points leads all too readily to programmes of education for which quite unwarranted claims are made. It is sometimes said, for instance, that the study of one major science can in itself provide the elements of a liberal education— that it can lead to the development of such abilities as effective thinking, communication, the making of relevant judgments, and even to some extent, discrimination among values. But this facile view is seen to be quite untenable if it is once understood how these abilities are defined, and how any one form of knowledge is related to them. Much more plausible and much more common is the attempt to relate directly the study of particular subjects to the development of particular unitary abilities. The Harvard Committee do this with subdivisions of 'effective thinking' when they suggest that, roughly speaking, logical thinking is developed by the sciences, relational thinking by social studies, and imaginative thinking by the humanities. This, of course, could be said to be true by definition if logical thinking were taken to be just that kind of thinking that is developed by the study of the sciences. But such a straight and limited connection is not at all what is indicated in the Report. The forms of thinking there are much more generalised. It follows then that logical, relational and imaginative thinking must be independently defined. Because of the vagueness of the terms it might appear that this would be simple enough. But in fact this very vagueness makes the task almost impossible, for any one of the three terms might, with considerable justice, be applied to almost any example of thinking. (And the appropriateness of using such a term as 'imaginative' to describe a distinct type of thinking rather than its manner or style is very debatable). Even if this most serious difficulty were overcome somehow, there would remain the problem of establishing empirical evidence, for asserting both the existence of such an ability, and that a particular study leads to its development. Generally speaking there is little such evidence. What there is on transfer of training suggests that it occurs only where there is marked logical similarity in the elements studied.[6]

Finally the characterisation of a liberal education in these terms is misleading owing to the tendency for the concept to be broadened so that it is concerned not only with the development of the mind that results from the pursuit of knowledge, but also with other aspects of personal development, particularly emotional and moral, that may or may not be judged desirable. This tendency can be clearly seen in the Report's comments on the abilities of communication, making relevant judgments and discriminating among values. Stretching the edges of the concept in these ways leads to a much wider, more generalised notion of education. It then ceases to be one defined directly in terms of the pursuit of knowledge as liberal education originally was, and thus cannot be justified by justifying that pursuit. But this is surely to give up the concept in favour of another one that needs independent justification. The analysis of such a concept is beyond our present concern.

## Paul H. Hirst

On logical grounds, then, it would seem that a consistent concept of liberal education must be worked out fully in terms of the forms of knowledge. By these is meant, of course, not collections of information, but the complex ways of understanding experience which man has achieved, which are publicly specifiable and which are gained through learning. An education in these terms does indeed develop its related abilities and qualities of mind, for the mind will be characterised to a greater or less degree by the features of the understanding it seeks. Each form of knowledge, if it is to be acquired beyond a general and superficial level, involves the development of creative imagination, judgment, thinking, communicative skills, etc., in ways that are peculiar to itself as a way of understanding experience. To list these elements, picking them out, as it were, across the forms of knowledge of which they are part and in each of which they have a different stamp, draws attention to many features that a liberal education must of course include. But it draws attention to them at the expense of the differences among them as they occur in the different areas. And of itself such listing contributes nothing to the basic determination of what a liberal education is. To be told that it is the development of effective thinking is of no value until this is explicated in terms of the forms of knowledge which give it meaning: for example in terms of the solving of problems in Euclidean geometry or coming to understand the poems of John Donne. To be told instead that it is concerned with certain specified forms of knowledge, the essential characteristics of which are then detailed explicitly as far as possible, is to be given a clear understanding of the concept and one which is unambiguous as to the forms of thinking, judgment, imagination and communication it involves.

In his Gulbenkian Foundation Report: *Arts and Science Sides in the Sixth Form*, Mr. A. D. C. Peterson comes considerably nearer than the Harvard Committee to the definition of a liberal education (once more termed here a 'general education') by proceeding in just this fashion. Being concerned that this should not be worked out in terms of information, he shies away from any direct use of the term 'knowledge' and defines the concept modestly as one that 'develops the intellect in as many as possible of the main modes of thinking'.[7] These are then listed as the logical, the empirical, the moral and the aesthetic. The phrase 'modes of thinking', it is true, refers directly to forms of mental activity, and Mr. Peterson's alternatives for it, 'modes of human experience', 'categories of mental experience' and (elsewhere) 'types of judgment', all look in the same direction. Yet the 'modes' are not different aspects of mind that cut across the forms that human knowledge takes, as the Harvard Report's 'abilities' are. They are, rather, four parallel forms of mental development. To complete this treatment so that there is no ambiguity, however, it must be made clear in a way that Mr. Peterson does not make it clear, that the four forms can only be distinguished, in the last analysis, in terms of the public features that demarcate the areas of knowledge on which they stand. Logical, empirical, moral and aesthetic forms of understanding are distinguishable from each other only by their distinctive concepts and expressions and their criteria for distinguishing the true from the false, the good from the bad. If Mr. Peterson's 'modes' are strictly explicated on the basis of these features of knowledge, then his concept of education becomes one concerned with the development of the mind as that is determined by certain forms of knowledge. This is to be in sight of a modern equivalent of the traditional conception of liberal education.

But the reassertion of this concept implies that there is once more the acceptance of some kind of 'harmony' between knowledge and the mind. This is, however, not now being maintained on metaphysical grounds. What is being suggested, rather, is that the 'harmony' is a matter of the logical relationship between the concept of 'mind' and the concept of 'knowledge', from which it follows that the achievement of knowledge is necessarily the development of mind—that is, the self-conscious rational mind of man— in its most fundamental aspect.

Whatever else is implied in the phrase, to have 'a rational mind' certainly implies experience structured under some form of conceptual scheme. The various manifestations of consciousness, in, for instance, different sense perceptions, different emotions, or different elements of intellectual understanding, are intelligible only by virtue of the conceptual apparatus by which they are articulated. Further, whatever private forms of awareness there may be, it is by means of symbols, particularly in language, that conceptual articulation becomes objectified, for the symbols give public embodiment to the concepts. The result of this is that men are able to come to understand both the external world and their own private states of mind in common ways, sharing the same conceptual schema by learning to use symbols in the same manner. The objectification of understanding is possible because commonly accepted criteria for using the terms are recognised even if these are never explicitly expressed. But further as the symbols derived from experience can be used to examine subsequent experience, assertions are possible which are testable as true or false, valid or invalid. There are thus also public criteria whereby certain forms of expression are assessable against experience. Whether the 'objects' concerned are themselves private to the individual like mental processes, or publicly accessible like temperature readings, there are here tests for the assertions which are themselves publicly agreed and accepted.

It is by the use of such tests that we have come to have the whole domain of knowledge. The formulating and testing of symbolic expressions has enabled man to probe his experience for ever more complex relations and for finer and finer distinctions, these being fixed and held for public sharing in the symbolic systems that have been evolved. But it is important to realise that this progressive attainment of a cognitive framework with public criteria has significance not merely for knowledge itself, for it is by its terms that the life of man in every particular is patterned and ordered. Without its structure all other forms of consciousness, including, for example, emotional experiences, or mental attitudes and beliefs, would seem to be unintelligible. For the analysis of them reveals that they lack independent intelligible structure of themselves. Essentially private though they may be in many or all of their aspects, their characteristic forms are explicable only by means of the publicly rooted conceptual organisations we have achieved. They can be understood only by means of the objective features with which they are associated, round which they come to be organised and built. The forms of knowledge are thus the basic articulations whereby the whole of experience has become intelligible to man, they are the fundamental achievement of mind.

Knowledge, however, must never be thought of merely as vast bodies of tested symbolic expressions. These are only the public aspects of the ways in which human experience has come to have shape. They are significant because they are themselves the objective elements round which the development of mind has taken place. To acquire knowledge is to become aware of experience as structured, organised and made meaningful in some quite specific way, and the varieties of human knowledge constitute the highly developed forms in which man has found this possible. To acquire knowledge is to learn to see, to experience the world in a way otherwise unknown, and thereby come to have a mind in a fuller sense. It is not that the mind is some kind of organ or muscle with its own inbuilt forms of operation, which if somehow developed, naturally lead to different kinds of knowledge. It is not that the mind has predetermined patterns of functioning. Nor is it that the mind is an entity which suitably directed by knowledge comes to take on the pattern of, is conformed to, some external reality. It is rather that to have a mind basically involves coming to have experience articulated by means of various conceptual schema. It is only because man has over millennia objectified and progressively developed these that he has achieved the forms of human knowledge, and the possibility of the development of mind as we know it is open to us today.

A liberal education is, then, one that, determined in scope and content by knowledge itself, is thereby concerned with the development of mind. The concept is thus once more clearly and objectively defined in precisely the same way as the original concept. It is however no longer supported by epistemological and metaphysical doctrines that result in a hierarchical organisation of the various forms of knowledge. The detailed working out of the education will therefore be markedly different in certain respects. The distinctions between the various forms of knowledge which will principally govern the scheme of education will now be based entirely on analyses of their particular conceptual, logical and methodological features. The comprehensive character of the education will of course remain, since this is essentially part of the definition of the concept, but any question of the harmonious organisation of its various elements will depend on the relationships between them that are revealed by these analyses.

But if the concept is reasserted in these terms, what now of the question of its justification? The justification of a liberal education as supported by the doctrines of classical realism was based on the ultimacy of knowledge as ordered and determined by reality, and the significance of knowledge for the mind and for the good life. Having weakened these doctrines, the Harvard Committee's justification of their concept ignores the question of the relationship between knowledge and reality, and there is a specific rejection of the view that knowledge is in itself the good of the mind. They assert, however, the supreme significance of knowledge in the determination of all human activity, and supplement this, as is certainly necessary because of the extended nature of their concept, by general considerations of the desirability of their suggestions. When once more the concept is strictly confined so as to be determined by the forms of knowledge, the return to a justification of it without reference to what is generally thought desirable on social or similar grounds becomes possible. And such justification for the concept is essential if the education it delineates is to have the ultimate significance that, as was earlier suggested, is part of its raison d'être. This justification must now however stem from what has already been said of the nature of knowledge as no metaphysical doctrine of the connection between knowledge and reality is any longer being invoked.

If the achievement of knowledge is necessarily the development of mind in its most basic sense, then it can be readily seen that to ask for a justification for the pursuit of knowledge is not at all the same thing as to ask for the justification for, say, teaching all children a foreign language or making them orderly and punctual in their behaviour. It is in fact a peculiar question asking for justification for any development of the rational mind at all. To ask for the justification of any form of activity is significant only if one is in fact committed already to seeking rational knowledge. To ask for a justification of the pursuit of rational knowledge itself therefore presupposes some form of commitment to what one is seeking to justify. Justification is possible only if what is being justified is both intelligible under publicly rooted concepts and is assessable according to accepted criteria. It assumes a commitment to these two principles. But these very principles are in fact fundamental to the pursuit of knowledge in all its forms, be it, for instance, empirical knowledge or understanding in the arts. The forms of knowledge are in a sense simply the working out of these general principles in particular ways. To give justification of any kind of knowledge therefore involves using the principles in one specific form to assess their use in another. Any particular activity can be examined for its rational character, for its adherence to these principles, and thus justified on the assumption of them. Indeed in so far as activities are rational this will be possible. It is commitment to them that characterises any rational activity as such. But the principles themselves have no such assessable status, for justification outside the use of the principles is not logically possible. This does not mean that rational pursuits in the end lack justification, for they could equally well be said to have their justification written into them. Nor is any form of viciously circular justification involved by assuming in the procedure what is being looked for. The situation is that we have here reached the ultimate point where the question of justification ceases to be significantly applicable. The apparent circularity is the result of the inter-relation between the concepts of rational justification and the pursuit of knowledge.

Perhaps the finality of these principles can be brought out further by noting a negative form of the same argument. From this point of view, to question the pursuit of any kind of rational knowledge is in the end self-defeating, for the questioning itself depends on accepting the very principles whose use is finally being called in question.

It is because it is based on these ultimate principles that characterize knowledge itself and not merely on lower level forms of justification that a liberal education is in a very real sense the ultimate form of education. In spite of the absence of any metaphysical doctrine about reality this idea of liberal education has a significance parallel to that of the original Greek concept. It is an education concerned directly with the development of the mind in rational knowledge, whatever form that freely takes. This parallels the original concept in that according to the doctrine of function liberal education was the freeing of the mind to achieve its own good in knowledge. In each case it is a form of education knowing no limits other than those necessarily imposed by the nature of rational knowledge and thereby itself developing in man the final court of appeal in all human affairs.

As here reformulated the concept has, again like the original, objectivity, though this is no longer backed by metaphysical realism. For it is a necessary feature of knowledge as such that there be public criteria whereby the true is distinguishable from the false, the good from the bad, the right from the wrong. It is the existence of these criteria which gives objectivity to knowledge; and this in its turn gives objectivity to the concept of liberal education. A parallel to another form of justification thus remains, and the concept continues to warrant its label as that of an education that frees the mind from error and illusion. Further, as the determination of the good life is now considered to be itself the pursuit of a particular form of rational knowledge, that in which what ought to be done is justified by the giving of reasons, this is seen as a necessary part of a liberal education. And as all other forms of knowledge contribute in their way to moral understanding, the concept as a whole is once more given a kind of justification in its importance for the moral life. But this justification, like that of objectivity, no longer has the distinct significance which it once had, for it is again simply a necessary consequence of what the pursuit of knowledge entails. Nevertheless, liberal education remains basic to the freeing of human conduct from wrong.

### CERTAIN BASIC PHILOSOPHICAL CONSIDERATIONS

Having attempted a reinstatement of the concept without its original philosophical backing, what of the implications of this for the practical conduct of education? In working these out it is necessary first to try to distinguish the various forms of knowledge and then to relate them in some way to the organisation of the school or college curriculum. The first of these is a strictly philosophical task. The second is a matter of practical planning that involves many considerations other than the purely philosophical, and to this I will return when certain broad distinctions between forms of knowledge have been outlined.

As stated earlier, by a form of knowledge is meant a distinct way in which our experience becomes structured round the use of accepted public symbols. The symbols thus having public meaning, their use is in some way testable against experience and there is the progressive development of series of tested symbolic expressions. In this way experience has been probed further and further by extending and elaborating the use of the symbols and by means of these it has become possible for the personal experience of individuals to become more fully structured, more fully understood. The various forms of knowledge can be seen in low level developments within the common area of our knowledge of the everyday world. From this there branch out the developed forms which, taking certain elements in our common knowledge as a basis, have grown in distinctive ways. In the developed forms of knowledge the following related distinguishing features can be seen:

(1) They each involve certain central concepts that are peculiar in character to the form. For example, those of gravity, acceleration,

hydrogen, and photo-synthesis characteristic of the sciences; number, integral and matrix in mathematics; God, sin and predestination in religion; ought, good and wrong in moral knowledge.

(2) In a given form of knowledge these and other concepts that denote, if perhaps in a very complex way, certain aspects of experience, form a network of possible relationships in which experience can be understood. As a result the form has a distinctive logical structure. For example, the terms and statements of mechanics can be meaningfully related in certain strictly limited ways only, and the same is true of historical explanation.

(3) The form, by virtue of its particular terms and logic, has expressions or statements (possibly answering a distinctive type of question) that in some way or other, however indirect it may be, are testable against experience. This is the case in scientific knowledge, moral knowledge, and in the arts, though in the arts no questions are explicit and the criteria for the tests are only partially expressible in words. Each form, then, has distinctive expressions that are testable against experience in accordance with particular criteria that are peculiar to the form.

(4) The forms have developed particular techniques and skills for exploring experience and testing their distinctive expressions, for instance the techniques of the sciences and those of the various literary arts. The result has been the amassing of all the symbolically expressed knowledge that we now have in the arts and the sciences.

Though the various forms of knowledge are distinguishable in these ways it must not be assumed that all there is to them can be made clear and explicit by these means. All knowledge involves the use of symbols and the making of judgments in ways that cannot be expressed in words and can only be learnt in a tradition. The art of scientific investigation and the development of appropriate experimental tests, the forming of an historical explanation and the assessment of its truth, the appreciation of a poem: all of these activities are high arts that are not in themselves communicable simply by words. Acquiring knowledge of any form is therefore to a greater or less extent something that cannot be done simply by solitary study of the symbolic expressions of knowledge, it must be learnt from a master on the job. No doubt it is because the forms require particular training of this kind in distinct worlds of discourse, because they necessitate the development of high critical standards according to complex criteria, because they involve our coming to look at experience in particular ways, that we refer to them as disciplines. They are indeed disciplines that form the mind.

Yet the dividing lines that can be drawn between different disciplines by means of the four suggested distinguishing marks are neither clear enough nor sufficient for demarcating the whole world of modern knowledge as we know it. The central feature to which they point is that the major forms of knowledge, or disciplines, can each be distinguished by their dependence on some particular kind of test against experience for their distinctive expressions. On this ground alone however certain broad divisions are apparent. The sciences depend crucially on empirical experimental and observational tests, mathematics depends on deductive demonstrations from certain sets of axioms. Similarly moral knowledge and the arts involve distinct forms of critical tests though in these cases both what the tests are and the ways in which they are applied are only partially statable. (Some would in fact dispute the status of the arts as forms of knowledge for this very reason.) Because of their particular logical features. it seems to me necessary to distinguish also as separate disciplines both historical and religious knowledge, and there is perhaps an equally good case, because of the nature of their empirical concepts, for regarding the human sciences separately from the physical sciences. But within these areas further distinctions must be made. These are usually the result of the grouping of knowledge round a number of related concepts, or round particular skills or techniques. The various sciences and the various arts can be demarcated within the larger units of which they are in varying degrees representative in their structure, by these means.

But three other important classifications of knowledge must in addition be recognised. First there are those organisations which are not themselves disciplines or subdivisions of any discipline. They are formed by building together round specific objects, or phenomena, or practical pursuits, knowledge that is characteristically rooted elsewhere in more than one discipline. It is not just that these organisations make use of several forms of knowledge, for after all the sciences use mathematics, the arts use historical knowledge and so on. Many of the disciplines borrow from each other. But these organisations are not concerned, as the disciplines are, to validate any one logically distinct form of expression. They are not concerned with developing a particular structuring of experience. They are held together simply by their subject matter, drawing on all forms of knowledge that can contribute to them. Geography, as the study of man in relation to his environment, is an example of a theoretical study of this kind, engineering an example of a practical nature. I see no reason why such organisations of knowledge, which I shall refer to as 'fields', should not be endlessly constructed according to particular theoretical or practical interests. Secondly, whilst moral knowledge is a distinct form, concerned with answering questions as to what ought to be done in practical affairs, no specialised subdivisions of this have been developed. In practical affairs, moral questions, because of their character, naturally arise alongside questions of fact and technique, so that there have been formed 'fields' of practical knowledge that include distinct moral elements within them, rather than the subdivisions of a particular discipline. Political, legal and educational theory are perhaps the clearest examples of fields where moral knowledge of a developed kind is to be found. Thirdly, there are certain second order forms of knowledge which are dependent for their existence on the other primary areas. On the one hand there are the essentially scientific studies of language and symbolism as in grammar and philology. On the other hand there are the logical and philosophical studies of meaning and justification. These would seem to constitute a distinct discipline by virtue of their particular concepts and criteria of judgment.

In summary, then, it is suggested that the forms of knowledge as we have them can be classified as follows:

(I) Distinct disciplines or forms of knowledge (subdivisible): mathematics, physical sciences, human sciences, history, religion, literature and the fine arts, philosophy.

(II) Fields of knowledge: theoretical, practical (these may or may not include elements of moral knowledge).

It is the distinct disciplines that basically constitute the range of unique ways we have of understanding experience if to these is added the category of moral knowledge.

## THE PLANNING AND PRACTICAL CONDUCT OF LIBERAL EDUCATION

Turning now to the bearing of this discussion on the planning and conduct of a liberal education, certain very general comments about its characteristic features can be made though detailed treatment would involve psychological and other considerations that are quite beyond the scope of this paper.

In the first place, as liberal education is concerned with the comprehensive development of the mind in acquiring knowledge, it is aimed at achieving an understanding of experience in many different ways. This means the acquisition by critical training and discipline not only of facts but also of complex conceptual schemes and of the arts and techniques of different types of reasoning and judgment. Syllabuses and curricula cannot therefore be constructed simply in terms of information and isolated skills. They must be constructed so as to introduce pupils as far as possible into the interrelated aspects of each of the basic forms of knowledge, each of the several disciplines. And they must be constructed to cover at least in some measure the range of knowledge as a whole.

In a programme of liberal education that is based directly on the study of the specific disciplines, examples of each of the different areas must of course be chosen. Selection of this kind is not however simply an inevitable practical consequence of the vast growth of knowledge. It is equally in keeping with what a liberal education is aiming at. Though its aim is comprehensive it is not after the acquisition of encyclopaedic information. Nor is it after the specialist knowledge of the person fully trained in all the particular details of a branch of knowledge. Such a specialist can not only accurately employ the concepts, logic and criteria of a domain but also knows the skills and techniques involved in the pursuit of knowledge quite beyond the immediate areas of common human experience. Nor is liberal education concerned with the technician's knowledge of the detailed application of the disciplines in practical and theoretical fields. What is being sought is, first, sufficient immersion in the concepts, logic and criteria of the discipline for a person to come to know the distinctive way in which it 'works' by pursuing these in particular cases; and then sufficient generalisation of these over the whole range of the discipline so that his experience begins to be widely structured in this distinctive manner. It is this coming to look at things in a certain way that is being aimed at, not the ability to work out in minute particulars all the details that can in fact be discerned. It is the ability to recognise empirical assertions or aesthetic judgments for what they are, and to know the kind of considerations on which their validity will depend, that matters. Beyond this an outline of the major achievements in each area provides some grasp of the range and scope of experience that has thus become intelligible. Perhaps this kind of understanding is in fact most readily distinguishable in the literary arts as critical appreciation in contrast to the achievement of the creative writer or the literary hack. But the distinction is surely applicable to other forms of knowledge as well.

This is not to assert that 'critical appreciation' in any form of knowledge can be adequately achieved without some development of the understanding of the specialist or technician. Nor is it to imply that this understanding in the sciences, the arts or moral issues can be had without participation in many relevant creative and practical pursuits. The extent to which this is true will vary from discipline to discipline and is in fact in need of much investigation, particularly because of its importance for moral and aesthetic education. But it is to say that the aim of the study of a discipline in liberal education is not that of its study in a specialist or technical course. The first is concerned with developing a person's ways of understanding experience, the others are concerned with mastering the details of knowledge, how it is established, and the use of it in other enterprises, particularly those of a practical nature. It is of course perfectly possible for a course in physics, for example, to be devoted to a double purpose if it is deliberately so designed. It may provide both a specialist knowledge of the subject and at the same time a genuine introduction to the form of scientific knowledge. But the two purposes are quite distinct and there is no reason to suppose that by aiming at one the other can automatically be achieved as well. Yet it would seem to be true that some specialist study within a discipline, if it is at all typical of the discipline, is necessary to understanding the form of knowledge in any developed sense. The study of a discipline as part of liberal education, however, contributes practically nothing directly to any specialist study of it, though it does serve to put the specialism into a much wider context.

A liberal education approached directly in terms of the disciplines will thus be composed of the study of at least paradigm examples of all the various forms of knowledge. This study will be sufficiently detailed and sustained to give genuine insight so that pupils come to think in these terms, using the concepts, logic and criteria accurately in the different domains. It will then include generalisation of the particular examples used so as to show the range of understanding in the various forms. It will also include some indication of the relations between the forms where these overlap and their significance in the major fields of knowledge, particularly the practical fields, that have been developed. This is particularly important for moral education, as moral questions can frequently be solved only by calling on the widest possible range of human understanding. As there is in fact no developed discipline of moral knowledge, education in moral understanding must necessarily be approached in a rather different way. For if it is to cover more than everyday personal matters this has to be by the study of issues that occur in certain particular fields of knowledge. The major difficulty this presents will be referred to briefly later. The important point here is that though moral understanding has to be pursued in contexts where it is not the only dominant interest, the aim of its pursuit is precisely the same as for all other elements in a liberal education, the understanding of experience in a unique way. What is wanted (just as in the study of the disciplines *per se*) is, basically, the use of the appropriate concepts, logic, and criteria, and the appreciation of the range of understanding in this form.

It is perhaps important to stress the fact that this education will be one in the forms of knowledge themselves and not merely a self-conscious philosophical treatment of their characteristics. Scientific and historical knowledge are wanted, not knowledge of the philosophy of science and the philosophy of history as substitutes. A liberal education can only be planned if distinctions in the forms of knowledge are clearly understood, and that is a philosophical matter. But the education itself is only partly in philosophy, and that is only possible when pupils have some grasp of the other disciplines themselves.

Precisely what sections of the various disciplines are best suited to the aims of liberal education cannot be gone into here. It is apparent that on philosophical grounds alone some branches of the sciences, for instance, would seem to be much more satisfactory as paradigms of scientific thinking than others. Many sections of physics are probably more comprehensive and clear in logical character, more typical of the well developed physical sciences than, say, botany. If so, they would, all other things being equal, serve better as an introduction to scientific knowledge. Perhaps in literature and the fine arts the paradigm principle is less easy to apply though probably many would favour a course in literature to any one other. But whatever the discipline, in practice all other things are not in fact equal and decisions about the content of courses cannot be taken without careful regard to the abilities and interests of the students for whom they are designed.

Yet hovering round such decisions and questions of syllabus planning there is frequently found the belief that the inherent logical structure of a discipline, or a branch of a discipline necessarily determines exactly what and exactly how the subject is to be taught and learnt. The small amount of truth and the large amount of error in this belief can only be distinguished by clarifying what the logic of a subject is. It is not a series of intellectual steps that must be climbed in strict order. It is not a specific psychological channel along which the mind must travel if there is to be understanding. This is to confuse logical characteristics with psychological processes. The logic of a form of knowledge shows the meaningful and valid ways in which its terms and criteria are used. It constitutes the publicly accepted framework of knowledge. The psychological activities of the individual when concerned with this knowledge are not in general prescribed in any temporal order and the mind, as it were, plays freely within and around the framework. It is simply that the framework lays down the general formal relations of the concepts if there is to be knowledge. The logic as publicly expressed consists of the general and formal principles to which the terms must conform in knowledge. Coming to understand a form of knowledge involves coming to think in relations that satisfy the public criteria. How the mind plays round and within these is not itself being laid down at all, there is no dragooning of psychological processes, only a marking out of the territory in which the mind can wander more or less at will. Indeed understanding a form of knowledge is far more like coming to know a country than climbing a ladder. Some places in a territory may only be get-at-able by a single specified route and some forms of knowledge may have concepts and relations that cannot be understood without first understanding certain others. But that countries are explorable only in one way is in general false, and even in mathematics, the most strictly sequential form of knowledge we have, many ways of coming to know the territory are possible. The logic of a subject is relevant to what is being taught, for its patterns must be accepted as essential to the form of knowledge. But how those patterns are best discerned is a matter for empirical investigation.

School subjects in the disciplines as we at present have them are in no way sacrosanct on either logical or psychological grounds. They are necessarily selections from the forms of knowledge that we have and may or may not be good as introductions for the purposes of liberal education. In most cases they have developed under a number of diverse influences. The historical growth of the subjects has sometimes dominated the programmes. The usefulness of certain elements, the demands of higher specialist education, certain general 'psychological' principles such as progressing from the simple to the complex, from the particular to the general, the concrete to the abstract, all these factors and many others have left their marks. This being so, many well established courses need to be critically re-examined both philosophically and psychologically before they can be accepted as suitable for liberal education. Superficially at least most of them would seem to be quite inappropriate for this purpose.

Though a liberal education is most usually approached directly in the study of various branches of the disciplines, I see no reason to think that this must necessarily be so. It is surely possible to construct programmes that are in the first place organised round certain fields of knowledge either theoretical or practical. The study of aspects of power, natural as well as social and political, might for instance be one element in such a scheme: or a regional study that introduces historical, geographical, industrial and social considerations: or a practical project of design and building involving the sciences, mathematics and visual arts. In this case, however, it must be recognised that the fields are chosen because together they can be used to develop understanding of all the various forms of knowledge, and explicit steps must be taken to see that this end is achieved. There will necessarily be the strongest tendency for liberal education to be lost sight of and for the fields to be pursued in their own right developing the techniques and skills which they need. These may be valuable and useful in many ways, and perhaps essential in many a person's whole education. (Certainly liberal education as is here being understood is only one part of the education a person ought to have, for it omits quite deliberately for instance specialist education, physical education and character training.) But a course in various fields of knowledge will not in fact be a liberal education unless that aim is kept absolutely clear and every opportunity is taken to lead to a fuller grasp of the disciplines. Again some fields of study will be better for this purpose than others but all will demand the highest skill from the teacher, who must be under no misapprehension as to what the object of the exercise really is. Yet it is difficult to see how this kind of approach can be fully adequate if it does not in the end lead to a certain amount of study of the distinct disciplines themselves. For whatever ground may have been covered indirectly, a satisfactory understanding of the characteristically distinct approaches of the different forms is hardly possible without some direct gathering together of the elements of the disciplines that have been implicit in all that has been done.

Whatever the pattern of a liberal education in its later stages, it must not be forgotten that there is being presupposed a broad basic education in the common area of everyday knowledge where the various disciplines can be seen in embryo and from which they branch out as distinct units. In such a basic primary education, the ever growing range of a child's experience and the increasing use of linguistic and symbolic forms lays the foundation for the various modes of understanding, scientific, historical, religious, moral, and so on. Out of this general pool of knowledge the disciplines have slowly become ever more differentiated and it is this that the student must come to understand, not confusing the forms of knowledge but appreciating them for what they are in themselves, and recognising their necessary limitations.

But is then the outcome of a liberal education to be simply the achievement of a series of discreet ways of understanding experience? In a very real sense yes, but in another sense not entirely. For one thing, we have as yet not begun to understand the complex interrelations of the different forms of knowledge themselves, for they do not only have unique features but common features too, and in addition one discipline often makes extensive use of the achievements of another. But we must also not forget that the various forms are firmly rooted in that common world of persons and things which we all share, and into this they take back in subtle as well as simple ways the understanding they have achieved. The outcome of a liberal education must therefore not be thought of as producing ever greater disintegration of the mind but rather the growth of ever clearer and finer distinctions in our experience. If the result is not some quasi-aesthetic unity of the mind neither is it in any sense chaos. Perhaps the most suggestive picture of the outcome is that used by Professor Michael Oakeshott, though for him it has more literal truth than is here intended. In this the various forms of knowledge are seen as voices in a conversation, a conversation to which they each contribute in a distinctive way. If taken figuratively, his words express more succinctly than mine can precisely what it seems to me a liberal education is and what its outcome will be.

'As civilized human beings, we are the inheritors, neither of an inquiry about ourselves and the world, nor of an accumulating body of information, but of a conversation, begun in the primeval forests and extended and made more articulate in the course of centuries. It is a conversation which goes on both in public and within each of ourselves. Of course there is argument and inquiry and information, but wherever these are profitable they are to be recognized as passages in this conversation, and perhaps they are not the most captivating of the passages.... Conversation is not an enterprise designed to yield an extrinsic profit, a contest where a winner gets a prize, nor is it an activity of exegesis; it is an unrehearsed intellectual adventure....
... Education, properly speaking, is an initiation into the skill and partnership of this conversation in which we learn to recognize the voices, to distinguish the proper occasions of utterance, and in which we acquire the intellectual and moral habits appropriate to conversation. And it is this conversation which, in the end, gives place and character to every human activity and utterance'.[8]

## NOTES

1. *General Education in a Free Society*: Report of the Harvard Committee (London: Oxford University Press, 1946).
2. *Ibid.*, p. 58.
3. *Ibid.*, pp. 64–65.
4. *Ibid.*, pp. 65–73.
5. *Ibid.*, p. 67.
6. Precisely the same criticisms might be made of some remarks by Professor P. H. Nowell-Smith in his inaugural lecture, *Education in a University* (Leicester University Press, 1958), pp. 6–11. In these he suggests that the prime purpose of the study of literature, history and philosophy is that each develops one of the central powers of the mind—creative imagination, practical wisdom, and logical thought. Once more we are up against the question of the definition of these 'powers' and if that problem can be solved, the question of sheer evidence for them and the way they can be developed.
7. *Arts and Science Sides in the Sixth Form*: Gulbenkian Foundation Report (Oxford University Department of Education, 1960), p. 15.
8. Michael Oakeshott, *Rationalism in Politics and Other Essays* (London: Methuen, 1962), pp. 198–199.

# CONCEPTIONS OF TEACHING

P. H. HIRST'S paper, which closes the previous section, deals generally with the justification of subjects and the applications of them to educational practice. Professor Corbett proceeds by considering what one subject, namely philosophy, *is*, and how it can and ought to function as part of a liberal education. The problem is not treated in the abstract, but rather through example, by discussing what is involved in, and aimed at, in *teaching* philosophy now. By examining the kinds of knowledge and skills that are actually aimed at in the course of teaching the subject, Corbett defines the subject and its value for the present culture, and, by implication, hints at a characterisation of philosophy of education. His is a clear statement of what it means, at least in one subject, to teach something to somebody.

Professor Wilson's concern is with teaching *per se*. In the course of his analysis of two types of teaching (that in which the method is clear, as distinguished from those areas in which there is real difficulty in the method), he develops a thesis that is basically consistent with that of Peters: that the context and manner of instruction are crucial factors in properly describing the activity of education. This is particularly relevant to the area of moral education.

Professor Atkinson's primary concern is moral education. His procedure is to characterise this activity by defining the contrasting teaching contexts in which instruction and indoctrination take place. Taking issue with Peters, he notes that although questions of manner are central to educational decisions, a consideration of manner alone might well lead us to the erroneous conclusion that the principles upon which the manner is decided are obvious or self-evident, or in some way do not require choice. Since there are no self-evident moral imperatives, conflict is essential to genuine moral speculation. The recognition of this conflict, and the search for ways of containing and accommodating it in a rational fashion are, he says, the concerns of the moral educator.

# TEACHING PHILOSOPHY NOW

## J. P. Corbett

WHAT makes thinking philosophical, and a man who habitually thinks in that way a philosopher?

The modern philosopher is not directly concerned with animals, vegetables or minerals; he is not a scientist. It is true that men who called themselves 'philosophers' in earlier days did ask and try to answer questions that we now think scientific; but the work of describing and explaining the phenomena of nature has long been seen to be different from that of thinking philosophically. The philosopher is indeed some kind of systematic thinker; but the questions that he asks and the answers that he tries to give are not those to which observations in the laboratory or in the field are directly relevant. So much is negative; what then positively distinguishes philosophical thinking from thinking of other kinds?

We can take a step forward by saying that philosophy is concerned with man. But if the philosopher is not a scientist then his concern with man cannot be that of the physiologist or the biochemist. He must have some other interest and approach. A further step forward is to say that the philosopher is concerned with man as a thinking animal, in particular as an animal that thinks in signs by which he can utter and record his thought. But even this is much too wide. A philosopher is not a phonetician, studying the characteristic sounds out of which a language is constructed; he is not a grammarian, studying the rules according to which the signs of a language must be put together; he is not a psychologist or a sociologist, studying the ways in which symbolic thinking works and is related to the structure and development of the organism, of personality and of society. To mark out the philosopher's concern with man from that of all such specialists we have to say that he is concerned with human thinking in so far as that thinking lays claim to validity. We men are constantly making statements, passing judgments, taking decisions, expressing preferences. In doing these things and many others like them we make the claim, explicitly or implicitly, that what we have said—our statement, judgment, decision or preference—is justified. Very often we get involved in arguments about these claims. It is here that the philosopher enters on the scene. To make a claim and to enter into argument about it is to assume that there are principles by which the claim can be justified and the argument settled. It is in the detection of these principles, the study of their mutual relations, and the examination of their solidity that philosophical thinking consists; it is the habitual scrutiny of these issues that makes a man a philosopher. As such he is not concerned with the justification of any particular claim. It is not up to him, as a philosopher, to determine whether a particular description is correct, a theory sound, a decision prudent, a preference rational. His business is with the principles of valid thought that underlie all such particular issues.

But that last sentence is ambiguous. We might read it as meaning that the business of the philosopher is to discover what principles people actually do use, and, in so far as those principles vary, to describe the alternatives. Or else we might read it as meaning that the work of the philosopher is not only to describe but to examine. He must indeed discover what principles are or have been used, in a given field of human activity; but he must then consider whether those principles are sound. It seems that this second interpretation is forced upon us. We do in fact find, when we examine human thinking in all its forms, that the principles that are latent in it at different times and places are not merely diverse but conflicting; indeed the great turning points of history seem to involve the replacement of one set of principles by another. Galileo established some important natural laws; what he also established was a comprehensive idea, not indeed new but never before predominant, of what a law of nature has to be. The utilitarians advocated many particular reforms; but what they also advocated was the principle that in matters of personal conduct and social organisation we should always and only have regard to the effects on human happiness of the practices we are considering, and should rule out as irrelevant any appeal to tradition, authority or God's supposed commands. Such shifts of principle as these, from the Aristotelian to the Newtonian conception of what physics ought to be, or from the traditionalistic or religious to the utilitarian view as to how moral and political issues should be determined, are facts of which the philosopher, in his capacity as an historian of ideas, must take note. But he cannot be content with taking note of them. They compete for his allegiance and, as the spokesman of his age, he must decide between them, or against them both. Any account of such principles which fails to assess and pass judgment on their claims evades the crucial issue. Thus philosophical thinking proves to be that kind of thinking which is concerned to discover and describe, but also to assess and judge, the general claims to validity which are implicit in the intellectual history of the race and in all our daily actions, however simple and obvious these may seem to be. I have made a date with a friend and turn up on time. I do not give the matter a thought. But all the same, implicit in my action is the principle of keeping one's word, and implicit in that is the whole issue as to how we may determine whether a suggested principle such as that of keeping promises, or whether indeed any principle whatever, is binding on us.

If we consider only such simple cases as that of keeping an engagement when nothing stands in the way, the work of the philosopher in disentangling and scrutinising principles seems needless and tiresome; needless because no issue has arisen, tiresome because it seems to waste time on subtleties when there are things to do. People who lead untroubled lives consequently find the philosopher's ceaseless probing of the obvious very little to their taste; and if all life were as simple as keeping a desired, easy and innocent engagement we should not hear much about philosophy. But life, of course, is not so simple or so kind as that; long before the philosopher gets to work, hard facts of experience have raised his questions for him. I am asked by a child what would happen if a nuclear bomb went off above his home. I have to decide whether to tell or to suppress the truth. If I tell the truth I may do lasting damage to his confidence and sensitivity by the shock of what I say; if I suppress the truth I will, in a plainer term, have told a lie. Two principles which I hold and believe to be important have collided. I cannot evade the issue. I must say something. I must choose. But in choosing one way or the other I must presumably rely upon some further principle; if I have the time and the inclination to think the matter out I may seek to formulate that principle and apply it explicitly to the case in hand. In other words, my practical dilemma forces me to ask and try to answer a philosophical question. Or, to take an example from a different field of thought, suppose I am a nuclear physicist. In the course of framing explanations for phenomena that have been observed I am forced to postulate particles whose properties are such that, unlike the particles of classical physics, they and the processes in which they are involved cannot be represented in the imagination. No picture is possible. It follows that I am forced to raise the question whether the possibility of constructing an imaginable model of the invisibly small is an essential part of anything that can properly be called a scientific explanation, or whether it was only deemed to be part of scientific explanation during a certain limited phase of scientific development, and can and must be dropped when scientific problems have taken on the shape that they have now. The practical scientist, however unphilosophical he may believe himself to be, is forced in such a situation to make a decision of principle about what scientific thinking ought to do.

Philosophical problems are not, in fact, the tiresome inventions of philosophers. They force themselves upon us at every turn. Whenever thought and action become really difficult, one or more philosophical problems are at work. What is peculiar about the philosopher is his special sensitivity to such deep, inpalpable issues. While the man of action will just tell or suppress the truth without qualms, and while the physicist will postulate and use his particles with the least possible attention to the changes that he is making in the idea of scientific explanation, the philosopher is fascinated by the issues that are thus passed over. He goes around the world noticing the snags, uncertainties and dislocations of human thinking; not the small ones, but those of such a radical kind that, when they are taken seriously, they threaten to upset great areas of what men normally take for granted. The philosopher tends therefore to be an unpopular figure. He is the nagging guilty conscience of the intellectual world.

But having raised nasty doubts about things that are usually assumed, what does the philosopher then do? To this question there is no single answer. One thing that great and not so great philosophers have attempted is to produce a systematic set of answers to all the questions they have raised. Inspired by a sense of the unity of things, they have sought to unfold that sense into a vision and that vision into an orderly concatenation of concepts and propositions, defining the structure of reality itself in such a way that everything of which we have experience, whether in ordinary life or science, and including our own thinking, with its restless search for complete validity, can be located in it. Such was the work of an Aquinas, a Descartes, a Hegel. Indeed the history of philosophy for the most part consists of the record of such systems, in their relation to one another and to the world in which they arose. But underlying this manifest structure and development of philosophical thought is the restless, remorseless, radical probing of validity that we associate with Socrates. Philosophy can never be understood unless that probing is recognized for what it is; philosophy can never be practised by anyone who does not respond to its fascination and submit his life to its discipline.

That being what philosophy is, the inference seems natural that it should play an important part in the studies of any university. For a university has the job of transmitting and developing just those fundamental intellectual traditions that the philosopher tries to express as principles of validity. But before one draws this inference a note of caution should be sounded. While philosophical thinking is an essential part of the intellectual life of a civilisation, it does not follow directly that there must be a special class of persons who devote themselves expressly to such thinking and are, therefore, to be called philosophers, still less that places should be established for such persons in a university. Perhaps good philosophical thinking can only be done by people who are themselves immediately involved in applying the principles which, in their philosophical moments, they study; perhaps only the active historian or physicist is competent to say anything significant about the methodology of those enquiries; perhaps only the man who is personally involved in politics can know sufficiently what political activity implies to be able to grasp and scrutinise its principles. And when we examine the history of philosophy in modern times we do in fact find that the great majority of those who have made important contributions to philosophical thinking have not only lived and worked outside universities, but have been severely critical of the philosophy that was being done within them. The only exceptions to this rule seem to be Kant and Hegel; and the fact that they did their great work inside universities was certainly due to the exceptionally dynamic part that was played by universities in a society whose other institutions were out of date. These facts suggest that doing philosophy inside a university may be more difficult than at first appears.

## J. P. Corbett

Notwithstanding this, philosophy is practised in almost all universities and is prominent in some. Oxford is a striking example. There philosophy plays an important part in three undergraduate schools of study, in Greats, where it is combined with Ancient History, in Philosophy, Politics and Economics, and in Psychology, Philosophy, and Physiology. The idea behind these courses is that in studying another civilisation, or in studying anything so complicated and obscure as modern society or the human mind, attention to the principles of validity that were current in that civilisation or are involved in those branches of theory is not only useful but essential. If that is granted then the further inference must be drawn that philosophy should be a component of all courses in arts, social and psychological studies. With support from a further premise, the argument can be extended to the point of saying that philosophy should accompany every other study. The case for this ambitious proposal may not be very strong if philosophy is considered only in its role as the investigation of the principles and methods of other branches of study. Historians and physicists seem in fact to get on very well without formal investigation of the nature of their subject. But if we add the further premise that philosophy is not only concerned with the methodology of other studies, but with the principles of morality, politics and religion, the case—if our warning note is disregarded—seems much stronger. For after all, students are active individuals, having responsibilities and ideals; they are citizens in the making who must take their part in the direction of their countries' policies; they are finite beings who are conscious of their finitude and must come to terms with it. Surely, therefore, it is essential to their education that they should have the opportunity to think, not occasionally and fugitively, but often and with care about the principles by which they regulate or ought to regulate those segments of their lives. However, rather than appraise this claim in abstract terms it will be more profitable to see what happens when we accept it and act upon it. Supposing one does try to teach philosophy, not only to the minority of students who have a passion for it, but to students of all kinds and tastes: how is the teaching to be done? what can be taught? what effects does it have? what are the gains and losses? And while these questions are very general, this essay sticks to experience that is being gained in a single university, in England, now.

When one tries to teach philosophy to the run of undergraduates in England at the present time, every factor from the most immediate and practical to the most abstract and theoretical leads one to teach a certain manner of philosophising, and in a certain way. The most practical consideration is simply that undergraduates, most of whose time is taken up with history, physics or any other major interest, can give relatively little time to philosophical studies. That fact alone makes certain approaches to philosophy impossible. Even if one believed in the truth of some philosophical system it would be impossible to teach it in the time available without making it so crude and boring that, whatever its merits, it would take no hold upon the student's mind. Again, even if one believed that the royal road to the subject is by a study of its history, so that the ideal course is to take students through the great succession of Greek and European thinkers, one would find that this road also is barred. An attempt to follow it would give the student no more than the crudest textbook knowledge of a few philosophical formulae, without any understanding of their origins, significance and influence. If philosophy is to be widely taught in a modern university, where most students must give other subjects the lion's share of their time, some other method must be found than that of expounding either a system or the history of the subject.

But much more fundamental factors count against a systematic or historical treatment of philosophy. The truth is that whatever may be the case with the foundations of science, the foundations of morality and politics are, in a society like that of England, highly controversial. The same is true of religion. In these fields there is no single set of principles which has only to be discovered and set out to be universally accepted. On the contrary, there are a number of different sets of principles. This society contains communists as well as liberals, believers in Catholic morality as well as moral anarchists, agnostics and atheists as well as true believers. All these frames of thought exist; and they are variously represented in every university amongst both teachers and students. But the modern university, usually in virtue of its statutes, but anyway in virtue of the climate of opinion to which it belongs, is precluded from taking sides between them. That means in practice not only that the university disowns the aim of teaching any such single view of life, but implicitly demands of its teachers that they should not use their position to inculcate what view of life may happen to be theirs. It does not, of course, require them to conceal, let alone to abandon—if that were possible—what convictions they may have; but it does require them to observe detachment in their teaching. If they speak from their convictions they must make it plain that this is what they are doing and that there are other possible positions which the student might adopt. If the student has convictions with which the teacher disagrees, he may bring arguments to bear upon them; but if these arguments are ineffective, the teacher must not make an issue of the matter or try, by other means, to get his way. It is in fact supposed to be the most fundamental principle of the modern university, a principle which is supposed to distinguish it from the universities of an earlier age when the churches were officially and explicitly predominant, and from universities in communist countries now, that it, as such, stands for no single doctrine, but permits and welcomes the discussion of them all. This principle must apply to the philosopher with special force. Of course, the scrupulous historian, who is also a Marxist or a Catholic, must observe a proper caution in the use he makes of those systems in the work of teaching; but just because the philosopher is concerned wholetime and expressly with such issues he is most nearly touched by this supposed neutrality in matters of belief. It follows that while in teaching undergraduates he may, indeed to be honest must, argue for whatever position he believes to be true or for whatever system he thinks he can establish, he is nevertheless bound by his environment to observe a considerable detachment. His main effort, merely for this reason, must rather be to raise issues than to offer answers.

But deep though this reason is, there is a deeper reason still why, in teaching philosophy to undergraduates in a modern university, the emphasis cannot fall on a systematic or a historical presentation. This reason is difficult to state shortly; but the fact is that human knowledge has now taken on a form which cannot be systematised in the grand manner of earlier philosophers. This is partly because the immense specialisation of knowledge has produced so many and so technically difficult conceptual problems that no single man, be he ever so accomplished, can study and elucidate them all. Kant could still reasonably take all human thinking for his province; within a few decades of his death the very idea of doing so had come to look absurd. But more important still than the complexity of modern knowledge is its dynamism. It has been said that 90% of the scientists who have ever lived are still alive. This registers the formidable growth of intellectual effort that has taken place over the last decades. And the effort delivers the goods. The structure of the intellectual world now changes almost visibly year by year, as new facts are discovered and new frames of theoretical explanation are evolved to comprehend them. In such a dynamic situation the idea of the philosopher as the master of all who know, weaving all men's principles of validation together into a single, coherent and enduring scheme, has lost what sense it ever had. Philosophical work must be piecemeal. The philosopher can neither assume nor achieve a point of vantage from which everything can be seen and understood. He can only work at the discovery and elucidation of these principles of validity which interest him most and which he is most competent to understand; and he must follow them out as far as he can, drawing comparisons and making connections with others. He must reconcile himself at once to the fact that he can only scrutinise a few and that, as even those few are changing in the onward rush both of science and of the society to which science belongs, such formulations as he gives will have but a transitory significance. Human beings, or some human beings anyway, cannot but try to discern the most general and most important principles of validity amidst the welter of thought and action; they must go after freedom and justice, necessity and cause; but nowadays their endeavour must be modest from the start.

If then one remains convinced that undergraduates, like other intelligent people, should sometimes carefully reflect on the principles of validity that they normally assume, the only way forward is to adopt a Socratic method. Ideally one must try to discover in what region of his intellectual world an individual feels that strong and restless interest which indicates that here at least the principles on which he works are really active; one must then invade the region, obliging him to produce the principles on which he normally relies and, when these have been produced, revealing the difficulties and contradictions that are implicit in his thought. It is remarkable how greatly people vary in this matter. Some are easily and deeply interested in questions that leave others cold. Social justice troubles one, the freedom of the will another, religious arguments a third, physical explanation a fourth. But of course there cannot be complete liberty of choice amongst such topics. Whatever the system of teaching, students must be prepared for a common examination and must therefore work on common problems. One obvious choice is the complex of problems surrounding the value-judgments and freedom in both morality and politics. Very few students fail quickly to discover soon a strong interest in some part of this large field; and it is remarkable how many of them soon become fascinated by the epistemological problems, notably those attending the concept of mind, that are immediately connected with it. If you start in this way you can carry most students with you; but what you then find is that you have only carried them with you to bring them up short against a very difficult and striking problem which has both human and philosophical sides.

What must be faced, both humanly and philosophically, are the consequences of bringing forcibly to bear upon the ordinary student the influence of sustained philosophical scepticism. We have seen that the work of philosophical education must begin by raising radical doubts. The teacher must apply his energy and skill to throwing the convictions of his student into disarray. He must personify the malignant demon of Descartes and stir up every doubt he can. This is the only way in which accepted principles of validity can be dredged up to the surface of the mind for examination. But principles of validity do not rest inside a personality, detached from the emotions and the will. They are an integral part of the personality; they are, in a very real sense, what a man is and how he lives. It follows that to play the malignant demon is to do more than play. If the operation is to be anything more than a trivial exercise in logical versatility it must bring the individual man or woman, and the society to which he belongs, under a corrosive influence. To put the matter in this way is, of course, to put it dramatically. No doubt most teachers will not press their questions quite so firmly home. And yet there is no doubt at all that except in proportion as they do so the teaching of philosophy is worthless. There is absolutely no point in making people collect a variety of opinions about the logical nature of the value-judgment unless they feel that the issue matters, and unless they have some living experience in terms of which the theories may be judged. They must realise the existence in the world of that ruthless egoism that Plato personified in Thrasymachus. And human nature is such that no one can realise the existence of such people in the world if they are not aware of the same qualities within themselves. Ethics is a pointless study to anyone who has not yet caught a glimpse of the Nazi within. But that realisation is a strenuous business. To achieve it one must abandon the comfortable opinions by which we conceal our natures from ourselves; and most of us, naturally enough, are unwilling to do that for a moment, let alone often, or for long.

With this the human implications of a real philosophical education become obvious. In the first place we can see more clearly why it is that philosophy is an awkward thing to fit in to the regular pattern of a university. Even less than literature or history can it be taught as a purely intellectual activity, raising no personal problems. Unless the personal problems are raised, it cannot be taught at all. But this puts both the teacher and the taught in a quandary. The real philosophical spirit blows where it lists; the real philosopher is an outsider. The capacity to admit and face the chaos which we attempt to reduce to order by means of our principles of validity is rare as between men and fitful in any one of them. Even those of us who have looked down into the abyss that a Hobbes can open up beside us cannot do so all the time; and many of those who have taken one look are disinclined to take another. There is therefore a standing temptation for the man for whom philosophy has been made a job to reduce his teaching of the subject to the level of playing games and solving puzzles. He is inclined to play with the paradoxes of human reason and to skirt the obscurity into which it falls, rather than to press these facts severely home. That is his first quandary, brought on by his own emotions. But if he is tough and enterprising enough to pour corrosive doubt into his pupil's minds, he must consider what the effect may be. The temperaments of students vary as much as those of teachers. Some are stolid; on them scepticism, however fierce, has small effect. Others have a conceptual versatility which lets them deal with the disturbance by moving nimbly from one answer to the next. Others can live with doubt. But to others, who are neither stolid, agile nor robust, vigorous philosophical teaching comes as a shock, and sometimes as a harmful shock. It is no good raising doubts in people's minds about what they have hitherto implicitly believed if you cannot help them to a new position, and they are not able to live without some articles of faith. The teaching of philosophy, if it is to be more than an arid formality, or to produce more than the odious skill that Descartes described as the ability to talk on all topics with an appearance of truth, therefore raises serious moral problems for all those who are involved in it.

But the piecemeal, sceptical approach to the teaching of philosophy, which we have seen to be implied by the circumstances of our universities and culture and which leads on to these moral problems, is also in itself philosophically problematic. Whatever the moral consequences may be, can one really be content, as a philosopher, with the ceaseless raising of doubts, the piecemeal suggestion of tentative solutions, and the careful preservation of ideological neutrality, to which we seem to be committed?

In fact, this ideological neutrality is a gigantic piece of bad faith. The official theory of the liberal university, reflecting the official theory of liberal society, is that it offers an open forum in which all opinions can be aired and all positions argued for. Their merits are supposed to be an open question. Let every view be expressed, and let the truth prevail! But this is really hypocritical. He who is not for Catholicism or Marxism is against them; for an essential ingredient of such doctrines is the contention that they are, and can be proved to be, the truth. To say therefore that all doctrines may be voiced but none taught is really to say that their claim to truth has not been made good, so that whatever interpretation is put upon them, it cannot be the interpretation that they put upon themselves. Liberalism is not in fact an impartial referee in the struggle of ideas; it is a leading contender in the struggle, claiming, implicitly at least, to rule the others out. But the paradox of liberalism is that this claim has usually been implicit and no more. Officially, liberal society keeps an open mind towards such rivals as Catholicism and Marxism; in reality it denies precisely what those doctrines hold to be the most distinctive things about themselves, their clarity and certainty. And it is this hypocrisy of liberalism that creates the fundamental problem of teaching philosophy in an English university at present. In English society at large the individual with religious or communist convictions is not directly attacked because he holds them. What is done to him is both more subtle and more powerful: he is obliged to keep his convictions on the shelf even when he is dealing with practical issues to which they are directly relevant, since it would be both ineffectual and imprudent to argue from them. In the university the same thing happens, but with the extra twist that when ideological issues become the topic of debate they do so on the assumption, which everyone who joins a liberal university implicitly if unwillingly accepts, that the case for any side has not been made. The fundamental weakness of liberal society, and so of its microcosm, the liberal university, is just that this assumption is not plainly asserted, and therefore that its consequences have not been drawn. For some reason or other liberal-minded people have been diffident, not to say cowardly, about seeking out rigorously and setting out plainly the positive view of life which underlies their rejection of its rivals.

It is this equivocal condition of thought which underlies the moral embarrassment of philosophical teaching. The sceptical, piecemeal method of philosophising, which we have seen that the modern teacher of the subject must adopt, is simply the theoretical form of the practical scepticism of liberal social life. In our philosophical operations, as in our social practice, we take grand views of man and of the world to pieces, but, ostensibly, put nothing in their place. It is this that makes the situation of a teacher of philosophy, who sets out vigorously to work upon his students, equivocal and, indeed, unpleasant.

The most extreme form of this philosophical position is that of what may be called crude positivism, strikingly represented by Ayer's book *Language, Truth and Logic*.[1] According to this theory, the only genuine thinking is that which occurs in mathematics and natural science; all other kinds of discourse, although they may be couched in linguistic forms of genuine theory, are really nothing of the kind. When people make value-judgments, for example, they are doing nothing but expressing their feelings in a misleading form; ethics consists simply in saying that ethical concepts are pseudo-concepts and therefore unanalysable. All that remains to be done after that is to describe the feelings so expressed, and to analyse their relations to the structure of personality and society. But this is empirical work for psychologists and sociologists. We cannot therefore think out how to live; we can only express the actual promptings of our nature and, as scientists, examine them together with those of other people, times and groups. A similar treatment is accorded to religious and metaphysical utterances. They are allowed emotional significance, but nothing more.

Philosophers who have maintained these views have generally denied that they are cynical, implying a deflation or destruction of morality. In a direct sense, this is no doubt true; it is unlikely that anybody has been led by Chapter 6 of *Language, Truth and Logic*, to break a rule that he would otherwise have kept. But, in an indirect sense, this theory does have a practical effect. If our judgments of value are mere expressions of our feelings they cannot properly be said to contradict or to imply each other; it follows that we cannot logically think them out. It does not make sense on this basis to ask and systematically to try to answer the question as to how one ought to live. The practical upshot of the theory is therefore equivocal. It either makes people acquiesce in their existing preferences or makes them feel that no preferences really matter. It conduces to conservatism or indifference. If this were the last word on the topic the rôle of the philosopher in the university and in society at large would be curious indeed.

But the most striking thing about the development of philosophy in England over the last decades is just that, while it has stuck to the broad programme of empiricism, it has seen that the crude positivist view of moral, religious and metaphysical discourse is untenable. Value-judgments can contradict and imply each other exactly as can statements of fact; no hard line separates the metaphysical from the empirical. The view that all human life is sacred contradicts the view that it is right to hang murderers; and metaphysical statements, such as that the world is a machine, while they do not belong to science in the sense of being able to be verified by observation, are yet relevant, indeed essential, to science in some more recondite way. Once these points have been made the road is open to admitting that rationality has a wider scope than that of empirical and formal science; the business of philosophers is seen to be that of scrupulously examining all the actual and possible provinces of reason and considering how they may all be related to each other and the world. This development is highly relevant to the problem of philosophical teaching. The empiricist who takes this broader-minded view about variety of rational discourse, while he is not prepared to say that religious or political doctrines which claim to have laid bare the essence of the human situation can really be accepted as they stand, yet will not go so far as to say, with the crude positivist, that they are literally meaningless. He has realised that meaning is diverse and wants to fathom its diversity. And seen from the standpoint of the evolution of liberal society, what the broad-minded empiricist has really been doing, although for the most part without knowing it, is to try to improve upon the doctrine of the open forum with its implication, flatly put by positivism, that those who raise their voices in it on any topics other than scientific or mathematical are talking nonsense. He has been trying to find a way of regarding doctrines which, while not allowing them just the sense they claim, yet does not deprive them of all sense whatever. If the development of philosophy is in this respect a true indicator of the development of society, the age of liberal equivocation is drawing to an end and a new, candid and positive liberalism is coming to the fore. And if this were true the position of the philosophical teacher would be less unpleasant than at first it seems to be; for, besides having much to take away, he would begin to have something to give.

The essence of the matter seems to be this. In science we have long accustomed ourselves to the situation in which no finality is claimed for the most abstract concepts and propositions in terms of which phenomena are explained. We do not think it an affront to reason that the framework of our physical thought should always be vague and always changing. We have discovered that there is a middle path between total scepticism and final certainty, a middle path that consists in constantly extending and modifying the web of knowledge by agreed procedures. In moral, political and religious matters, however, this revolution has not yet taken place. The ordinary man is inclined to believe that one must have absolute principles or none at all. To think of moral and political principles in the way we think of scientific knowledge, as something in constant evolution, its rationality being guaranteed, not by finality of content but by the way in which the evolution occurs, is an insight to which common sense has not yet come. But come to it it must, not just by pure philosophical illumination but by the pressure of the facts. Industrial society is dynamic; the environment in which we have to live is therefore always changing; consequently, our principles of conduct must constantly be thought out anew. There is no doubt that this revolution in human circumstance, bringing with it a revolution in the conduct of practical moral thinking, is finally bringing with it also a revolution in our philosophical insight into the nature of practical rationality.

Marx was the first to get this new idea in his famous aphorism: 'Philosophers have hitherto only interpreted the world in various ways; the point however is to change it.' In the changing of the world the philosopher has his special rôle to play. It is not for him to unravel new secrets of nature, to devise new applications of scientific knowledge, to invent new institutions, or to shape new policies. His business lies at a deeper level. As knowledge grows and practice changes, and does so with ever greater speed over an ever wider front, so the deeper intellectual assumptions and procedures upon which the enterprise has been conducted get out of step with the new powers and circumstances which have been produced. The work of the philosopher, called forth by these profound contradictions, is to fashion new assumptions and procedures in whose terms the contradictions can be overcome. Abandoning the old hope that human reason can finally be reconciled to itself, he accepts the task of ceaseless partial reconciliation; and at the personal as at the social level he discovers that to march hopefully is better than to arrive.

Given this conception of philosophical work, both the destructiveness of philosophical scepticism and the hypocritical neutrality of liberal society fall into their place, as essential parts but not the whole of man's new intellectual world. They are essential parts because all claims to a complete and certain picture of the human situation need to be broken; they are not the whole because we men, each and all of us, do need to have fashioned for us or to fashion for ourselves some vision of our individual and social nature in whose terms to think and work together, even if we can no longer claim that those visions are final, clear and comprehensive. I believe that there is work for the philosopher which is neither the mere corrosion of doubt, nor the construction of illusory dogmatic systems, nor the complacent acceptance of common sense and common language. But I also believe that this new style of philosophical work, belonging to a new style of life, is not to be invented easily or quickly. Rather, teaching philosophy in a liberal society now is an adventure: we must embark upon it, but the first results of doing so properly are drastic, and we cannot see the end. 'On s'engage, et puis on voit.'

### NOTE

1. A. J. Ayer, *Language, Truth and Logic,* 2nd Ed. (London: Gollancz, 1946).

# TWO TYPES OF TEACHING

## John Wilson

EDUCATION does not dictate to society: society dictates to education. Most pupils know that schools and universities are primarily factories, whose end products are the passing of examinations, social status and economic security. Teachers and professors also know this, in their saner moments, but they pretend otherwise. Either they have taken Socrates too seriously and Thrasymachus not seriously enough: or, more probably, it suits them to acquiesce in the face-saving theory that education is devoted to truth. This no doubt helps to compensate them for their low salaries.

It is therefore not surprising that what is taught, and the way in which it is taught, has rarely been subjected to any radical criticism. When it has, the criticism has been still-born: for the two factors chiefly responsible for both curriculum and teaching methods overwhelm it. These factors are: first, the basic demands of society, which insist that children and adolescents be taught to read, write, and count, control machines at the appropriate technological level, and be indoctrinated with the current social morality: and second, the willingness of a sophisticated and leisured society to permit those subjects to be taught which by academic tradition are regarded as 'cultural' or 'scholarly'.

Naturally these demands are rationalized. By a curious coincidence, now that our technology demands more scientists, we are told that science ought *de iure* to be part of every cultured human being's education. We must be 'numerate' as well as literate; and it is as bad, says Sir Charles Snow, for a man not to know the second law of thermodynamics as never to have read Shakespeare. Similarly all the traditional academic subjects are bitterly defended, often for reasons which earlier ages would never have dreamed of, as soon as they come under fire: Latin 'trains the mind': the learning of French irregular verbs 'is a good mental discipline': learning

Greek is 'useful for understanding scientific terminology'. (There are some Englishmen who scrape the bottom of the barrel in a similar way in trying to defend the English system of weights and measures against the metric system.)

Even such rationalizations as these may, of course, be *per accidens* good reasons: but they are none the less rationalizations, because it is society and an uncritically accepted academic heritage—technology and tradition—which really make the wheels turn. Just as no parent wants his child brought up in a different religious or moral code from his own, so no society is as yet prepared to allow its youth to be educated primarily as human beings, if there is any risk of lowering the standard of living thereby, or if the nation's security is otherwise threatened; and so also no professor who gains a living —and, more important, an identity—by the study of Provençal verb-endings is going to admit that this study has little advantage over Scrabble or (let us be fair) chess.

Most of what is written on the 'philosophy of education' is monumentally dull, because it refuses to face these rather obvious home truths. Educationalists spend most of their time either trying to justify the curriculum as it stands, or escaping into vague talk about educating 'the whole man', 'the mature individual', 'the responsible citizen', 'the lover of truth', and so on. Hence in this subject, if it is a subject, the gap between theory and practice is appallingly wide. As any teacher knows, as soon as you get in a classroom most of what educationalists have written seems utterly divorced from reality. Few educationalists seem to know what children and adolescents are actually like, and neglect such obvious truths as, for instance, that adolescent girls are chiefly interested in boys and not in French grammar, or that some children are just too stupid to understand Shakespeare. Since it is impossible to hold sane views on what children should be like, and hence on what and how to teach them, unless you know what they are like, and hence what they want to learn, it is not strange that writers on education allow their imagination to body forth the forms of things unknown, and give to airy nothing a local habitation and a name.

Let us, for a few glorious minutes, suppose that we are going to educate human beings as human beings, for that part of our time at least which we can spare from the demands of society (many of which are of course quite reasonable). Let us further suppose that we make no doctrinaire or *a priori* assumptions about what human beings ought to be like or ought to learn: let us not try and make them saints or scholars, 'cultured' or 'civilized', gentlemen or good middle-class citizens. Let us see what they *want* to be like, what they want to learn. Of course this is vague. But if we forget to be clever or high-minded for a minute, we might make some such sketch as this:—

Human beings want to be happy. (This is not a tautology unless we care to make it so: and if we do, it is a tautology worth remembering.) They want pleasure, money, good health, people to be loved by and people to love. Some want power: most want a sense of achievement. Boys want to get girls and girls want to get husbands. They want to feel at ease with their parents, with their wives and husbands, and with their employers and employees. They want to avoid war, and other less unpleasant forms of interference. Quite a few are interested in whether or not there is a God, and in what is right and wrong. A lot enjoy some form of music or literature. Many like tinkering with machines, or making things, or playing games. A very few are intellectuals or highbrows. I happen to like Palestrina, Donne, Greek grammar and logical puzzles. But this is peculiar. Nor can it plausibly be argued that Palestrina and the rest are in any significant sense more important or more 'worth while' than the more usual human interests which I have just mentioned. Indeed, they are not even more important to me, since health, pleasure, love, and so on affect me far more. Palestrina is really just a sideline.

Appropriate techniques for fulfilling some of these wants can hardly fall under the heading of 'education'. They must be satisfied by physics, medicine, economics, improved technology, and so on. These wants are logically simple (though often difficult to satisfy in practice) because they are dealt with by expertises whose methodology is on the whole clear. You have a headache: you go to a doctor. We want a higher standard of living: we consult economists. Doctors may not be able to cure cancer, and economists may disagree. But this has nothing to do with the education of human beings: it concerns education only in so far as we need people with special skills, people who are masters of various useful τέχναι—and of course this is very important. But there are other wants, just as important and even more widely shared, for which we have no properly developed expertises. The problem of satisfying these wants faces every human being: and the education of human beings as such consists in enabling them to master techniques—they will hardly merit the term 'expertises'—which will help in this satisfaction.

To make this perhaps boringly clear:—If you need to master chemistry or Greek grammar in order to get a certain job, or to help society, or just because you happen to enjoy them, that is understandable. But it would be odd to say that chemical knowledge or knowledge of Greek is an essential tool for the construction of your happiness as a person. On the other hand, the ability to talk, walk, make friends, live at peace with your neighbours and express yourself sexually might be regarded as essential tools. It now becomes clear that, as one might expect, most of the essential tools are *skills*. (Many of them, such as walking, eating, talking, keeping ourselves clean and so on, we learn at home when we are young.) A great many of the other tools, at least as they figure in the curriculum, consist not of skills but of *factual knowledge*. (We learn science, history, languages, and so forth.)

The distinction between learning which is essential to a human being (I shall call this 'human') and learning which is not, which is the really important distinction, does not correspond exactly with the distinction just made between the learning of skills and the amassing of facts (between 'knowing how' and 'knowing that', if you like). Plainly, if there are any hard facts of psychology, human beings ought to know them: and conversely, knowing how to play the flute or how to behave in a laboratory are non-human skills, not solely matters of fact. But they do correspond to some extent: enough for me to speak in my title of 'two types of teaching'.

The first type of teaching, then, relates to subjects which are not essential to human beings as such. It consists mostly of factual knowledge, and does not require any very sophisticated form of communication between teacher and pupil. I can learn most of my mathematics, my history, my science, and so on from a book, or from a closed-circuit television lecture. I do not *have* to like my professor, nor does he have to understand me as a person. As I have already (rather broadly) hinted, quite a lot of this learning may not only be inessential to human beings as such, but of little value in any context: particularly when we remember that we have only so many man-hours and so much money to spend on education, and that we do not want to waste any of it. Obviously we must have scientists, doctors and technicians: but when the basic wants of human beings are not satisfied—when they find it hard to make friends, to live at peace, to love, to be sane—it seems just a little odd to spend so much time on irregular verbs and the Anglo-Saxons. Nor, if one is not going to be an electrician, need one know about electricity simply because other people are going to be electricians and because electricity is very important. It is important as a τέχνη, not as a tool for happiness in the sense I have tried to give it. (Personally I have long believed that electricity is caused by little men running very fast up and down wires. I know it isn't really, but I get by O.K.)

The second type of teaching, on which I wish to spend more time because it is neither properly recognised nor properly practised, is the teaching of those 'subjects' which each human being needs to master. I have put 'subjects' in inverted commas for obvious reasons. Skills are not subjects in the sense that chunks of factual knowledge can be subjects: and the majority of tools for human happiness, as we have seen, are skills. There is a tendency amongst sophisticated people to look down on things like 'the philosophy of education', 'group relationships', 'citizenship' and the like on the ground that they are not subjects. Nor are they: but they may be convenient titles for groups of skills. 'Philosophy' itself is perhaps no more than such a title: so perhaps are 'literary criticism' and 'psychology'.

If we look at our list of basic human wants, it should strike us that a great many of them are essentially concerned with communication. Learning that skill, or that group of skills, which we may call 'getting on with people' or 'having a happy marriage', is essentially learning to communicate in certain ways. To extend Wittgenstein's metaphor, it is like learning to play certain games: and linguistic ability, the ability to communicate in certain ways, forms a large part of these games. In important respects learning to obey the laws of the land, the laws of polite society, and the laws of cricket are similar. Just as most children learn to talk, so most adults need to learn how to talk better: in particular, how to adjust the rules of their talk to different contexts and different purposes.

Approaching this from another angle, it is clear that a great deal of what we call 'philosophy', 'religion', 'psychology', 'literary criticism', 'sociology', and 'history' is a matter of acquiring skills. These skills too are closely bound up with communication. To do philosophy or literary criticism properly we have first to learn, by practice and precept, what sort of talk is required of us: we have to learn the rules of the game. Often, when we are confronted by (say) the talk of a depth psychologist, or a deeply religious person, we experience a feeling of bafflement: we are not sure what to make of it: we don't understand what *sort* of talk it is. When we are told that we all want to kill our fathers or that *Lady Chatterley's Lover* is a deeply moral book we may be worried because we don't know what's meant: we're not in the game. To borrow an example from a non-human subject, it is like trying to make the jump from arithmetic to algebra, learning that $x$ stands for any number but not for any particular number, attempting to grasp a whole new language.

Human skills all ultimately concern the human self: and this is why communication plays such a large part. For though practice, imitation, and direct precept are important, we can only control the self by understanding it and by training ourselves in awareness and self-consciousness. This is done through talk. The model case here is psychoanalysis, as it is alleged to be practised by true-blue Freudians: i.e. with the objective of promoting awareness in the patient, and not with the objective of making him a good citizen, 'adjusted', 'mature', 'sane', etc. Psychoanalysis itself, however, depends on the patient knowing how to talk. (Playing with dolls' houses and clay figures à la Melanie Klein may be jolly good, but is certainly more arduous.)

Traditionally we still divide the curriculum into subjects, on the analogy of languages or the physical sciences. Just as there are living things and hence biology, and subtle things like light and heat and hence physics, so there are supposed to be individual human beings and hence psychology, human beings *en masse* and hence sociology, 'ultimate truths' and hence philosophy (or religion as a soft option), and so on. Of course this does not even begin to look plausible. The methodology of these 'subjects' is doubtful: in fact discussion of methodology forms perhaps the kernel of them. (I once did a sociology essay for a student, who had it marked by two professors. One of them gave it 21 out of 100: the other gave it 89. Something is funny somewhere.) What we can extract from these 'subjects' is a number of approaches or techniques. Often these need to be combined to answer certain questions: to take a simple example, 'Is there poetic truth?' needs both a philosopher, and a literary critic, and perhaps a poet as well—even a psychologist would not be out of place.

It should not surprise us that many of these techniques arise, not from prolonged thinking in ivory towers, but from a close context of communication which for one reason or another gives rise to them. We may think here of the Vienna Circle, the Leavis school of literary criticism, and the cross-fertilisation of physics in the later '30s. The skills are imparted more by personal teaching, group conversation, and example than by lecture-notes or learned books. Indeed we might almost venture on a totally new approach to education, and say that instead of thinking first of the content of education and only afterwards of the context, we should reverse the order. Suppose we decided what were good contexts of communication and established those, and then waited to see what techniques developed from this. Certain contexts we know or take for granted: the home, the summer camp, and some would say the boarding school. But apart from these we are rather at a loss. Everyone is a bit worried about pupil-teacher relationships, suicides at the university, teenagers, and so on, but very little is actually done about this. The ability to communicate with pupils of all sorts in various contexts is not one of the things which, in practice, we appoint professors or teachers for. As one might expect, we retire into our academic shells and appoint them for academic ability and 'scholarship' which in nine cases out of ten are totally useless both to their pupils and to society. The general impression is of people taking in each other's washing in a highbrow sort of way. No wonder so many people don't like eggheads.

What we teach must not be retained because it is 'cultural', 'scholarly', 'traditional', etc.: nor on the other hand must it be scrapped because it is not of immediate and direct utility. ('Useful' is far too vague a word for educationalists.) It must be scrutinised to see what bearing it has on human beings. Plainly the techniques of philosophy, psychology, history, literature, and so on can be brought to bear: but it is the business of educationalists to see how this can be done and to do it, not to leave them under glass cases for fear of revolutionary moths. Above all, the 'subjects' must be geared to the interests and wants of the pupils: this is just another way of saying that they must be taught as skills which the pupil will want to use, not just as 'cultural facts'.

Let me consider one example to give coherence to what I am trying to say—the teaching of moral philosophy. Now here we have something which ought *par excellence* to provide the pupil with skills that will be useful to him in running his life, which ought to give him increased understanding and hence control of himself and his own destiny. I think most instructors would agree, however, that as it is taught it does nothing of the kind. The opinions of those philosophers who are studied rarely seem to the student to be relevant to his own decisions: he is not usually able to discuss them fully: he has to pass his course chiefly by memorising what they have said, adding a veneer of criticism for form's sake; and consequently they leave his practical reason, in the Aristotelian sense, quite untouched. Most students still seem to think if one challenges their own personal beliefs, either that morals are 'just a matter of taste' or that there are unshakeably correct answers to all moral questions which they, the students, know. Significantly, in neither case is there any place for discussion of morality; and this bears horrid witness to the failure of moral philosophy to present itself as something worth discussing. Much the same applies to the teachings of religion: students either think they know already, or else think there is nothing *to* know. The propositions that it is possible to get closer to truths of which we are at present uncertain, and that philosophy can provide one with skills which help in this process, do not commend themselves to most students.

Plainly this is a failure in communication. If you have a student who, perhaps like most ordinary people, is what we might call a naive intuitionist in his morality, you are not going to affect his moral decisions without questioning his own brand of intuitionism: and you are not going to question *his* intuitionism by making him read Hume and Mill, or even Ayer and Hare: even if he can understand them, they will not seem immediately relevant. You have to start with his own attitude, and then try and show him that he needs to learn, and that what he needs to learn can be found in the writings of others. This is a long business, and depends entirely on close personal contact with the student. Plenty of students will, by themselves, use philosophical literature to equip themselves with 'answers' to life, 'philosophies', cultural knowledge, and smart quotations: but most of this simply builds more barriers round their entrenched positions. To educate them is a different process: it involves doubt, uncertainty, questioning and a feeling of inadequacy—not, as so many students have, a feeling that they are not 'intellectual' enough and have not read enough of the World's Great Books, but a feeling that they do not have a proper mastery of the skills by which they need to live. This feeling necessarily involves emotion as well as reason, and set lectures are inadequate to deal with it.

## Two Types of Teaching

Not only in philosophy, but in most other 'subjects' which relate to human skills, the student has continually to be referred to his own experience, and has to move back and forth from the felt reality of that experience to the unknown skills and knowledge that will help him to make sense of it and generalise from it. In the teaching of English literature, for instance, we can give the pupil culture (and perhaps pleasure) by making him learn the jollier bits of *Paradise Lost*, and we can save him from the epithet 'illiterate' by teaching him rules of grammar and punctuation, although many of these are obsolete and irrational. But what he needs as a human being is, amongst other things, to be able to feel characters and situations in literature as real and relevant to himself, and to be able to express himself, to understand, and be understood, both orally and on paper: to be able to write and to be able to talk. How many students who have had, let us say, ten thousand man-hours of 'English', can actually do this?

To be able to talk and understand is basic to almost all of these skills; and it is very difficult to teach. The obstacles are not so much that the student has not read enough, or does not command a wide vocabulary or a high I.Q. They are psychological. People are frightened to speak, prejudiced, bewitched, over-eager, fanatical, and so forth. The difficulties can only be overcome by practice in small groups (with about four to six members, let us say) run by a competent instructor. Herein lies the real problem: adults are not much better at talking than students. The image of the professor or the teacher, as it exists in the minds of pupils, is not such as to encourage communication. Perhaps the ultimate reason why this type of teaching is not popular is that we, the teachers, are frightened of doing it. For it is difficult and painful.

At this point I ought perhaps to make clear that I am considering these skills or 'subjects' only in the context of education, not in the context of research or in any other context. Failure to make this distinction is perhaps responsible for much of the trouble. Take history, for instance: plainly a subject which can shed much light on human behaviour. Now there are a few people on the one hand who are gifted with the aptitude for historical research: they pore over documents, balance probabilities, make nice judgments from a wide background of knowledge, and so on. For them the context of human communication is not so essential. There are somewhat more people, on the other hand, who are historically curious: not many, because intellectual curiosity and an interest in intellectual problems for their own sake is a rarity. They too may learn a great deal from books, or otherwise by their own efforts. But the vast majority will only be interested in so far as historical knowledge can be shown, and (more important) *felt*, to be relevant to their own lives.

Of course it is easy to *say* that the Greeks and the Anglo-Saxons are relevant to the modern world: and so they are. But to make them so is a Herculean, and often an impossible, task. A response from the fair-minded student such as, 'Oh yes, that's very interesting, I see it all starts with the Greeks', is not by itself adequate. In so far as it has made any impact at all on him, it has done so as a hobby, an amusement, a nice piece of knowledge to carry around. But now suppose the student has strong Protestant or puritan feelings, and we are able to show him (say, by going realistically into the history of Luther and others) how these feelings arise and under what conditions—how the battles of the human self have been fought on a large scale on the map of history—his reaction will be different. We will have given him a glimpse of a technique for becoming more aware of his own feelings, and for setting them in proportion, regarding them more objectively, and just possibly being able to do something about them.

All these human skills are, in a sense, techniques for becoming aware of the human self; and communication is essential because it is each individual student's own self that he has to become aware of. If we now go on to consider briefly what 'subjects', as they normally figure in the curriculum, are or could be of value in this task, it should be clear that the manner rather than the content of the teaching is by far the more important. There is hardly any arts subject which, if properly angled, cannot shed the sort of light we require: though some are obviously better than others. Psychology and the social sciences study man directly: philosophy examines the concepts of his thinking: history illumines his past behaviour: languages show the thought and feelings of other peoples in action. None of these subjects as usually taught, however, is of much use, because they are taught as subjects: that is, the educators assume a subject-matter and want the student to acquire a comprehensive and scholarly grasp of it. For people who are by nature intellectually curious this is admirable. They may succeed in their academic work and become scholarly, cultured, clever, well-informed and all the rest of it. But they are not any the better *educated* for it; and certainly there is no indication that they conduct their lives any better.

If I may be permitted a little more autobiography:—I am by nature intellectually curious. Being good at problems and getting things right, I did well at classics and philosophy. But for any techniques that I have begun to master I am indebted, not to the educational system, but to the accidental benevolence of my friends and an occasional teacher and tutor. A friend taught me to look at literature in a way which can enlarge one's awareness: other friends taught me to make some kind of sense out of Freudian and other depth-psychology: tutors taught me to look at concepts and language philosophically: and so on. None of these techniques were written into the system, although the system had room for some of them. I am reminded of being taught to swim when I was fourteen. Hitherto, being by nature nervous and frightened of the water, I had pretended illness or evaded it by other means. One intelligent schoolmaster who actually noticed what I was feeling took me up on this in a kindly way: after about three days' communication with him, during which he helped me to get the feel of the water, I learned to swim.

Since learning these human skills is essentially like learning to swim in that it consists of 'getting the feel' of particular techniques, educationalists should devote their research to the conditions of communication which facilitate this. I am only a philosopher, but there are some suggestions I can make and others I would like to endorse. First, it is too often assumed that people want to be rational, and want to be made more aware of themselves in a critical way. They don't. The radical objection to, or at least handicap for, books about straight thinking, how to win friends and influence people, how to be happy though human, etc., is that people only partly want to achieve these objectives. Listen to any discussion which lies close to the hearts of the participants: it is quite evident that nearly everyone thinks that the rules of rationality (whatever these may be) do not and should not apply to him in certain contexts. His wife is being so *obviously* silly: Mr. Bloggs is so *patently* hostile and superior in his manner: everyone *knows* there is a God: the rules of courtesy just aren't *meant* to apply when arguing with Communists. It's rather like when people apologise, and say 'I'm very sorry I lost my temper, but . . .' and then follows a justification for their having lost it. Or it's as if they continually excused themselves for special cases, as if whenever they did a murder it ought to count as a *crime passionel*. Most people are non-rationalists: they express this in remarks like, 'Logic isn't everything', 'My instincts tell me ...', 'The human reason cannot comprehend ...' 'Every decent person knows ...' and many others.

The teacher's first job is to have this out and to demolish the inner complacency which we all have: otherwise the student simply sits inside his castle, taking a benevolent interest in what the teacher has to say, but not letting it affect him at any vital point. Proper education, like proper psychoanalysis, is *disturbing*. There is bound to be a transference of some kind between pupil and teacher, because if the teacher does his job properly emotions will be let loose. He has to handle them benevolently and with reasonable detachment. Without some degree of transference, identification, aggression and imitation no effective human education can be carried on. This, I think, is the basic truth which educators are reluctant to accept, even though parents have practised it for millennia.

Secondly, we need to use obvious ways of objectifying the student's thoughts and feelings. Consider the merits of tape-recording discussions and playing the tape back, commenting on it and discussing the discussion: of taking movies of groups of people in action and commenting on those: of making students act parts, defend theses, deliver mob-swaying orations, give extempore and prepared talks. Such methods will sound time-wasting to some and naive to others: they can be both, unless competently handled by the instructor. But they can also be intensely illuminating. The stock remark about how terrible it was to hear one's voice on a tape recorder for the first time covers a multitude of fears and problems. It wasn't until I heard my own voice on a recorder, becoming more and more drawling and 'Oxford' the more my disputant grew heated, that I realised how maddeningly calm my way of speech must sound in such a context.

Thirdly, we need to inspect different language-games much more closely, and try to lay down the rules for each. The phrase 'rational discussion' alone includes a multitude of such games: for the criteria of reason vary according to the game. Thus in discussing a moral problem, a work of art, a psychological proposition, a historical thesis, and a matter of empirical fact quite different criteria apply in each case. Then there are contexts of discussion which approximate much more to psychoanalysis, though they may still be quite far from it. One often wants to say to a student, for instance, 'Look, isn't it really that at the back of your mind you feel so-and-so?', or 'Surely underneath you're frightened of such-and-such, aren't you?' Discussions may be more or less *ad hominem*: and legitimately so. What is important is to distinguish the games, and not to play two of them on the same board.

Finally, although my whole thesis has been a plea to formalise the communication of human skills, it must be recognised that until we get much better at doing this most of the work will be informal: the best educators can do is to provide time, money, the right kind of staff and the right kind of *milieu* for this informal instruction to occur. This is not only because we have not made much progress in this field. It is also because this kind of communication should, ideally, arise out of the context of life itself. It is when the student is actually making a moral decision that he needs the help of a moral philosopher or a psychologist—that is, if moral philosophers and psychologists really have anything to teach of educational value. Unfortunately moral problems do not always coincide with classes or tutorials in moral philosophy. They arise, or at least can be discussed, at meals, in the bar, while walking or drinking, and on a host of other occasions. Without a properly-organised community that makes allowances for this sort of thing I doubt if, at present, the kind of teaching I have tried to outline can be done very effectively, because it is bound to seem unreal. To seat two or three utterly unknown people before you in a study, office or lecture-room and say 'Right, now we're going to Communicate' is to give the kiss of death to any such enterprise. Such communication must arise naturally out of a particular context. Here again we see that the provision of appropriate *milieux* of communication is more important for educators than the content of communication. And in case anyone is afraid that the whole business will reduce itself to good-natured but aimless chats, with the students doing no work and having to meet no standards of scholarship or anything else, let me say at once that this is a false fear. For instructors to be in close personal contact with their students does not mean that they have to be weak-minded: though perhaps many teachers fear that it will entail this.

Can modern philosophers help here? Their strongest card, I think, which they picked up from Wittgenstein, is the desire to investigate particular cases and to clarify the rules of particular games. Some of the games played in education—and I include football as well as learning the multiplication tables—we know, more or less, how to play. Others we do not. Clarification of them is essentially clarification of concepts: and I regret that I have not had space to do this as fully and precisely as might be wished. Educators need the help of analytic philosophers to decide, in particular contexts of teaching and learning, exactly what (logically) is going on. What sort of teaching is this? Does it count as education? Is the student learning a skill? Or facts? What sort of facts? What are the criteria of success in learning this subject? Is it useful? What are the criteria of utility? The philosopher delineates the logic of games, where the sociologist or psychologist delineates their empirical natures. Educational research needs both: and both, perhaps, need each other more than either is willing to admit.

# INSTRUCTION AND INDOCTRINATION

## R. F. Atkinson

THERE is too little communication between academic moral philosophy and the philosophy of education. They are separate countries, and a citizen of the one finds himself an alien in the other. The language change is confusing, and it is hard to feel altogether confident of one's judgment of what is and is not worth saying once one has crossed the frontier. So, at any rate, it has come to seem to me. In the present paper what I have tried to do is to proceed, by way of a discussion of instruction and indoctrination, to the consideration of a prominent theme in recent moral philosophy whose implications for moral education are, it seems to me, insufficiently appreciated in much that is written on the topic. There seems still to be point in emphasizing the sense in which there are open options in morality and consequently in moral education.

I

The distinction I have adopted the terms 'instruction' and 'indoctrination' to mark is clearly important in many educational discussions. What is less clear is how firm a distinction it is, and over what range of things taught it can be maintained. There would seem to be no great difficulty in drawing it with respect to academic and vocational education, but can it be drawn in the field of moral education? It is here that I, at least, am disposed to object most strongly to indoctrination, but I am not at all sure that there is a basis for instruction here either. There can, obviously, be instruction *about* morals: it is instruction *in* morals that is in question.

'Instruction' and 'indoctrination' are not the only, and may well not be the best pair of terms for the distinction intended. Sometimes 'education' is the term opposed to 'indoctrination', whilst 'instruction' is used for a rather direct sort of telling of people what is and

171

is not so, a telling that smacks rather of indoctrination than education proper. Again, Scheffler, in his illuminating study *The Language of Education*,[1] adopts a much narrower usage for 'instruction' than I have elected to do. It is possible, of course, that there is here a difference between British and American usage. Such linguistic matters are not, however, of very great importance in themselves. The distinction required is simply a special case or reflection of that between the rational and the irrational or a-rational. It is that distinction applied to the teaching process.

'Instruction', though probably not 'indoctrination', is perhaps most naturally applied to theoretical teaching, to teaching *that* as opposed to teaching *how*. But the distinction we are concerned with can perfectly well be drawn with respect to teaching how, which cannot in any case be wholly separated from teaching that. Quite apart from the fact that, so far as language goes, it is very frequently a matter of choice whether we speak of teaching how or that, it is clear that academic teaching as ordinarily understood is not exclusively theoretical, nor vocational purely practical. Vocational training normally involves the mastery of some fact and theory, academic the acquisition of a variety of skills.

Instruction, then, is essentially a rational process, both at the giving and, in so far as it is successful, at the receiving end. It involves, for instance, providing adequate support, by way of proofs, reasons, evidence, whatever may be appropriate to the field in question, for the conclusions it is sought to impart. No higher degree of conviction is sought than is warranted by the nature of the support available. Not conviction by itself, but justified conviction, rational assent is the aim. The imparting and acquiring of an understanding of what is taught is consequently involved in its realisation. Because of this, and in so far as it succeeds, instruction puts its subject in the way of making progress in the field by his own efforts. Indoctrination, on the other hand, need not. It is subject to no such restrictions. Conviction or assent is all that is sought, and any teaching procedure is acceptable provided only that it is or is thought to be effective in achieving this end. Understanding, awareness of the grounds upon which opinions ought to rest, is not required. If knowledge consists in justified (full) conviction, then the object and result of instruction may be knowledge; whereas of the man who is indoctrinated merely, although what he believes may be true and capable of justification, it will not be possible to say that he knows it.

## Instruction and Indoctrination

With regard to teaching and learning how, the instruction/ indoctrination distinction manifests itself as that between, say, training and drilling. The trained man knows how to achieve a certain sort of result. The well-drilled man only knows how to carry out certain routines which will, no doubt, in appropriate circumstances, be effective in producing the results. The former operates intelligently, whereas the latter does not. The trained man knows what he is about, knows not only the rules of procedure but also the reasons for them, and hence knows how to adapt the rules to non-standard conditions. The man who is merely well drilled has to make do with rules of thumb which he mechanically applies.

This does not pretend to be an account of teaching methods. I am not maintaining that teaching should or can consist entirely in instruction and training as I have described them. Even where the ultimate aims are knowledge and intelligent practice, it seems inevitable that some recourse will have to be had to non-rational teaching methods, that it will sometimes be necessary to try to impart information and techniques beyond the recipients' understanding, that there will be some learning by rote or drill. Nor, moreover, can anybody have a full grasp of all the information, techniques, etc., that he puts to use. We have all taken a vast amount on trust, and must continue to do so.

Instruction and indoctrination, training and drilling—this sort of distinction, whatever words may be used to express it, is, I believe, commonly taken for granted in discussions of the aims and practice of education. On what basis does it rest? Once the question is raised it becomes apparent that the distinction presupposes that there are clear criteria of truth, cogency, correctness in any field to which it applies. It is not required that there should be a body of established truths, facts, laws, practices, in the field, only that there should be criteria for determining what is and what is not acceptable. Instruction, training, is then a matter of teaching with due regard to the criteria appropriate to the field in question: indoctrination, drilling, the reverse. Accordingly, the more fugitive the criteria may be in a particular field, the harder will it be to distinguish instruction and indoctrination.

It is, moreover, on this basis easy to understand why we are inclined to discriminate morally between instruction and indoctrination. Since the process of instruction is governed by criteria which are in principle accessible to any rational person, it is, to use the traditional, imprecise, but perhaps sufficiently well understood language, a matter of treating a person as an end in himself: it is not putting him to use, exploiting him, treating him as a mere means, as indoctrination so clearly is. And further, so long as the instruction/indoctrination distinction can be drawn within a field, we have, as it were, ready-made, a basis for evaluating and regulating the non-rational teaching procedures that we may be obliged to use, whether for lack of time or competent teachers or because of the immaturity and/or incapacity of the taught. We can restrict ourselves to the inculcation of information and practices which could be the content of rational teaching and, with regard to the young especially, employ only those non-rational methods which do not or as little as possible impair the recipients' capacity for subsequent instruction and training.

Before turning to the main enquiry how moral education stands with regard to the instruction/indoctrination distinction, it might be worth while to take a look at two cases in which the need for such an enquiry has been overlooked—once very obviously, in the other case less so. No one can fail to see that in the following passage, which one must hope to be fairly untypical of ecclesiastical pronouncements on education, a relevant question has been begged:

> Every education system makes use of indoctrination. Children are indoctrinated with the multiplication table; they are indoctrinated with love of country; they are indoctrinated with the principles of chemistry and physics and mathematics and biology, and nobody finds fault with indoctrination in these fields. Yet these are of small concern in the great business of life by contrast with ideas concerning God and man's relation to God, his neighbour and himself, man's nature and his supernatural destiny.[2]

But John Stuart Mill's much weightier and in so many ways justly celebrated defence of the liberty of thought and expression suffers, it seems to me, from a similar defect. The chief ground on which Mill supports this liberty is that it is the necessary condition of people's acquisition and full understanding, which alone secures stable possession, of 'the truth'.[3] This is no doubt the case where truths of fact (scientific truths) are concerned, but the argument is meant to apply to thought and expression in morals, religion and politics too. It has to be asked, therefore, whether there are truths of anything like the same sort to be discovered in these fields. Mill in his essay betrays an altogether inadequate awareness of the possibility of radical differences among the various fields of enquiry, speculation and practical judgment. He appears to think that they can readily be placed on a simple scale of increasing complexity, running from mathematics, where 'all the argument is on one side', through natural philosophy (science), to morals, religion and politics. So very far is Mill from according any special status to moral 'truths', which presumably must by their nature have some specially close relation to conduct, that he allows that they, along with all other opinions, lose their immunity when so expressed as to be direct instigations to action,[4] as if people were to be allowed any moral opinions they liked so long as there was no danger of them or anybody else acting upon them. It may be that sense can be found for the idea of truths in morals, politics and religion, but unless and until it has, nobody is entitled to advocate liberty of thought and expression in these fields on the ground that it is a necessary means to securing the truth.

II

Is there then a firm enough basis for drawing the instruction/indoctrination distinction with respect to moral education? In many treatments of the topic attention is directed on to the contrast between direct moral teaching by explicit precept on the one hand, and reliance on example, on the candid discussion of moral issues as and when they arise in the teaching of other subjects, on the other. On the face of it at least, this contrast relates primarily to the method of moral teaching, whereas the present concern is with its content, or rather with the question whether there is a possible content for moral instruction. It is true that indirect methods of moral teaching, in so far as they engage the attention and judgment of the taught, to that extent differ from indoctrination as described above. All the same our question about the content of moral education remains to be answered.

What then is there to teach in morals? Not, it is clear, information in any ordinary sense, nor practical skills. As to the latter, moral progress is frequently understood in contradistinction from the acquiring of such skills as are necessary or helpful for achieving economic or social success, and, even if one takes more presentable candidates like promoting other people's welfare, there is no getting round the fact that immorality is never viewed as a matter of lacking or losing a capacity. Incapacity is indeed a defence against charges of immorality. And as to moral information—what could this be? Take any moral position and its opposite can be maintained without logical error or factual mistake. It can, of course, be taught and learnt (is a possible object of knowledge) that a certain moral position is held by certain people, but, whatever adequate grounds for holding a moral position might be, it is clear that this is not among them. There can be moral teaching, instruction in, as opposed to instruction about morality, only if there are criteria of truth, cogency, correctness, in the field. Are there such criteria?

Manifestly it is impossible even to list all the more important sorts of answer that have been given to this question. All I shall attempt is to illustrate a type of view which seems to be dominant among contemporary philosophers of a, very broadly, empiricist or, less happily, linguistic persuasion. There is no one who seriously entertains the hope of being able to establish a substantial moral criterion, a touchstone of moral truth. The possibility of formulating a criterion for applying the term 'moral' is, of course, another and less momentous affair. Morality, it is asserted or conceded, cheerfully or sadly, is a field in which there are irreducibly open options.

It has to be recognized, of course, that the difficulties in the way of establishing a moral criterion are inherent in the empiricist position, which excludes, among other things, the possibility of recognizing necessary or self-evident (non-tautological) truths in morals. And further, it is not at all impossible that contemporary empiricistically minded moral philosophers have operated with an unduly simple notion of what a moral criterion could be. It can be a matter of great difficulty to find words to express the ideas people have of what is and is not morally acceptable, ideas which are very often much more complex and subtle than the 'principles' to which lip-service is paid, and which are quoted as examples in the moral philosophy books. But the obstacles to establishing a moral criterion are not problems of formulation. Morality is not unique in that its first principles are not susceptible of proof. What distinguishes morality from the formal and natural sciences is that in it different and opposed first principles are readily conceivable, and are in fact accepted by morally serious people.

Although contemporary moral philosophers differ from Hume on many important matters they are with him on the point of present concern. Hume in effect suggested that, provided no errors of logic or fact were made, any moral position was as much or as little reasonable as any other. Conduct is reasonable or otherwise in so far as it does not tend to achieve the satisfaction of the agent's desires. But desires themselves cannot be reasonable or unreasonable. "'Tis not contrary to reason to prefer the destruction of the whole world to the scratching of my finger'.[5] The way Hume expressed his insight is highly exceptionable. It is simply untrue, now and in Hume's day, as he did in fact rather oddly notice, that such terms as 'reasonable' and 'rational' are never applied to desires or ends.[6] But this leaves the substantial point untouched. Choice of means can be reasonable or rational in a sense in which choice of ends cannot. Mistakes can be made about means in a way they cannot about ends. Agreement is achieveable in principle about the means to given ends, as it is on any other matter of fact. There is not the same basis for agreement on ends.

The historical Hume had many other observations to make about morality, and started some lines of thought which lead away from the view described. It is, however, this possibly somewhat over simple interpretation of him that has been remembered and reflected in current moral philosophy. Stevenson, for instance, follows Hume on the main point. He too, despite some few appearances to the contrary, maintains that there can be logically irreducible differences on moral matters. He is prepared to allow that moral judgments may be held to be 'true', but it turns out that he regards this as merely an idiomatic, perhaps debased usage in which the word functions simply as a mark of assent.[7] He does not hold that disagreements whether a moral judgment is true can be settled in principle. And, although Stevenson is willing to talk of people arguing from matters of fact to moral judgments, and of their offering factual statements as reasons for moral judgments, he has scruples about applying the term 'valid' to such arguments.[8] Even if ordinary usage permitted this application of the term, it would be misguided to go along with it for fear of suggesting that the quoting of factual reasons somehow served to establish a moral judgment.

Moral teaching would presumably be regarded by Stevenson as a matter of influencing attitudes and, rather promisingly, he distinguishes between rational and non-rational (persuasive) methods of effecting this,[9] and again between moralists and propagandists.[10] Hopes of finding here a basis for the instruction/indoctrination

distinction are soon dashed, however. The discussion of moralists
and propagandists consists mainly in pointing out that the terms
overlap in application and consequently give scope for persuasive
definitions. The distinction between rational and non-rational
methods of influencing attitudes is equally disappointing. It turns
out to be the distinction between influencing attitudes by operating
on beliefs and influencing them direct, i.e. by overtly emotive talk.
The former procedure can indeed be called giving reasons for a
moral judgment, but this needs to be interpreted in the light of
Stevenson's doctrine that *any* belief about *any* matter of fact which
is *causally* efficacious in influencing attitudes may be adduced as a
reason.[11] It is not a very impressive species of rationality that Stevenson finds room for in morality. It is a rationality that has lost all
connection with truth or correctness, as they are ordinarily understood. Opposed conclusions can be reached from the same premisses
by equally rational methods. The emotive theory of ethics, of which
Stevenson is perhaps the most thorough and serious exponent, is, it
is true, now largely abandoned, in part because it seems to allow too
little scope for rationality in morals. More fashionable views, though
from within the tradition they appear very different from Stevenson's, do not, it will transpire, differ significantly from his on the
point at issue.

Hare, in a by now well known passage in his *Language of
Morals*,[12] gives an account of what he calls justifying a moral decision completely by showing that it is in line with a way of life to
which one is committed. This need not be conceived as a simple
exercise in deduction, a matter of mechanically applying general
principles to particular cases. It is explicitly recognised that our principles are made what they are by, and are modified in the light of,
our decisions in particular cases. But once a decision has, so to say,
been fitted into a complete pattern of living, the view is that there is
no more to be said by way of justification of it. Different and
opposed ways of life are held to be possible and, as Hare recognises,
the question arises whether the choice of a way of life is to be considered completely arbitrary. Manifestly it cannot be justified in the
way that a decision is justified by being referred to a way of life.
Hare denies that such choices are necessarily arbitrary on the
grounds that a person considering what is involved in the choice of
a way of life may be considering *everything* that could conceivably
bear upon the matter, and that a choice consequent upon such

comprehensive deliberation cannot correctly, i.e. in accordance with usage, be called arbitrary or unfounded. In so far as these words connote haste or inadequate consideration of relevant matters then Hare is undoubtedly correct. But this should not be allowed to obscure the fact, which of course Hare does not deny, that opposed choices of ways of life may be equally well-founded and non-arbitrary. It follows that opposed decisions in particular cases may be equally susceptible of 'complete justification'.

No recent moral philosopher has found a way round the point that irreducible differences are possible in morality, that 'justifications' in this field have the remarkable property of failing to exclude opposed alternatives. Such writers as Toulmin[13] and Baier,[14] for instance, do no more than reduce the emphasis given to the point, and perhaps even obscure it by conventionalist manoeuvres. And the most thorough discussion of the topic that has appeared, by Taylor in *Normative Discourse*, though it is clearly intended to advance the discussion beyond the point at which Hare left it, seems in the end to amount to no more than a more elaborate restatement of Hare's position.[15]

In this work Taylor undertakes to specify the necessary conditions, which are I suppose held to be jointly sufficient, for the choice of a way of life to be rational. There turn out to be three of them, those of freedom, enlightenment and impartiality.[16] But, it transpires, we can never in practice know that these conditions have been fulfilled. We do not and never will know that one way of life is rationally preferable to another.[17] It is moreover allowed that there may be irreducible differences among people's rational preferences.[18] Indeed in one place Taylor explicitly asserts that it is a 'fundamental error' to overlook or deny the 'element of decision' which underlies all normative, and hence all moral, assertions.[19]

If, with Hume, we emphasize the distinction between appraisals of means and appraisals of ends, we are likely to come to think that the former can be 'objective' in a way the latter cannot. If, somewhat similarly, we make much of the distinction between proximate and ultimate justifications, between justifications *within* a certain accepted framework and justifications of the framework itself, we can hardly fail to conclude that completeness is achievable in the former case in a way it cannot be in the latter. The setting of questions about justification in morality so far determines the answers to them that it is natural that attempts should from time to time be made to see whether they cannot be set differently. Such writers as Dewey[20] and Myrdal,[21] for example, have in their different ways, and perhaps not always with sufficient attention to the logic/ psychology ambiguity of questions about the ways we think and argue, tried to break out from the means/ends, fact/value frameworks. Peters' recent discussions of moral education (1959 and 1962)[22] will bear examination from this point of view. Not that he was, as I understand him, so much concerned with questions of justification as with emphasising the possibility of appraising the manner of education as well as its aims and content. It is all the same worth enquiring whether this re-direction of emphasis affects the matter of justification.

Peters' central contention is that the more general problems of education are not means/ends problems at all. Mill's *Logic* (Book vi, chap. 12),[23] first published over a century ago, is perhaps the classical statement of the view that all practical problems have this form, but Mill is followed in all essential respects by so recent and philosophically sophisticated a writer as O'Connor.[24] Such scepticism as O'Connor expresses in chapter 5 of his book about the adequacy of the education/applied science analogy does not derive from any doubts about the appropriateness of applying the means/ ends category here, but rather from his doubt whether the social sciences have developed to a point at which they are clearly of more use to the educator than is commonsense, 'psychological' lore. Peters is much more radical. The more general aims of education, such objects as 'self-realisation', 'character', 'citizenship', are, in his view, neither goals nor end products. Like 'happiness' they are high-sounding ways of talking about doing some things rather than others and of doing them in a certain manner. Statements about the aims of education are better to be understood as expressing views about *how* rather than *what* we should teach, views about the procedure rather than the content of education. Values are involved in education less in the shape of goals or end products than as principles implicit in certain manners of proceeding.

I have no doubt that this distinction between values as ends or goals and values as rules of procedure is a useful one, and that Peters is right in suggesting that some educational pronouncements, though ostensibly about *what* is to be taught, are better conceived as pronouncements about *how* any subject matter should be taught. No doubt, too, moral education can be thought of as a matter of teaching people a manner of conducting their practical lives, rather than as one of teaching them substantive principles of conduct. Such a shift of emphasis might well furnish a basis for co-operation in moral education for people who are divided with regard to substantive principles of conduct. It is moreover possible that some of the stress one finds in discussions of moral education on the importance of indirect methods, example as opposed to precept, should be interpreted as a somewhat confused way of making a point like Peters'. That is to say, it might be interpreted not as it appears to be intended and as I suggested above, as a view about the method of teaching a given subject matter, but rather as the view that the problem is to teach people how to grapple with the 'subject matter' for themselves, to teach them how to go about making practical decisions and not to present them with practical conclusions. 'Character' in 'character training' could then be understood in the third of the senses distinguished by Peters in the works referred to, the sense in which it refers to the *style* rather than to the *content* of a person's rule-following.[25]

My one worry here is that such an attempt to exhibit the problems of moral education in a fresh light may distract attention from the fact that there are substantial moral issues calling for decision. By all means let us consider the manner as well as the matter, both in teaching and practical life. But we must not forget that there are choices to be made about the manner too. As with all other practical choices, there are no rules laid down to make them for us, though we can decide to adopt whatever rules commend themselves to us. Nor is there any method given, though we can decide to adopt one.

### III

It might well be thought that the impossibility of establishing an ultimate moral criterion has received at least as much emphasis as it deserves in recent moral philosophy. I have, however, been struck by the absence of much reflection of it in most of the discussions of moral education I have seen. There is undeniably a widespread belief in the importance of moral education, and some attention is given to questions of method and approach, but it seems to be assumed that there is no room for serious dispute about what is to be taught. This assumption—but perhaps it is really a conspiracy of silence—needs very little consideration to be seen to be quite extraordinary. There is obviously widespread disagreement on the moral issues of daily life, on the 'details' of morality, and, as I have tried to show, there is little enough reason to suppose that a greater measure of agreement can be reached on fundamentals.

This reluctance to take account of the possibility of moral conflict may, in Britain, be partly explicable on historical grounds. Morality seems most usually to be thought of as an appendage of religion, as that part of the teachings of the various religious bodies which can be regarded as common ground. Rather elaborate suggestions, which have in the main been carried out in the public educational system, are made in both the Spens (1938)[26] and Norwood (1943)[27] Reports for maintaining religious instruction and practice in the schools in the face of denominational disagreements. No need for any such arrangements with regard to moral teaching seems to be envisaged. I suppose it is feared that any serious consideration of morality might reopen the denominational quarrels of the past. Hence the constant lip-service to platitudinous ideals, whose bearing on any concrete issue of daily life is left wholly obscure. Hence the air of complete unreality that infects discussions of morality from official or otherwise respectable sources. Hence too the absurd public outcry when some prominent figure makes a candid observation, allows it to be known, say, that he is aware that there are conscientious and serious people who dissent from some article of the 'official' sexual code. To judge by what is said in public, a great many people in Britain have not grasped the possibility that people may differ in their views of what is right and ought to be done, and not merely in the extent to which they live up to or fall short of what the one 'true' view would require of them.[28]

I am very far from thinking that the point I have been pressing is the only important point about morality. Indeed I think moral philosophy may in recent years have been unduly preoccupied with questions of ultimate justification, and that the more recent reaction, change of emphasis, is to be welcomed. On the other hand, however obvious and familiar it may be to some, the point remains an important one, which needs to be taken account of, not least in connection with moral education.

## NOTES

1. I. Scheffler, *The Language of Education* (Springfield, Illinois: C. Thomas, 1962), pp. 76–77.
2. Quoted by J. S. Brubacher, *Eclectic Philosophy of Education* (Englewood Cliffs, New Jersey: Prentice-Hall, 1951), p. 326.
3. J. S. Mill, *On Liberty*, 1859, Chapter 2.
4. Mill, *op. cit.*, Chapter 3.
5. D. Hume, *A Treatise of Human Nature*, 1739–40 (Oxford, 1888).
6. Compare P. Edwards, *The Logic of Moral Discourse* (New York: Free Press, 1955), pp. 127–128.
7. C. L. Stevenson, *Ethics and Language* (New Haven, Connecticut: Yale University Press, 1944), p. 169.
8. *Ibid.*, pp. 153–154.
9. *Ibid.*, Chapter 6.
10. *Ibid.*, Chapter 10.
11. *Ibid.*, p. 114.
12. R. M. Hare, *The Language of Morals* (New York: Oxford University Press, 1952), p. 69.
13. S. E. Toulmin, *Reason in Ethics* (New York: Cambridge University Press, 1950).
14. K. Baier, *The Moral Point of View* (Ithaca, New York: Cornell, 1958).
15. P. W. Taylor, *Normative Discourse* (Englewood Cliffs, New Jersey: Prentice-Hall, 1961).
16. *Ibid.*, pp. 165–175.
17. *Ibid.*, p. 174.
18. *Ibid.*, p. 175.
19. *Ibid.*, p. 249.
20. J. Dewey, 'Theory of Valuation', *Int. Encyc. Unified Science*, II: iv (University of Chicago Press, 1939).
21. G. Myrdal, *Value in Social Theory*, trans. P. Streeton (New York: Harper, 1958).
22. R. S. Peters, *Authority, Responsibility and Education* (New York: Taplinger, 1960), and 'Moral Education and the Psychology of Character', *Philosophy*, Vol. XXXVII, No. 139, January 1962.
23. J. S. Mill, *A System of Logic*, 8th ed., 1898.
24. D. J. O'Connor, *An Introduction to the Philosophy of Education* (London: Routledge, 1957), p. 7.
25. Peters, 'Moral Education and the Psychology of Character', p. 43.
26. 'Spens Report', *Report of the Special Committee on Secondary Education* (H.M.S.O., London, 1938).
27. 'Norwood Report', *Curriculum and Examinations in Secondary Schools* (H.M.S.O., London, 1943).
28. The recent 'Newsom Report', *Half Our Future* (London: H.M. Stationery Office, 1963), I am glad to see, does show at any rate some awareness of the possibility of moral disagreements in the staff room.

# THE ESSENCE OF EDUCATION

USING the university as a context, Professor Griffiths here attempts to describe what education essentially consists in. In the process he considers most of the major issues that are discussed in the other articles in this volume: educational aims, the manner of instruction, the nature and justification of subject matter, the definition of teaching, and the meaning of moral education. His aim is to separate the merely accidental characteristics of the university from the essential ones. He proceeds through an analysis of the logic of activities, arguing that some are more exciting and interesting than others because the object of the activity possesses reciprocity, i.e., it presents new challenges to the agent. He distinguishes two kinds of activities—those having particular objects which are peculiarly the possession of the agent, and those having universal objects. From this he argues that the disinterested pursuit of universal objects is the central function of the university.

This pursuit has many by-products. Yet the production of these should not be construed as the proper aim of the university.

In drawing out the applications of this central notion, Griffiths presents a consistent and persuasive view of a wide range of educational problems. The comprehensiveness of approach, and the implicit points of agreement and disagreement with the other essays make it an appropriate closing piece for this volume.

# A DEDUCTION OF UNIVERSITIES

## A. Phillips Griffiths

### INTRODUCTION

I SHALL try to show what a university essentially is. I shall then discuss how its essential nature is related to those further functions which it sometimes performs, or are thought by some that it should perform: which, not being a part of the essence, may be called accidents.

No philosopher is in a position nowadays to set forth gaily on discussing the essence of something. To many 'essentialism', even with regard to institutions, is a methodological Sin against the Holy Ghost. Essentialism—the idea that we must set out to discover the necessary characteristics of things in order to know them—may often be nothing more than the examination of our own definitions. The essences we discover may be merely nominal. Something more than our own classifying activities must be related to the thing if we are to say not merely what it as a matter of fact is, but what it must be. The idea of the end or purpose of a thing may supply this: if we conceive men, trees, the world, as somehow aiming at perfection in their own kind, it becomes possible to speak of their essential nature at least in terms of potentialities. But we do not any longer conceive natural objects in this way, and we do not talk of their essences. Institutions, however, are not natural objects. In their case, essentialism, while still having dangers for the careless, may be unavoidable.

Even though institutions are not as Mill claimed[1] 'at every stage of their existence made what they are by voluntary human agency', they are what they are at any time of their existence because of the quality of the thought of their members. What an institution is, what differentiates it from others, cannot be explicated in terms of empirically observable factors such as physical movements. These may in principle be the same in different institutions; and the differentia can only be the way the members themselves conceive it.[2] If so, for institutions the essence—the idea—is prior to existence: not, of course temporally prior in all or even many cases, but logically prior; in that, unlike stones and the sea, institutions cannot logically be unless they are conceived as such-and-such.

I am not of course suggesting that we can make institutions come and go, appear and disappear, by the magic of thinking; or that we can by thinking make social institutions be whatever we like—even where 'we' means not you or me but all of us. For we cannot think whatever we like, and we cannot do whatever we like, and in consequence there are limits on what institutions are possible, and surprises about what institutions become actual. The limits of possibility are set by the (cultural and not merely logical) limits of thought, and by the (physical, cultural, social, economic, etc.) limits of practice. The inner demands of thought may, especially in the face of the pressures of the world, transform the mind that thinks it and revolutionise the institution that embodies it. This is above all true of the institution whose idea is an Ideal which involves values. Where the institution is conceived as aiming at the perfection of some activity, the perfect realisation of which is open, and could not be known until it is long pursued, it may develop according to what seem, in retrospect, inevitable steps, which could never have been predicted from its earlier nature. On the other hand, those institutions whose 'end' is limited by articles, such as a project to build a war memorial or to prevent a road running through a park, having clear and definite criteria for deciding when their activities are successful or unsuccessful, complete or incomplete, may be regarded as the product of conscious human will, but incapable of producing the surprises or development that is characteristic of more 'open' institutions.

This openness of those institutions whose essence is related to an ideal explains how it is possible both that their nature depends on how men conceive them, and yet at the same time men may argue interminably about what their nature is. What they are arguing about is very often what would count as satisfying the Ideal which constitutes the essence. For this reason the fact that people say the most diverse and even contradictory things about what some institution such as a university is for, does not necessarily mean that they are not all trying to talk about the same thing. And for this reason also, we should not be misled by this bewildering variety of views to think that there is nothing for it but to give up talking about what a university is for and talk only about what it does. What all universities, without exception, do, is warm the air slightly in their immediate vicinities. As soon as we say that it would be idiotic and irrelevant to mention this as an account of what universities do, we are entering on the road to essentialism. We have given up merely observing practices, and are beginning to prescribe them.

What then I propose to do is to present a 'deduction' of the idea of a university; attempting to understand the institution in terms of a justifiable Ideal. I shall try to show that there is a region in the firmament of values that must be filled; and that, in general, it is the institution which people tend to call a university that serves to fill it. I shall be saying at once what a university is and what it ought to be. I shall then, in the last section, go on to discuss some of the things which, while remaining itself, a university may or may not also be.

### ESSENCE

What makes an activity valuable considered as an end rather than a mere means?

This question is a vast one. To deal with it in all philosophical rigour, we should first enter into what are called 'meta-' questions about the logic, epistemological status, and justification of value judgments. This would take us a long way from the immediate topic and, judging by past efforts, we should probably never get back again. Here, I can make only certain suggestions, based on a consideration of the nature of an activity as such, which I hope will have some plausibility as a general account.

I am speaking of *activities*, and not other states of being or states of mind: of action rather than passion. Many things, such as warmth, pleasure, serenity and excitement, are thought to have value but are not activities at all.

Activities are things people engage in, which they may or may not know how to do. Not all the things people do are activities. If asked 'What are your spare time activities?' a man could answer 'Oh, breathing, blinking and sneezing', rather than 'none', only as a snub or a bad joke. Nor would we normally speak of 'knowing how' to breathe (unless we are talking about operatic singers or swimmers), or how to blink, or how to sneeze; because not being activities these things are not pursued in accordance with rules or standards. We do not do them well or badly, we simply either do or do not do them. If anything is to be an activity it must allow the possibility of effort, for the presence of standards implies the possibility of success or failure, and hence trying. No activity is of much value in itself unless it presents the need for effort to the degree that it is in some way strenuous: standards too easily followed cease to involve conscious attention and become mere habits (e.g. counting, amusing when one first starts on it as a child but a bore after a while). It would be a mistake quite obviously to have a simple linear scale of the value of an activity based only on its degree of difficulty. The more valuable difficulty differs qualitatively rather than quantitatively from the less valuable one. The specific terms of value we use in respect to activities are 'absorbing', 'interesting', and 'fascinating'. It would seem that the difficulties an activity presents in order to be satisfying in this sense must be varied, unpredictable in detail, and requiring constant adjustment and the exercise of new modes of action. This must have something to do with the fact that activities are valuable only as modifications of consciousness, and more valuable as these modifications are richer and capable of indefinite development without mere repetition. They are not those that can be done with half a mind, mechanically, or passively. The objects of valuable activities must possess a quality which we might call *reciprocity*. In acting on it, it bounces back again and one may miss it or it may bump one in the nose; or it may return from an unexpected angle which presents itself as a discovery demanding a new response. Bouncing a ball from an uneven wall is more interesting than from an even one. The responses required are more varied and unpredictable, and require more absorption and engagement. Practising boxing with a punchball is more interesting than pummeling a fixed leather bag; boxing with a man, more interesting and difficult still. It is true that if the punchbag is hard and heavy enough it may be even more difficult to hit it than to box with a man; but all this involves is a quantitative increase in one of the many difficulties involved in boxing a man, not the increase in quality of difficulty which arises from the manifold variety of a human opponent's responses. Playing chess against oneself is less satisfactory than playing it with someone else roughly as good; on one's own one gets less or none of the challenging surprises provided by a good player. Activities involving personal relationships, such as fatherhood, possess this quality in the highest degree: every action may elicit a response which requires a new adjustment. An artist in paint or words is, again, frustrated and at the same time satisfied by the response of his material. The permanence and fecundity of the reciprocity of the object of an activity seems to determine much of its value.

Of course the relative difficulty of an activity may present in addition a positive disvalue. It must not be so difficult as to be impossible even to attempt, and it must not be utterly and quickly exhausting. But this does not affect my point; everyone would probably agree that the lazy, the easily tired, the relatively inactive, miss a great deal in life. We pity the weak and the unable, and perhaps try to make up for the poverty of their lives by giving them more from the passive sources of contentment, such as a rubber teat.

Some very important activities derive their value from their effects rather than what they are in themselves. We may continue with them very wisely when they are mechanical, uninteresting, effortless or dull; but unless we are mad this will only be because we are concerned with some further end they happen to serve. Emptying dustbins (trashcans) neatly might, just possibly, be an interesting task at first, but it would make an odd permanent hobby. Nevertheless, the efficient disposal of waste is undoubtedly of the utmost value. But we must not, because impressed by the important by-products of human activity, forget that some human activities have a value of their own. Emptying dustbins will, we hope, one day be done entirely by machines; but not our dancing or our conversation.

Any activity which is pursued as an end in itself is an expression of love. Activities are pursued according to standards, and the objects proper to them are either (as an ideal to be attained) sought or (as in some degree already actual) improved on. For a man to regard something as an end to be sought or cherished or improved rather than harmed, not because of other things but for its own sake, is for him to love it. His activity may be explained by some further end, in which case it is that and not the object of the activity he loves; or he pursues the object because he loves it. Otherwise, his behaviour is unintelligible. To learn to pursue an activity as an end in itself is, then, to learn to love it. I mention this point because the account I have given may seem somewhat soulless. Why should these formal characteristics, so cerebrally detected, have anything to do with what is of value to people? Surely, to be valued,

A. Phillips Griffiths

something must be liked or loved as well? My answer to this is 'Not
*as well*; I am trying to articulate what it *is* to love'.

Now the pursuit of learning—the study of physics, history or
philosophy—is clearly an activity whose objects possess reciprocity.
They provide the kind of interest which is not readily exhaustible,
and which provides challenges at every stage which cannot be satisfied except by digging more deeply. Every acquisition of knowledge
seems to reveal a host of new and often more subtle and difficult
problems. Without care, we get no answers or misleading answers
when we put nature to the question, and the next question we ask
will be determined by the last one we got. In history, literary criticism, and philosophy, we are engaged in a dialogue with other men,
in which we value the unpredictability of their responses and—at
least ideally—the unexpected upsetting of our own views. These
activities differ, however, from many other valuable ones in one
most important respect. Two men who are pursuing them both
pursue the same object. Their objects are universal, and at the same
time concrete, in that what each man gets is not an instance of, but
a relation to, the same thing as his fellow. (All such objects are
qualitatively and not numerically identified). The object of the
activity of conversation, or fatherhood, is an individual person
(conceived under a limiting description) in which every situation is
concrete and unique, shared, if at all, by at most a few. The tennis
player is faced with an individual opponent, and he faces a series
of new situations defined in terms of the numerically distinct participants and hence peculiarly his. They cannot be shared or passed
on. Where the object of a non-universal activity—such as a mistress
—is passed on, it is pre-empted. But physics, history, or philosophy
are not diminished for me if others pursue them. I may be jealous,
or, more reasonably, envious, of the better philosophical achievements of others, but I cannot be jealous because there are other
philosophers as I might be if my wife had lovers; for I cannot, even
mistakenly, conceive philosophy as *mine* in the way that I might—
possibly mistakenly—conceive a woman as mine. I cannot speak of
my history, my physics, as I can speak of my singing, my son, or
my tennis match. As universal and public, physics or history must
be pursued under different conditions from those under which
non-universal objects are pursued. It is not only that these objects
*can* also be pursued by others; they *must* be, if I am to pursue them
myself. And I cannot pursue them properly and seriously if I ignore

the work of others. They require the check of the opinions of others. and this is possible as well as necessary because they are public and objective in a way that other activities are not. They all involve the pursuit of truth.

The pursuit of learning is, then, an activity having value as an end in itself. But because its objects are distinguished from others by their universality, they can be sought only in a certain kind of environment. It must be one in which there is time to pursue the activity; for the universal objects of the highest excellence are those which demand most systematic attention, and are practically inexhaustible. It must provide the freedom within which the new challenge can survive, in which whether an argument or some fact is considered depends on the standards of the activity rather than any external criterion, such as its social acceptability or its political convenience. It must be an environment in which communication is possible with others who are engaged in the same pursuits.

This environment is one which has been traditionally provided by universities, especially for their senior members. While other societies may have fulfilled this function, such as classical Athens, it was only because they, too, provided the required environment. Leisure in Athens made the pursuit of learning possible; freedom, of the kind idealized by Pericles in his funeral speech, made it live; and the smallness of the community made its sharing easy. The leisure that made learning possible in Athens was, of course, a consequence of the exploitation of others who were not permitted to share in it: the slaves on the land and in the mines, the over-taxed colonies and tributaries, and everyone who was taken advantage of by the commercial superiority of Athens. In this too Athens was similar to the modern university, for there also the pursuit of learning is carried on at the expense of those who have no part in it.

The centre of learning, existing as it must outside Eden, demands a great deal from the community in which it exists. It demands its keep; and (what may be more difficult to give) it demands its indulgence, for it is a place where the most important prejudices, which may be essential for the stability or even the existence of its surrounding community, may have to be questioned, and perhaps destroyed.

As I have described it, there seem to be cogent reasons why anyone who is not a member of a centre of learning should not want it to exist, and no reason why he should. To him, the centre of learning could be justified only in terms of its by-products. Before going on to discuss these, two things need to be said. First, that we, who for our own selfish purposes (or in concern for the selfish purposes of others who love learning) want to defend universities, should be careful, in our zeal for pointing out their useful by-products, that we do not end up forgetting what we were essentially concerned with, rather than the mere by-products. Secondly, we must not too quickly reject the value and importance of selfish activities.

It is only a kind of lunatic puritanism that would condemn all selfish activities. If an activity is supposed to have value only in its contribution to the well-being of others, then value can reside only in effects, only in what is suffered and not in what is done. This is to ignore the value of activities as such altogether. Furthermore, the pursuit of mathematics or history is not *viciously* selfish in the sense that greed is. Pursuing them does not prevent, but rather enhances, their pursuit by another. Except that a mathematician withdraws his hands from the production line, he diminishes no one.

The relevance of the last point might be disputed on the grounds that in practice the pursuit of learning can be the privilege of only a few. It is sometimes said that the pursuit of universal activities as I have described them requires much time and energy; so those who engage in them must be the few who can be spared in the community's productive effort. In any case, only a very few are intellectually capable of the pursuit of universal objects.

Certainly, if history or physics or philosophy are to be advanced, there must be some people who dedicate a considerable part of their lives to them. But once the pursuit of physics or philosophy exists as an institution, others who have much else to do may participate in it. Thus the selfishness of the few is a condition of the satisfaction of the many. That only a few are intellectually capable of the pursuit of universal objects is simply not in accordance with the facts.[3] It will require the presence of those more practised in such pursuits, but it is possible for many to reach a point (as many do who are awarded bachelor's degrees, or attend three-year extramural classes) where they produce the guessing, insight and argument that must take place at the growing point of a subject.

# A Deduction of Universities

There can be no doubt that universities often provide the environment necessary to the pursuit of learning as I have described it. But it is not enough to say this if I am to show that a university must *essentially* be a centre of learning. For universities do other things too. They usually set up to teach; they preserve and even further culture; they help people to acquire useful arts which later enable them to increase productivity, decrease productivity, and perform other desired economic functions; they may be supposed to turn people into better citizens. In addition to these things, which may be and indeed all have been mistaken for the essential function of the university, they do other things too. They are thought by some to be incomparably the best, if the most expensive, marriage bureaux on earth. They are in some places essential to the maintenance of good semi-professional football teams. They are often decorative, places of tourist resort and, as I remarked before, they all warm the air slightly. I shall not think it necessary to concern myself with the second set of university functions. It would clearly be quite idiotic to suggest that they might be considered the essential functions of a university, because it would mean that universities are not at all distinct from correspondence clubs, sporting clubs, national parks or warming pans, respectively. This shows that we do not invent the concept 'university' to represent these functions (or we would not have a different concept), we do not conceive the institution in this way. And what it is is how it is conceived. So I need only concern myself with the first set of functions, because some people do conceive universities as essentially distinguished by them. To show that they are wrong, it will be necessary to show that these functions can be conceived as functions of the university only so far as they are dependent on the central function, the pursuit of learning. This however one can only do in so far as one believes they are possible; and as I shall argue, perhaps the last is not.

## (i) Teaching[1]

Some universities are said to have begun by scholars taking pupils in order to be able to live. Many universities today are full of teachers who are teachers because that is the only way they can get enough money and live in the right surroundings to pursue their subjects. This may be a sufficient explanation of why people who have as a major aim in life the pursuit of universal objects become university teachers (or, perhaps, monks). But it makes the matter look rather too accidental. The activity of teaching is peculiarly compatible with the pursuit of universal objects, in a way that other work, even part-time work, is not. For certain kinds of teaching, at any rate, are nothing but the practice of the activity in public; the pupil and the teacher form the community within which the universal object is publicly possessed. The dialogue between pupil and teacher need not be fundamentally different from that between scholar and scholar. Its avowed end is not the same: it is the initiation of another into a universal activity, not the discovery of truth. But this can be done only by treating the dialogue as if its end were the discovery of truth. The pupil is introduced to the activity by participating in it with someone more advanced who is for the moment more concerned for the state of mind of the individual than the advancement of his subject, but who shows the pupil what a concern for the advancement of his subject amounts to. It is true that even this is too much to ask of some; there are university dons who hate their pupils for interrupting their real work, until one as advanced and brilliant as himself obtrudes on his attention as would a colleague.

However, to say that teaching is peculiarly compatible with the pursuit of universal objects does not show that it is the pursuit of universal objects which is the essence of the university. It shows merely that university scholars may well teach, not that university teachers must be scholars. But for the latter it is enough to say that for anyone to be introduced to a universal activity, he must be in the presence of someone who practises it, and who does so in a way which shows most manifestly the standards and principles of the activity. There is no way of introducing people to these activities except by helping them to practise them. But no one can simply be *instructed* how to practise them. They possess reciprocity in the highest degree. At every stage they require the stance of doubt: the readiness to meet challenge. Every step must be questioned and one must always be prepared for—indeed look for—refutation. One cannot be prepared for refutation unless one knows what refutation is, and that means knowing what it is to refute. The pupil is from the beginning the critic of his teacher's work, and his aim is to overthrow it if possible (as indeed it must be the scholar's aim, if he is concerned for truth, to see his work overthrown). From the beginning the pupil must take an active part:[5] it is the teacher's cross to bear with initially simple-minded and half-baked objections so that he may eventually be proved wrong with good ones.

So the teacher must be concerned for his pupil as well as for his subject; but if he is teaching history, for example, his concern must be for his pupil as a possible historian rather than as a future wage-earner.[6] What he has to do, whether he himself loves his own subject or pursues it only for some further end such as making a living, is to lead the pupil to act as if the pupil loved the subject: for only in this way can he bring the student to see what this love consists in. It is only in this way that the pupil can come to pursue the subject properly, that is, by the standards internal to it, rather than as a mere means which may be restricted to serve an external end. (More about this in section iii). In these circumstances it would be reasonable to expect what does indeed seem to be the case, that the best teachers tend to be those who do love their subjects, for whom their subjects are ends in themselves. Such people will want to be at a centre of learning rather than an institution which does not satisfy this description. They will want people to talk to on their own academic level, the leisure to pursue their subjects, and the freedom to do so not so much as they think fit but as they judge the subject demands. Introducing people to universal objects must be done then at centres of learning, because you must go where the people who can best do it are to be found.

## (ii) Education

To acquire the practice of a universal activity may not, perhaps, be to become educated. If we regard an educated man as someone who has the knowledge and sophistication which is common to some civilisation, his ability to pursue a universal object will not be sufficient for him to be educated. He may be a barbarian in most respects; and this means that every senior member of a university may be a barbarian and still be a satisfactory scholar in his own field. There may be philistine pure mathematicians, philosophers with no aesthetic sense, physicists who never read the newspapers, philologists who spend half their time glued to the telly, and mediaevalists who think science is some kind of hand-soiling tinkering with gadgets. To some extent, this seems to be becoming more generally true, especially of non-scientists: people interested in

A. Phillips Griffiths

the arts seem far less able to discuss or understand scientific interests than scientists are able to discuss and understand the arts. At any rate, the common mode of conversation throughout a whole university often seems to tend towards sheer gossip: for personalities seem to be all that each man can talk about other than his own subject.

If this is inevitable, we have a choice: universities either as centres of learning or centres of culture, it would seem. Are universities for turning out educated men of culture, or for turning out people who can do physics or history or philosophy? If the former then they are not essentially centres of learning. If the latter, and the gap is unbridgeable, they will not be centres of culture at all.

But let us now ask, if this is inevitable what, then, would a centre of culture be? It would be a place where people pursue not only physics, but philosophy; not only philosophy, but music; not only music, but engineering (nobody can understand our world and be an all-round cultured man without a knowledge of the nature and problems of engineering); not only engineering, but theology. It is difficult to see why, if they can do all of these things reasonably well, they cannot do one of them well. In which case, the centre of culture is a centre of learning too. But it is also difficult to see why, if they cannot do any one of them well, they should be expected to do all of them reasonably well. If it is inevitable that centres of learning cannot be centres of culture, then it is inevitable that there cannot be centres of culture: it means that our culture is not only fragmented, as C. P. Snow would have it: but that it is necessarily fragmented.

On the other hand, if this is not inevitable, then a centre of learning should provide the environment in which a man can acquire a general culture if he can acquire it at all. For it is there that the growing points of a culture—at least so far as it concerns universal objects—are; and it is there that he will come into contact with those who are most deeply immersed in some aspect of culture. What he may well not do is to meet those who are concerned with the growing points of culture so far as it concerns non-universal objects. He will not meet painters, poets, or international tennis players, and he will not meet many of the best composers. There is no reason why a university should not extend itself to being a patron of the non-universal arts, if it can afford it, as many American universities have done. (Such writers as Frost and Auden, such composers as Schoenberg, who hated teaching harmony, and such footballers as I cannot name, have found niches in American universities from time to time). This should not however be at the expense of its central function as a centre of learning. These other lonelier activities will go on somewhere whether the university environment is provided or not. The university environment, with its air of public criticism, is often inimical to the artist. Artists do not always fit well into institutions, especially ones not primarily dedicated to their purposes. Above all, we do not want to turn poets into literary critics, painters into art historians, or great musical innovators into teachers of elementary harmony: and this not for the sake of universities but for the sake of poetry, literary criticism, painting, art history, and Schoenberg.

## (iii) Useful Arts

In their *Dictionary of Contemporary American Usage* Bergen and Cornelia Evans say of the term 'liberal arts': 'It means, etymologically, befitting a free man. In practice it means a course of studies comprising the arts, natural sciences, social studies, and the humanities, which is not designed, as are courses in engineering, business administration, forestry, and so on, to have an immediate utility'.[7] There may seem to be no obvious connection between the etymology and the present meaning of 'liberal arts': can't an engineer, or a dentist, be a free man? But there is this interesting connection. There is a sense in which the pursuit of philosophy or physics or history is the pursuit of a free man whereas business administration or forestry is the pursuit of a slave or at least a servant. It is the sense in which the former pursuits are of value in themselves to those who pursue them,[8] as a pursuit of universal objects; whereas the latter are pursued as a means only, so that people will pursue them only (as slaves) under threat of punishment or (as servants) for the sake of reward. But if this is the reason for the distinction, the examples mentioned are dangerously misleading. The distinction is not really one of different studies. Painting, physics, psychology and Latin may all be pursued 'so as to have an immediate utility'; while engineering, business administration, forestry and dental caries may all be studied simply because they are interesting. If, in a university, the study of Latin as a language is robbed of its historical and philological interest because efficient schoolteachers of Latin, who are being processed in the university, have no need of such things, we are treating the students like slaves who have to be equipped with hoes or hammers. If psychology is studied just so far as it might be of use to those who later on will have to advise advertisers about the most efficient methods of deceiving the general public, it has ceased to be the pursuit of a universal object. What makes the distinction is not the field of study but the way it is pursued. It cannot be pursued as a valuable universal object if arbitrary limits are set on what determines the importance and relevance of any question within it; that is, if the standards of relevance become extrinsic to the activity, it loses the fecundity of reciprocity which makes it valuable.

To say that in universities subjects are pursued as ends in themselves is not then to say that they are all useless; it is only to say that their use does not determine the way they are studied. Confusion in this matter may account for the contemptuous attitude displayed by some members of arts faculties to their scientific colleagues; as if the latter were somehow engaged in trade. That their own subjects are largely useless, and many sciences undoubtedly useful, does not necessarily mark any difference in the way in which these subjects may be approached. The same may be said of those subjects coming under the heading of 'technology'. Technological problems are objective, public problems, which are related to those trying to solve them in exactly the same way as the problems of physics or literary criticism. That, in solving them, it becomes immediately possible to build a bridge does not mean that, in pursuing them, those who studied them would lose interest if they did not happen to want a bridge. Indeed, far from its being the case that such subjects are not 'liberal', their usefulness often depends on their being treated in a disinterested liberal way (as Bell Telephone Laboratories have shown). This is fortunate for universities and for those useless subjects pursued in them; were it not true there would undoubtedly be less of them.

Turning out people with technical abilities is not, then, incompatible with the essential function of a university; but it will become so if this aim is allowed to determine its activities. We may also say that when this aim does become the determinant of its activities, it fails to achieve this aim on the highest level.

### (iv) Preparation for Life

Education is often held to have as one of its primary aims the training of character; if so we might demand of institutions of higher education that they also have this aim. Not inevitably, however; for we may question, in the first place, whether we should think of universities as being very centrally concerned with *education*, rather than the pursuit and passing on of universal activities; or, in the second place, whether *all* education, at every stage, involves the training of character. But it is a hoary idea that universities should concern themselves with this aim; that they should be turning out good citizens and, indeed, as the highest reaches of the educational system, that they should be turning out the *best* citizens —the aristocrats who will lead.

I shall not concern myself here with the inegalitarian aspects of this view, or with the dangers to the ideals of democracy of leadership cadres. I am writing about universities, not the best way to run society. What I shall ask is whether this aim seems even possible in any institutions which look remotely like universities.

I am not going to argue that leadership, etc., cannot be learnt. But the context in which it is learnt seems as a rule a very different one from an academic institution. In the Army and Police force there are semi-academic institutions such as the Staff Colleges. But no one thinks that it is at such places that the qualities of leadership are developed. The students are those who are already some distance up the ladder of leadership and, being leaders, are acquiring certain specific information and skills. Trade unionists get sent to various educational institutions during their careers, but they acquire the qualities of a good trade union leader in the work of the union. Leadership, the ability to handle men and make decisions showing practical judgment, while requiring certain initial qualities of mind and character, seems to be developed by practising *it* and not something else.

On the other hand, graduates do not seem to possess these qualities of character strikingly more than anyone else. So if we are to regard universities as schools of leadership, we shall have to ask them to do rather different things from their present practice. It must not be too different or we shall not call them universities at all. This means that if anyone is going to put forward the Platonic view that certain studies ultimately produce the qualities needed in leaders of men, he will be required to make quite specific suggestions as to which studies, in what way pursued, will have this effect. Obviously I cannot deal with all such suggestions here. I shall content myself with the discussion of one such recent suggestion, that made by Professor Nowell-Smith in his inaugural lecture at the University of Leicester.[9] It is an interesting one because it involves a very explicit suggestion that university studies should be limited, in arts faculties, in just the way that technical subjects may be, by being supposed to have 'an immediate utility': the reverse view to that which takes a pride in the uselessness of arts subjects. Only here the 'immediate utility' is in terms of desirable effects on the characters and minds of the students, rather than on their economic value.

What the student should acquire at the university, according to Nowell-Smith, are the 'skills required for living';[10] since university students 'are marked out by their talents as leaders and it is they who will have most to contribute to the solution of our social, moral and political problems'.[11] The academic training should develop not special but general skills: 'creative imagination, practical wisdom, and logical thought'.[12] The view is directly in contradiction to the one I have been putting forward. These general skills are not simply valuable by-products but developing them is the essential function of the university. The aim of the university should explicitly *not* be 'to teach literature, history, or philosophy, but those skills that are required for living' to the majority of students.

I think this view is doubly dangerous. In the first place, it may lead us to neglect those valuable functions which, essential or not, can be performed only by a university. In the second place, and I conclude by arguing this point, the aim is not a possible one. It would be foolhardy to sell universities to the public on such grounds; one fears what might happen when it is seen that the Emperor is nothing but clothes.

Nowell-Smith's suggestion is that the 'skills required for living', creative imagination, practical wisdom, and logical power, may be developed by a (partial) study of literature, history and philosophy respectively. If these are skills, they are very odd ones. Notice that most ordinary skills—swimming, tight-rope walking, or carpentry —can be acquired only by practising them; you cannot acquire the skill of swimming without going to the water. But it seems that we can get practical wisdom by studying history and creative imagination by studying literature. Secondly, these skills seem to have no direct manifestation. We can tell that people can swim by seeing them swimming. We cannot tell they have practical wisdom by seeing them do any particular sort of thing. We may be misled on this point because there are sometimes good tests for the possession of qualities of this sort; intelligence tests are an example. But the relation between intelligence tests and intelligence is quite different from the relation between swimming tests and the ability to swim. One could actually learn to swim by doing lots of swimming tests, just as some people learn to play the piano by mastering a series of graded test pieces. One cannot acquire intelligence by doing intelligence tests. This suggests that it is a mistake to regard such qualities of mind as imagination, practical wisdom, and logical power as skills at all, for this will lead us to think they can be acquired in the same way that skills are acquired, and that once acquired they may have one uniform manifestation. In fact such concepts as intelligence or practical wisdom must be 'schematised' before they can be applied: that is, given a concrete sense in terms of some particular activity. For different activities performed by the same individual may manifest different degrees of intelligence or imagination. It *may* be true that an intelligent man is more likely to make an intelligent boxer than an unintelligent man; yet an intelligent boxer may be an 'unintelligent man'. You may be able to tell whether a man is a logical historian by seeing how well he is able to solve logical puzzles; but it is not conceptually impossible to find a brilliantly logical historian who in fact cannot do logical puzzles (for example he may be quite put off by too great a degree of abstraction). We know he is a logical historian because of the *way* he does *history*. Such qualities as logical power or imagination are not skills like the ability to ride a bicycle or blow smoke rings, and they are not manifested as pure intelligence or pure wisdom, as riding a bicycle and blowing smoke rings perfectly manifest the corresponding skills. They are manifested in the *way* some things are done; 'imaginative', 'wise', 'logical' and 'intelligent' are adjectives which derive their sense from the adverbial form. Intelligence, imagination and wisdom are the qualities needed to do things intelligently, imaginatively and wisely, and the force of these adverbs will depend on what they qualify (which may be understood by realising that the question 'Does an imaginative scientist need more or less imagination than an imaginative poet?' is a nonsensical one). Furthermore, all these qualities are needed to pursue any activity well.

I shall try to illustrate these points by looking at the suggestions Nowell-Smith makes more closely and in greater detail, before drawing my conclusion.

## A. Phillips Griffiths

He regards history as involving examples of practical wisdom and as capable of developing it. But the study of history surely already pre-supposes some practical wisdom, and a lot of imagination (sympathetic, if not creative imagination; but I am not too sure of the distinction). It would seem that the study of political institutions is an art: some people have a flair for understanding the nature and processes of such institutions as the Soviet Communist Party, a flair which is essential for any good political analyst. This is also true of understanding the past. If imagination is necessary to the study of history, no less is analytical intelligence. Nowell-Smith says 'the historian will be all the better as a historian for some philosophical training'. Perhaps. But a historian without considerable logical and analytical intelligence would be no historian worthy of the name. He must be able to detect inconsistencies in his theories, and to characterise the past in meaningful and viable concepts. Probably, he will not consult the philosopher about where he fails: he is more likely to be corrected by other historians, who know better what he is talking about.

The same sort of thing may be said for either literature or philosophy. In literary criticism we do not develop creative imagination, but we surely require that the critic should be imaginative, in that he is able to perceive connections, significances, ambiguities and comparisons of a non-obvious kind in the works he is studying. The connection with practical wisdom is at least as plausible as in the case of history. (It is perhaps more plausible. History might equally be regarded as the record of the manifold follies of men as of their wiser decisions. To distinguish the one from the other means bringing practical wisdom to it, not getting it from it.) In the novel, in drama and in epic and other poetry, there is not only often an abstractable set of situations which are of interest to the moral sense: the moral sense is essential to the appreciation of the work itself, to the significance of its images and its development. Anyone who reads *Lear* without realising its preoccupation with the idea of love and its demands and misuses misses a great part of the value of the work. Equally important to the critic is the capacity for logical thought and careful analysis. As in history, his second order concepts must be consistent, meaningful and viable; but the critic must also bring his logical sense to bear on the work itself. There are arguments in literature, world-views, the posing of problems, even though these are not its primary end; but they are elements of the

204

work, and it is impossible to appreciate or criticise them unless the critic has the necessary analytical equipment.

Again, all these qualities of mind are necessary to the philosopher. The reason why analytical thought is so much more important in philosophy is because it is an absolutely necessary condition of any philosophical view that it should be clear and consistent. It cannot put up with the openness and ambiguities of a literary work—which indeed are a part of the value of literature—and it cannot reflect the empirical modesty of history, which accepts concepts and hypotheses for their working value. So on the critical side in philosophy one can usually make do with analytical expertise. But this merely destructive criticism is not sufficient to a good philosopher. Philosophy never exists in a vacuum; philosophical thought always goes on against a background of other people's philosophical views. Sympathetic historical imagination is necessary to appreciate philosophical work of the past. Furthermore, the power of imagination is necessary to the development of one's own philosophical views: since seeing connections, picking out important and central concepts, and the perspicuous understanding of a language game are not matters of deduction or calculation or mere painstaking analysis.

Imagination, wisdom, and intelligence seem then to be necessary conditions of pursuing any of these three subjects, and, indeed, anything else, well. But it would be a mistake to think that they are *generally* developed by any activity requiring them. In pursuing history or physics, or philosophy, in facing the difficulties of these activities and overcoming them, one becomes better at history, physics or philosophy. Perhaps this means becoming a more intelligent, imaginative, and logical historian or physicist or philosopher. But it certainly does not mean becoming a more intelligent boxer or philologist or soldier, or a more imaginative poet or joke-teller, or a wiser father or trade union leader; or a wiser, more imaginative more logical and intelligent man.

There are human activities which need universities for their pursuit where one may acquire the ability to pursue them, and which require the possession of such qualities of mind as intelligence, imagination and practical wisdom. There is no reason to suppose that the consequence of learning to pursue these activities will be anything other than the ability to pursue them; but being able to pursue them is nevertheless a good thing.

## A. Phillips Griffiths

## NOTES

1. J. S. Mill, *Representative Government*, Chapter 1.

2. Consider, for example, what might make a ritual dance an attempt at magic, a form of amusement, or an act of public worship. For further arguments see P. Winch, *The Idea of a Social Science* (London: Routledge and Kegan Paul, 1958).

3. This will seem to some to be unwarrantable dogmatism. Here I can refer only to the investigations of the Robbins Committee (Committee on Higher Education, *Higher Education* [Report of the Committee under the chairmanship of Lord Robbins, 1961–63; London: H.M. Stationery Office, 1963], esp. Chapter VI), and earlier investigations of the British Association of University Teachers. It is, I fear, true, that very many dons in England have bitterly opposed the view that there is a pool of untapped ability, as the ghastly phrase goes. Generally however their remarks seem to have been made on a journalistic, intuitive level. Some now seem to have been convinced by the Robbins Committee report, but find new arguments to oppose the expansion of Universities (one prize example being the claim that while bigger Universities would not necessarily be academically bad, it would diminish the *moral* influence of the writer and other dons over his students. Enough said.).

4. My argument in this section has been considerably modified in discussion with Professor R. S. Peters.

5. This leads, at least in my own teaching of philosophy, to a pedagogical problem which I have never satisfactorily resolved. To teach students what it is to refute, it is sometimes necessary to give them practice by defending to them a not easily defensible position. A second reason for doing this is that they may be inclined themselves to reject a commonly rejected position—such as psychological hedonism—because it is commonly rejected and not because they have seriously worked through the reasons against it. But taking up the rôle of devil's advocate sometimes results in the student's doubting the sincerity and seriousness of the teacher. This I think illustrates what I have been saying. There is bound to be a kind of tension resulting from the fact that in teaching one is not primarily seeking truth but must at the same time present to the pupil an example of that search.

6. This is not a distinction without a difference. Only via such distinctions can one give the concept 'love of persons' any content at all. I should argue that there is no such thing as love of a person *as such*; only of a person under a given description. Forms of love of persons are thus discriminated in terms of the description under which their objects are conceived, and the activities which are their expression are consequently very different, as fatherhood differs from friendship, being a good daughter differs from being a good wife, and the love of a wife is different from the love of a Queen (which must lead to difficulties in the life of a Prince Consort).

7. B. and C. Evans, *Dictionary of Contemporary American Usage* (New York: Random House, 1957), p. 274.

8. Ignore the other dimension of meaning of the word 'liberal', that a liberal course is a *general course*. I have discussed this issue in the preceding section.

9. *Education in a University* (Leicester University Press, 1958).

10. *Ibid.*, p. 7.

11. *Ibid.*

12. *Ibid.*

# INDEX

*Entries in italics indicate bibliographical references*

209

# Index

McClelland, D., *111*
manner, importance of, 12, 95
Maritain, J., 28, 116
Marx, Karl, 155
metaphysics, 24
Mill, J. S., 174-5, 180, *183*, 187, 206
mind: development of, 125, 126; rational, 123
model, *see* situation, educational
Montessori, M., 63
moral education, and indoctrination, 171ff
morality, teacher and, 66
moral knowledge, 131, 134
moral philosophy, 171; teaching of, 163-4
moral statements, analysis of, 26
morals, relativity of, 32
Munroe, R. L., *85*
Myrdal, G., 180, *183*

neutrality, ideological, 148, 152
Newman, J. H., 115
Newsom Report, 90, *183*
Norwood Report, 182, *183*
Nowell-Smith, P. H., 6, *13*, 138, 202, *207*

Oakeshott, M., 106, 109, *111*, 137-8
O'Connor, D. J., 1, 7, *13*, 180, *183*
Oxford, philosophy at, 146

paradigms, use in liberal education, 133, 134
passiveness, in pupil, 69
Peel, E. A., *55*
perception, educational, 51-2
Perry, L. R., 2, 10, 11
Perry, R. B. 6, 13
personality, 72
Pestalozzi, J. H., 52, 69, 77
Peters, R. S., 7, 10, 11, *13*, *111*, 180-1, *183*
Peterson, A. D. C., 122-3

philosopher, what he is, 141ff
philosophy: current trends, 5; function of, 4-5, 17-18; meaning of, 23-4, 144-5; subject-matter of, 8; teaching of, 146ff; and universities, 145-6
philosophy of education: benefits of, 34ff; language of, 46ff; meaning, 26-7; and practice, 28, 31-32; purpose of, 52; synthetic, 3
physical education, 99
Piaget, J., 45
Plato, 2, 5, 6, 49, 97, 150
positivism: crude, 153; logical, 56
precision, incentives for, 110
principles, scrutiny of, 142-3
problems, philosophical nature of, 143-4
Progressive Education Movement, 94
psychoanalysis, 162
psychology, 1, 3, 7; educational purpose of, 41-2
pupil: in child-centred model, 72-74; in traditional model, 68

Quintilian, 44, 52, 63, 106

rationalization, of educational practice, 157-8
realism, 4; philosophical, 116
reciprocity, 190, 192
refutation, 196
Reid, L. A., 5, 10, 11, *37*, 49-51, 52, *56*
Robbins Commitee, 206
Rosmini, A., 52
Rousseau, J.-J., 49, 63, 91, 94
rules, application of, 30
Rusk, Robert R., 47, *56*
Ryle, G., 7, *13*, *111*

Sandford, P., 43, 55
scepticism, philosophical, 150-1, 153

211